Formu

technical analysis 2014/2015

CW00542175

The 2014 SEASON

With the 2014 season, F1 turned its back on naturally aspirated engines and welcomed the era of hybrid power units in an attempt, in a certain sense, to keep pace with the demands and developments of normal automotive mass production.
The Power Unit, the combination of a 1600 cc turbocharged engine with two electric motors for the recovery of energy from the brakes and the heat of the turbo meant sleepless nights for many a technical director from the various teams. Adrian Newey was one of them, he who would usually make remarkable progress every time he had to start from scratch when designing a new car. The RB10 even had to abandon testing at Jerez on its debut and things hardly went any better in the other two sessions in Bahrain, setting an unwelcome record with just 1609 km covered in 12 days of testing before the start of the World Championship. Never before in preparation for a Formula 1 season had so many problems kept the cars in the pits and forced teams to miss sessions before they were ready to try again. Not to speak of the issues that arose in this initial

period with the electronic management of the rear brakes. All this was perhaps only to be expected given the extent of the epochal revolution introduced by the FIA. An upheaval that affected all areas of the cars, with no exceptions and which had given grave cause for concern when in the first race of the World Championship less than half the cars that started reached the finish.
Only the Mercedes can be excluded from this discussion given that they practically laid claim to the title from the first test in Jerez in spite of the failure of the front wing immediately suffered by Hamilton in the opening laps.

MERCEDES DOMINATION

Once again Ross Brawn had called it right when, analysing the 2013 season in Austin, he had predicted, not without a certain regret as he was about to abandon the Stuttgart team, the Silver Arrows' dominion in 2014. A destiny that was written as soon as the decision was taken to launch the Power Unit project and the 2014 car well ahead of all the team's competitors. "What you will see at the

start of the World Championship is the second car designed, a car that has overturned the initial concept by also introducing brand-new features in other sectors that are not specifically concerned with the new Power Units." Almost as if to confirm this "prophecy", Paddy Lowe added in a candid admission, "what we fielded at the debut in Jerez was the 27th version of the cooling system designed for the W05". Later in the season, the team saw Rosberg take his car to 2nd place in the Canadian GP despite the total black out of his ERS (the two electric motors) and despite suffering severe braking problems, managing to lap at the same times as his rivals with the exception of Ricciardo in the Red Bull. This was evidence that the performance of the W05 was not solely a matter of the efficiency and the management of the Power Unit but also derived from the chassis, the suspension and the aerodynamics. In short, the W05 was one of the best-designed cars in the history of modern F1, together with the Red Bulls of recent seasons and the Ferrari F2002 and F2004 from the beginning of the millennium.

Mercedes W05

Red Bull RB10

THE RED BULL MIRACLE

Perhaps no one at all, not even within the team itself, would have bet on a Red Bull managing to finish in 2nd place in the first race of the season given the interminable series of misadventures the team had suffered in the testing ahead of the championship opener. The correct disqualification for the irregularity of the flow meter noted after that first race nullified the technical miracle performed in just two weeks at Milton Keynes but did nothing to diminish the great qualities of the of the RB10's chassis and aerodynamics. It was no coincidence that every time the Silver Arrows had a problem, it was Red Bull who grasped the opportunity and took the only three races (Montreal, Budapest and Spa) that slipped through the fingers of Hamilton and Rosberg. This was despite the chronic lack of power with respect to the Mercedes, a lack that obliged Newey and his team to radically revise the aerodynamics of the RB10. They had to sacrifice much of the downforce that made the cars so fast through corners, following other paths that allowed them to make up for the deficit in power of the Renault engines and overtake on the straights with decidedly more slippery wings. A policy that really did go against the tide with respect to recent seasons.

A YEAR TO FORGET FOR FERRARI AND McLAREN

It was from 2009 that Ferrari had not finished fourth in the World Championship, a season in which it had at least recorded a victory. To find a year with a similar lack of success, we have to go way back to 1993; these two facts alone reveal the extent to which the 2014 season was an uphill climb for the Prancing Horse. And yet the F14 T was born out of an ambitious project with daring and innovative choices such as that of the oil reservoir that returned after 16 years to the gearbox spacer behind the engine.
The objective was that of creating an extreme aerodynamics package that in the end actually penalised the engineering of the Power Unit in a season in which it became the key component in achieving performance.
Under fire were above all the undersized turbine and compressor, the efficiency of the MGU-H and the exhausts. Work was undertaken on the latter, with experiments also being conducted with Marussia in an attempt to avoid the dispersal of heat that compromised the effectiveness of the MGU-H.
McLaren had a remarkably poor season, with not a single victory despite the great advantage of being able to count on the best Power Unit of the moment, in effect the same that had got the Williams flying as the team returned to the top with the W36 under the direction of Pat Symonds.

NEW FEATURES

2014 saw all-new cars, especially with regards to the layout of the various accessories of the Power Unit, but with innovative features in all the other sectors too.
The first and one of the most interesting came to light just moments after the presentation of the Mercedes: the tuning fork shaped lower front wishbone. Then it was the turn of the McLaren rear suspension and its so-called "shutters" and the fixing of the rear wing assembly with a profile flush with the extractor on the Williams and Toro Rosso. Bahrain then saw the asymmetries of the Lotus: on the dual tusk nose, the sidepods and the exhaust. In Malaysia we saw the compressor positioned at the front of the Mercedes engine and the Ferrari intercooler in the V of the engine. In China came the discovery of the unusual positioning of the intercooler within the monocoque of the Mercedes and lastly, in Hungary, the revolutionary yet inefficient layout of the Ferrari F14 T which after 16 years returned to the positioning of the oil reservoir in the gearbox spacer rather than in front of the engine in a niche in the monocoque.

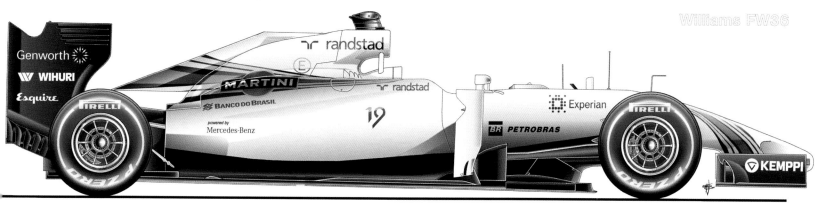

Williams FW36

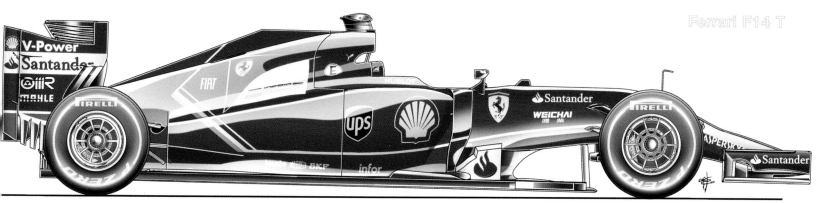

Ferrari F14 T

CONTROVERSIES

There was controversy or at least discontent on the eve of the World Championship and at the first race, above all for fear that reliability issues might have ruined the spectacle. The underwhelming sound of the turbo engines put the noses of many fans out of joint and was less than popular with those working in the sport and the drivers themselves. An attempt was even made to modify the single exhaust imposed by the FIA with a kind of megaphone, but in the end the season unfolded without any major problems and, in the face of the Mercedes dominion, the spectacle was enlivened by the internecine struggle between Hamilton and Rosberg that frequently led to some great racing. The Hungarian GP recalled some of

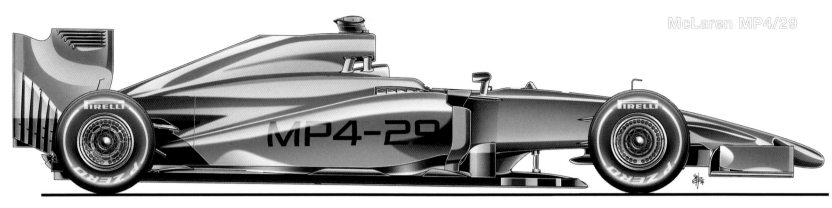

McLaren MP4/29

Force India VJM07

Toro Rosso STR9

Lotus E22

the epic races of F1's golden age.
The additional power provided by the electric motors resulted in counter overtaking out of the corners thanks to the scorching acceleration made possible by the motors.
Apart from the usual summer farce with the banning of the hydraulic interconnection between the suspension of the two axles, only two episodes of technical irregularity were noted. Curiously, they came in the first and last races of the season, with Red Bull the guilty party in both. The first was perhaps the less serious but led to Ricciardo's disqualification after finishing in second place in Australia; the second instead meant he had to start from the pit lane after irregularities were noted following qualifying (see the Controversies chapter).

ADIEU JULES

Traditionally, photographs have never been published in this book but the loss and the memory of Jules Bianchi took us back to the last great bereavements in F1 in the 1994 season at Imola, with the deaths of firstly Roland Ratzenberger and then Ayrton Senna. Since then, enormous progress has been made in terms of safety in Formula 1 and we had perhaps deluded ourselves into thinking that a similar tragedy could not happen again. What occurred at Suzuka, on that horrible, rain-drenched day, actually had little to do with the safety of the cars or their drivers' abilities. A sequence of circumstances arose that should not have happened and today, as unfortunately often happens, the sport is forced to take steps following a tragedy rather than anticipating and preventing it. Only thus could we have avoided the loss of that smile that always accompanied the brief career of Jules Bianchi and his talent, with the miracle at Monaco when he finished in the points, a miracle that represented Formula 1 survival for Marussia.

Lastly, the 2014 edition has again benefitted from the contribution of the author of the Engines chapter, Franco Nugnes, who has become an invaluable consultant for the book, and the work of the engineers Giancarlo Bruno and Kazuhito Kawai for the Tyres chapter.
Particular thanks go to the engineer Andrea Pellegrini (Brembo) for the data and the diagrams provided for the Brakes chapter.
In this edition too, assistance in the visual recounting of the technical developments over the season has been drawn from 3D animations.
The photos on the double page dedicated to Jules Bianchi are instead by Flavio Mazzi.

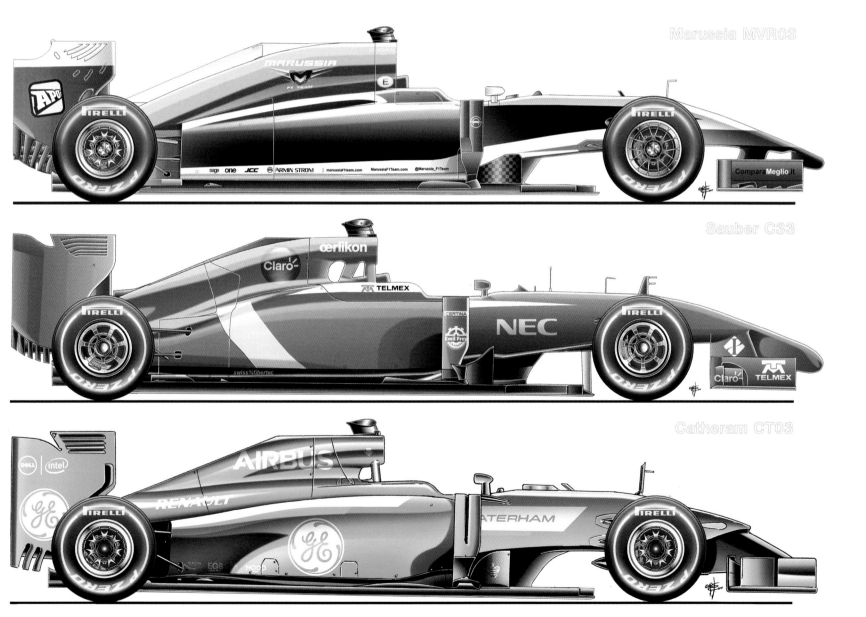

Marussia MVR03

Sauber C33

Catheram CT03

Chassis HYSTORY

Since the parc fermé between qualifying and the race was introduced in 2008 and the T-car was abolished, this section of the book has inevitably become much less interesting. We have therefore restricted the analysis to the three leading teams that, moreover, were unable to assemble their spare chassis in the 2014 season given that only two assembled cars were allowed in the pits. It should also be remembered that in the case of an accident in the initial laps of free practice in the morning, teams are not allowed to assemble the spare for the afternoon session but only for the following day or the race if the accident happens on the Saturday.

FERRARI

Ferrari was the team that constructed the most chassis, a total of seven chassis (306 used only for crash test) for the F14 T, closely followed by Mercedes and Red Bull with four, as in the 2013 season. Williams, the revelation of the 2014 season, also built four chassis.

CURIOSITIES

WINNING CHASSIS

Only three drivers won races in the 2014 season compared with the five in 2013 (the record of eight different drivers and six teams belongs to the 2012 season, when Vettel and Webber for Red Bull, Alonso for Ferrari, Hamilton and Button for McLaren Rosberg for Mercedes, Maldonado for Williams and Raikkonen for Lotus all won at least one race).

MERCEDES • *W05* • N° 44-6

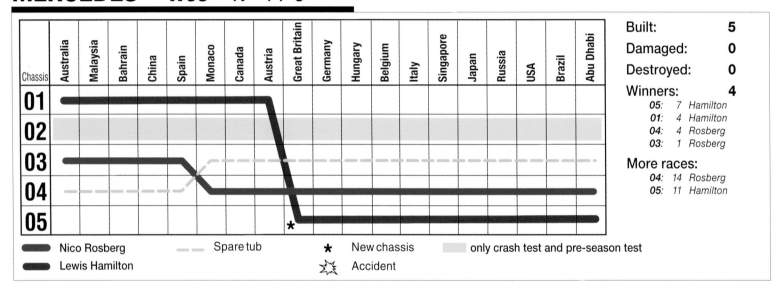

Built: 5
Damaged: 0
Destroyed: 0
Winners: 4
- 05: 7 Hamilton
- 01: 4 Hamilton
- 04: 4 Rosberg
- 03: 1 Rosberg

More races:
- 04: 14 Rosberg
- 05: 11 Hamilton

Nico Rosberg — Spare tub — * New chassis — only crash test and pre-season test
Lewis Hamilton — Accident

RED BULL • *RB10* • N° 1-3

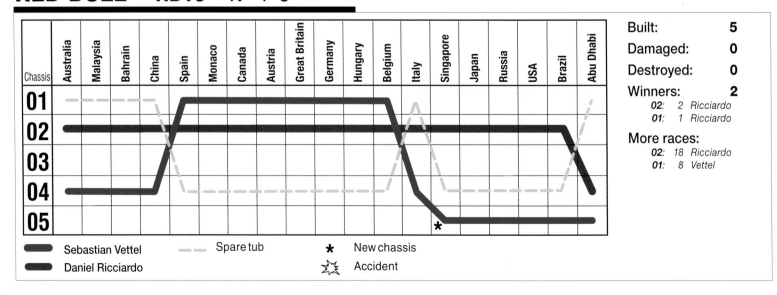

Built: 5
Damaged: 0
Destroyed: 0
Winners: 2
- 02: 2 Ricciardo
- 01: 1 Ricciardo

More races:
- 02: 18 Ricciardo
- 01: 8 Vettel

Sebastian Vettel — Spare tub — * New chassis
Daniel Ricciardo — Accident

FERRARI • *F14 T* • N° 14-7

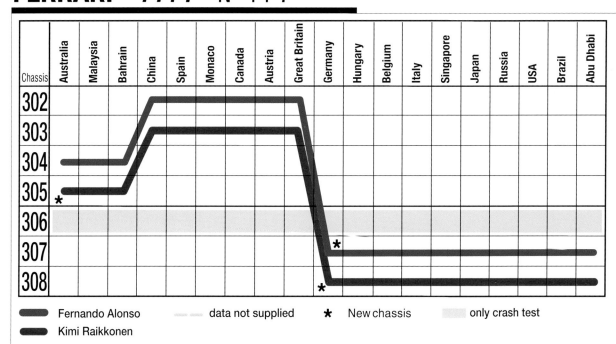

Chassis	Australia	Malaysia	Bahrain	China	Spain	Monaco	Canada	Austria	Great Britain	Germany	Hungary	Belgium	Italy	Singapore	Japan	Russia	USA	Brazil	Abu Dhabi
302																			
303																			
304																			
305	*																		
306																			
307									*										
308									*										

━━━ Fernando Alonso   - - - data not supplied   ***** New chassis   ▨ only crash test
━━━ Kimi Raikkonen

Built:	**7**
Damaged:	**0**
Destroyed:	**0**
Winners:	**0**

More races:
307: 10 Alonso
308: 10 Raikkonen

The drivers who won at least one race in 2013 were Vettel, Alonso, Hamilton, Rosberg and Raikkonen, with Red Bull's German driver dominating in the second half of the season. Mercedes' supremacy in the 2014 season was instead crushing, with no less than 16 victories in 19 races: Hamilton took 11 and Rosberg five. The three remaining wins went to Ricciardo in the Red Bull. The number of winning drivers thus dropped to three.

THE MOST RACES
Among the three leading teams, the chassis that competed in most races, 18 out of 19, was Ricciardo's Red Bull 02, followed by Rosberg's Mercedes 04, Webber's Red Bull 04 on 17 and Hamilton's Mercedes 04 with 14 races; the Mercedes 05 chassis instead competed in 11 races. The same number of races for the Williams 02 but divided between two drivers (seven for Massa and four for Bottas), while on 9 races was chassis 01 (six for Bottas and three for Massa).

WHEELBASES
In contrast with the situation over the previous three seasons, McLaren was not the longest car in the field, that honour going to Red Bull, with 3457.2 mm, followed by Mercedes with 3440 mm, Lotus 3420.7 mm, McLaren 3419 mm, Force India 3411 mm, Ferrari 3398.5 mm, Sauber 3396 mm, Williams 3358 mm, Toro Rosso 3337 mm, Caterham 3328 mm and Marussia 3318 mm. It should be noted that Mercedes, now in second place in this particular list, had fielded the shortest car in the 2011 season at just 3208 mm.

	laps completed	finishes	technical failures	accidents
McLaren	2231 (98,5%)	35	**3** (2) clutch - electronics	0
Ferrari	2144 (94,5%)	35	**2** MGU-K - electrics	0
Mercedes	2112 (93,1%)	33	**4** engine - brakes - gearbox - electrics	1
Red Bull	2065 (91,0%)	32	**3** engine - turbocharger - suspension	0
Williams	2064 (91,0%)	33	**1** engine	4
Force India	1926 (84,9%)	30	**3** hydraulics - gearbox - MGU-K	5
Toro Rosso	1895 (83,5%)	28	**10** (3) exhausts - chassis - undertrail - gearbox - brakes - puncture driveshaft - electrics	0
Lotus	1800 (79,3%)	24	**14** (5) engine - (2) MGU-K - (2) rear wing - (2) water leak gearbox - turbocharger - brakes	0
Sauber	1790 (78,9%)	23	**7** (2) battery - engine - gearbox - MGU-K - electrics - water leak	8
Marussia	1523 (67,1%)	24	**2** brakes - gearbox	5
Caterham	1432 (63,1%)	21	**11** (2) oil leak - (2) suspension - engine - brakes fuel pressure - electrics - electronics - vibrations	2

The most reliable team was McLaren with an incredible 98.2% of the total championship laps completed. Next came Ferrari with 94.5%, Mercedes with 93.1% and Red Bull and Williams both on 91%.; these figures were all the more significant given that this was the first season for the hybrid cars. The least reliable proved to be Caterham with 63.1%. The team that had the most accidents was Sauber with eight, followed by Force India with six and Williams with four.

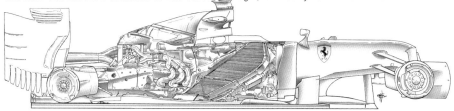

Chassis F14 T	302	303	304	305	306	307	308
First run	28/01/2014	18/04/2014	25/02/2014	14/03/2014		18/07/2014	18/07/2014
Track	Jerez	China	Bahrain	Australia	only	Germany	Germany
Km test	3230,1	0	1915,4	894,9	crash	0	972,5
Km race	4215,3	3765,8	2247,7	2227,5	test	6752,1	7648,4

Car TABLE

		44-6 MERCEDES	1-3 RED BULL	19-77 WILLIAMS	14-7 FERRARI	22-20 McLAREN
CAR		**W05**	**RB10**	**FW35**	**F14 T**	**MP4-29**
	Designers	Paddy Lowe Andy Cowell	Adrian Newey Rob Marshall	Pat Symonds	James Allison Pat Fry	Timo Goss Jonatan Neale Neil Oatley
	Race engineers	Tony Ross (6) Peter Bonington (44)	Guillaume Rocquelin (1) Simon Rennie (3)	Andrew Murdoch (19) Jonathan Eddolls (77)	Andrea Stella (14) Antonio Spagnolo (7)	Dave Robson (22) Mark Temple (20)
	Chief mechanic	Mattew Deane	Kenny Handkammer	Carl Garden	Francesco Ugozzoni	Jonathan Brookes
CHASSIS	Front track	1470 mm	1440 mm*	1480 mm	1470 mm	1470 mm*
	Rear track	1405 mm*	1410 mm*	1420 mm	1405 mm*	1405 mm*
	Front suspension	2+1 dampers and torsion bars	2+1 dampers and torsion bars	2+1 dampers and torsion bars	Pull-rod 2+1 dampers and torsion bars	Push-rod 2+1 dampers and torsion bars
	Rear suspension	Pull-rod 2+1 dampers and torsion bars	Pull-rod 2+1 dampers and torsion bars	Pull-rod 2+1 dampers and torsion bars	Pull-rod 2+1 dampers and torsion bars	Pull-rod 2+1 dampers and torsion bars
	Dampers	Sachs	Multimatic	Williams	Sachs	McLaren
	Brakes calipers	Brembo	Brembo	A+P	Brembo	Akebono
	Brakes discs	Brembo Carbon Industrie	Brembo	Carbon Industrie	Brembo CCR Carbon Industrie	Carbon Industrie Brembo
	Wheels	BBS	O.Z.	O.Z.	BBS	Enkey
	Radiators	Secan	Marston	IMI Marston	Secan	Calsonic - IMI
	Oil tank	middle position inside fuel tank	middle position inside fuel tank	middle position inside fuel tank	in gearbox	middle position inside fuel tank
GEARBOX		Longitudinal carbon	Longitudinal carbon	Longitudinal titanium	Longitudinal carbon	Longitudinal carbon
	Gear selection	Semiautomatic 8 gears	Semiautomatic 8 gears	Semiautomatic 8 gears	Semiautomatic 8 gears	Semiautomatic 8 gears
	Clutch	Sachs	A+P	A+P	Sachs	A+P
	Pedals	2	2	2	2	2
ENGINE		Mercedes PU106A hybrid	Renault energy F1 2014	Mercedes PU106A hybrid	Ferrari 059/3	Mercedes PU106A hybrid
	Total capacity	1600 cmc	1600 cmc	1600 cmc	1600 cmc	1600 cmc
	N° cylinders and V	6 - V90	6 - V90	6 - V90	6 - V90	6 - V90
	Electronics	Mercedes	Magneti Marelli	Mercedes	Magneti Marelli	McLaren el.sys.
	Fuel	Petronas	Total	Total	Shell	Mobil
	Oil	Petronas	Total	Total	Shell	Mobil
	Dashboard	Mercedes	Red Bull	Williams	Magneti Marelli	McLaren

[1] non official value   *extimated value

27-11 FORCE INDIA	25-26 TORO ROSSO	8-13 LOTUS	17-4 MARUSSIA	21-99 SAUBER	9-10 CATERHAM
WJM07	STR9	E22	MR03	C33	CT05
Adrew Green	James Key	Nick Chester	Jhon Mc Quillam	Eric Gandelin	Jhon Ileay
G. Lambiase (27) Bradley Joyce (11)	Xevi Pijolar (25) Marco Matassa (26)	Ayao Komastsu (8) Mark Slade (13)	Francesco Neri (17) Gary Gannon (4)	Marco Schüpbach (99) Graig Gardiner (21)	Angel Baena (9) Tim Wright (10)
Nicholas Howe Greg Borrill	Domiziano Facchinetti	Greg Baker	Richard Wrenn	Reto Camenzind	Stuart Cramp
1480 mm	1440 mm	1450 mm	1470 mm	1460 mm	1440 mm
1410 mm	1410 mm	1420 mm	1405 mm*	1400 mm	1410 mm
2+1 dampers and torsion bars	2+1 dampers and torsion bars	2+1 dampers and torsion bars	2+1 dampers and torsion bars	2+1 dampers and torsion bars	2+1 dampers and torsion bars
Pull-rod 2+1 dampers and torsion bars	Pull-rod 2+1 dampers and torsion bars	Pull-rod 2+1 dampers and torsion bars	Pull-rod 2+1 dampers and torsion bars	Pull-rod 2+1 dampers and torsion bars	Pull-rod 2+1 dampers and torsion bars
Sachs	Koni	Penske	Sachs	Sachs	Koni
A+P	Brembo	A+P	A+P	Brembo	A+P
Hitco	Brembo	Hitco	Hitco	Brembo	Hitco
BBS	O.Z.	AVUS	BBS	O.Z.	BBS
Secan	Marston	Marston	Secan	Calsonic	Marston
middle position inside fuel tank	middle position inside fuel tank	middle position inside fuel tank	in gearbox	in gearbox	middle position inside fuel tank
Longitudinal carbon	Longitudinal carbon	Longitudinal titanium	Longitudinal carbon	Longitudinal carbon	Longitudinal titanium
Semiautomatic 8 gears	Semiautomatic 8 gears	Semiautomatic 8 gears	Semiautomatic 8 gears	Semiautomatic 8 gears	Semiautomatic 8 gears
A+P	A+P	A+P	A+P	A+P	A+P
2	2	2	2	2	2
Mercedes PU106A hybrid	Renault energy F1 2014	Renault energy F1 2014	Ferrari 059/3	Ferrari 059/3	Renault energy F1 2014
1600 cmc	1600 cmc	1600 cmc	1600 cmc	1600 cmc	1600 cmc
6 - V90	6 - V90	6 - V90	6 - V90	6 - V90	6 - V90
Mercedes	Magneti Marelli	Magneti Marelli	Magneti Marelli	Magneti Marelli	Magneti Marelli
Petronas	Total[1]	Total	Shell	Shell[1]	Total
Petronas	Total[1]	Total	Shell	Shell[1]	Total
P.I.	Toro Rosso	Renault F1	Magneti Marelli	Magneti Marelli	P.I.

2014 REGULATIONS

The Federation decided to actuate what was an epochal revolution in F1 for the 2014 season, without doubt the greatest technical upheaval in the modern history of the sport. It was even more far-reaching than the one introduced after the dramatic accidents at Imola in '94 with the introduction of the stepped bottom, aerodynamic restrictions and the mass of safety regulations that represented a true turning point in the history of modern F1 and, obviously, the one introduced in '99 that principally concerned two sectors, aerodynamics and the introduction of KERS. This time the revolution concerned every sector of the car, from the 1.6-litre V6 engines now fitted with turbocharging and a dual KERS energy recovery system known as MGU-K with double the power and MGU-H, where the H stands for heat, this time associated with the heat generated by the turbine, through to the aerodynamic package and the installation of the components on the car. The end result was radically modified cars that were substantially more complex and in certain cases extremely unattractive.

We begin the analysis of the new regulations with the exterior appearance of the cars, without for now entering into the merit of the specific interpretations adopted by the individual teams even though, as is always the case when virtually starting over from scratch, the novelties were so numerous and of such magnitude as to make the 2014 season particularly interesting. In this section we have adapted, deliberately and without flights of fancy, the new regulations to the Red Bull that since 2009 had dominated the F1 scene, bullishly entering the realm of the milestones that have marked the technical development

of this sport. There were two new restrictions that made the 2014 cars completely different in their external appearance: the drastic reduction in the height of the chassis and noses and the 15 cm reduction in width of the front wing.

The first new regulation was dictated by safety concerns. It was intended to limit damage in the case of T-bone collisions between cars and above all to prevent cars from taking off in the case of collisions. There was not simply a return to the low noses seen in the past, the last of which being that of the Brawn GP from 2009, which for simplicity's sake we have exemplified in the drawing. Noses of bizarre shapes have appeared: ant-eater, tapir and proboscis, all attempts to find the least detrimental aerodynamic form possible that compensates for the loss of downforce associated with the new regulations. It has to be pointed out that a number of the new low noses aroused a degree of doubt and convinced the Federation to modify the regulations for the 2015 season. The loss of aerodynamic efficiency derived not so much from the reduction in size of the wings (both front and rear profiles were restricted), but from the elimination of the exhaust blowing that made the diffusers extremely efficient. In 2014 the blowing of the exhausts in the zone ahead of the rear wheels, a feature that had attracted extensive and expensive development the pre-

vious year, was effectively prohibited through the adoption of special sidepods designed to exploit the Coanda effect. In place of the blowing effect there is a single central duct that is long enough to exit behind the rear axle and thus denying any aerodynamic advantage. The complexity of the Power Unit tripled the problems faced by the designers in terms of heat dispersal with the introduction alongside the usual radiators of dedicated intercoolers for each component element of the Power Unit. For the same reason, the minimum weight was increased from 642 to no less than 690 kg given the increased bulk of the Power Unit (155 kg) and batteries (20-25 kg). Furthermore, at the front the sidepods had to enclose longer deformable protection structures that as per the regulations had to be identical for all cars and were designed on behalf of the FIA by Red Bull.

BATTERY PACK
The regulations dictated that the battery pack for the electric motors had to be had to be located in the fuel tank area, as on the Ferrari ever since the introduction of KERS way back in 2009 (highlighted in the drawing).

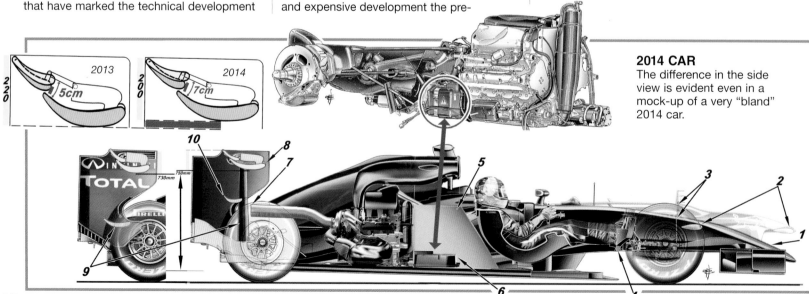

2014 CAR
The difference in the side view is evident even in a mock-up of a very "bland" 2014 car.

2013 5cm

2014 7cm

FRONT VIEW

A comparison between the two major vertical restrictions. The first concerned the initial rib of the chassis (A-A) that had to have a height from the reference plane of between 625 and 525 mm as well as possibly a similar reduction of 100 mm in the chassis floor, given that the section of the chassis had to remain unvaried. The second penalised the rear wing with a reduction in encumbrance of 20 mm that directly affected downforce.

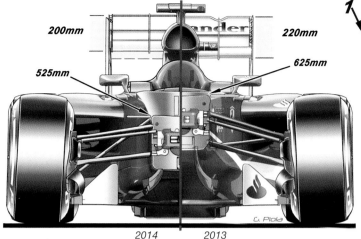

200mm 220mm
525mm 625mm

2014   2013

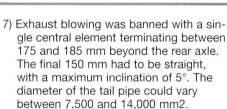

1 180cm
   165cm

2

2014   2013

SIDE PROTECTION STRUCTURE
ART. 15.4.3 AND ART 18.9.2

Again in terms of safety, the FIA modified the impact absorbing structures protecting the survival cell. Through to the 2006 season all teams used structures attached to the chassis, as seen in the drawing of the Ferrari chassis from that year. In the 2007 season, the Maranello-based team integrated them with the bottom of the car, a practice soon widely copied. For the 2014 season, not only did the FIA insist that the protections be fixed solidly to the chassis, but imposed structures (4) that were the same for all teams, choosing the Red Bull design after a kind of tender. Their greater length (highlighted in the Top View) made the front part of the sidepods more bulky.

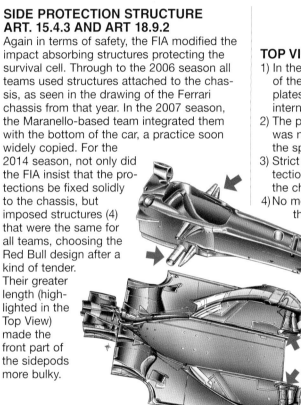

TOP VIEW

1) In the top view we can see how the reduction in width of the front wing eliminated the alignment of the end-plates with the front wheels, which now impacted internally by 65 mm more each side (art 3.4.1).

2) The positioning of the video cameras in the nose section was no longer free but strictly regulated, as illustrated in the specific drawing.

3) Strict regulations concerned the deformable chassis protection structures. They had to be longer, rigidly fixed to the chassis and the same for all cars.

4) No more blowing from the exhausts in the end section of the sidepods. The exhaust had to have a single tail pipe.

5) Strict limits on the single exhaust from the 1600 cc V6 turbo: the last 150 mm had to be straight and reach at least 1750 mm beyond the rear axle and be no more than 1850 mm in height (art. 5.8.2); The vertical limit was between 350 and 550 mm from the reference plane (art. 5.8.4) with an inclination tolerance of +5° and -5°.

6) In recompense, the so-called monkey seat, the mini-profiles in the area above the deformable structure, could have a width of 200 mm, 50 mm more than in the 2013 season.

3

4

175mm
185mm

5

6 100mm 75mm

1) The reduction in the height of the nose is notable, passing from 525 mm to just 185 mm at 700 mm from the front axle. As in 2013, the nose could now be extended with an overhang of up to 1,200 mm. The width of the front wing was reduced from 1800 mm, the same as the full width of the car, to 1650 mm (highlighted in the overhead view) while the 50 mm central section that had to be neutral for all cars remained.

2) The position of the video cameras was regulated, with the teams no longer free to interpret the rules like Red Bull and Williams with their hammerhead configuration; they instead had to be located at the start of the nose, at a height of between 325 and 525 mm from the reference plane.

3) The height of the chassis was reduced from 625 to 525 mm with its end section unvaried (A-A), while the bodywork could reach 625 mm, as in the 2013 season. This meant that the driver could have his feet placed 10 cm lower (5) as shown in this diagram. In reality in most cases the designers came up with configurations that maintained the lower part of chassis high.

4) In almost every case the driver had the same position.

5) The capacity of the fuel tank was severely restricted to just 100 kgs.
The batteries had to be in a single pack, located in the fuel tank area with no duplex elements as in the case of the Red Bull.

7) Exhaust blowing was banned with a single central element terminating between 175 and 185 mm beyond the rear axle. The final 150 mm had to be straight, with a maximum inclination of 5°. The diameter of the tail pipe could vary between 7,500 and 14,000 mm2.

8) The rear wing was also restricted to a box reduced in height by 20 cm. On the other hand, the adjustable flap DRS opening was enlarged from 50 mm to 70 mm.

9) Moreover, the lower profile to which the whole rear wing assembly was fixed was outlawed (art. 3.9.2)
In most cases long vertical supports returned.

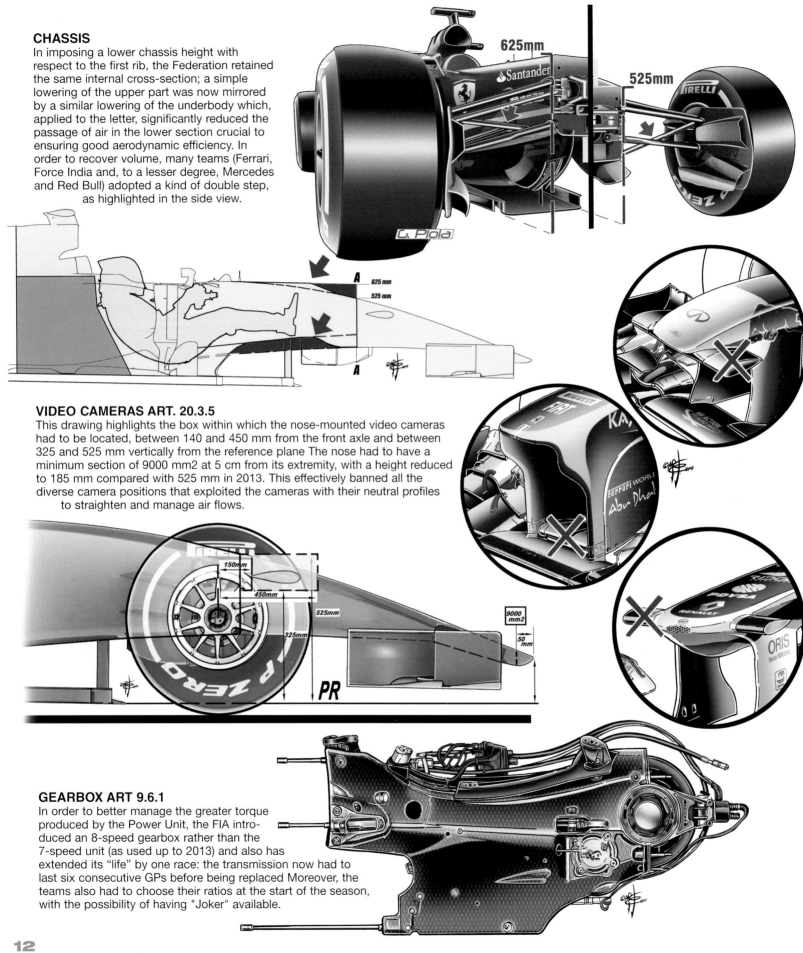

CHASSIS

In imposing a lower chassis height with respect to the first rib, the Federation retained the same internal cross-section; a simple lowering of the upper part was now mirrored by a similar lowering of the underbody which, applied to the letter, significantly reduced the passage of air in the lower section crucial to ensuring good aerodynamic efficiency. In order to recover volume, many teams (Ferrari, Force India and, to a lesser degree, Mercedes and Red Bull) adopted a kind of double step, as highlighted in the side view.

625mm

525mm

A
625 mm
525 mm
A

VIDEO CAMERAS ART. 20.3.5

This drawing highlights the box within which the nose-mounted video cameras had to be located, between 140 and 450 mm from the front axle and between 325 and 525 mm vertically from the reference plane The nose had to have a minimum section of 9000 mm2 at 5 cm from its extremity, with a height reduced to 185 mm compared with 525 mm in 2013. This effectively banned all the diverse camera positions that exploited the cameras with their neutral profiles to straighten and manage air flows.

150mm

450mm

525mm

325mm

9000 mm2

50 mm

PR

GEARBOX ART 9.6.1

In order to better manage the greater torque produced by the Power Unit, the FIA introduced an 8-speed gearbox rather than the 7-speed unit (as used up to 2013) and also has extended its "life" by one race: the transmission now had to last six consecutive GPs before being replaced Moreover, the teams also had to choose their ratios at the start of the season, with the possibility of having "Joker" available.

POWER UNIT ART. 5.1.2/3/4/5/6/7

The major novelty of the 2014 season was that the era of F1 cars powered by a single internal combustion engine (the last major change in this respect being the banning of turbos at the end of the 1988 season) came to an end with the introduction of a power unit composed of a turbocharged 90° V6 engine mated to two electric motors. The "old" KERS, with double the power, known as MGU-K and as ever associated with the recovery of energy from the rear brakes, was now joined by the new MGU-H in which the H stood for heat, with the system recovering energy from the hot gases exiting the turbine. The supplementary power virtually doubled, increasing from 60 kW for just 6.7 seconds per lap to no less than 120 kW for 30 seconds; at the same time, MGU-H could recharge the batteries as well as transfer energy directly to the other electric motor or adapt the turbine speed to the engine speed. The Power Unit had a minimum weight of 155 kg (art. 5.41) while the battery pack had to be a single unit of between 20 and 25 kg.

This drawing highlights the main components of the new Power Unit with their weights (blue) and the maximum operating temperatures (red) that must be respected via dedicated cooling systems in order for them to perform effectively.

The configuration is that of Renault and Ferrari, with the in-unit turbo assembly, while Mercedes instead provided for the separation of the two components. The MGU-H was connected to this assembly and was subject to greater thermal stress with respect to the Mercedes layout. The MGH-K, the KERS from 2013, was on the left-hand side of the engine As well as the weights listed, the inverters accounted for 3.5 kg and cables and other components another 10 kg for an overall weight for the entire Power Unit of around 50/60 kg

In order to reduce power outputs, the FIA imposed a drastic reduction of fuel tank capacity (just 100 kg) and a similar reduction in fuel flow that could not exceed 100 kg/h compared with around 130 kg/h in 2013. This parameter was controlled not via the injector jets, but with a flow meter built directly for the FIA by the American firm Gill.

Battery

25 Kg
80°

MGU-K

10 Kg
200°

MGU-H

5/6 Kg
200°

Compressor

200°

Turbo

1000°

MINIMUM WEIGHT (ART. 4.1)

In order to compensate for the increased complexity of the power unit and its in-car installation, the FIA increased the minimum weight from 642 to 690 kg. The distribution between the two axles was unchanged with 314 kg on the front axle and 369 kg on the rear. The drawing also shows the larger lateral protection structures (art. 15.4.3).

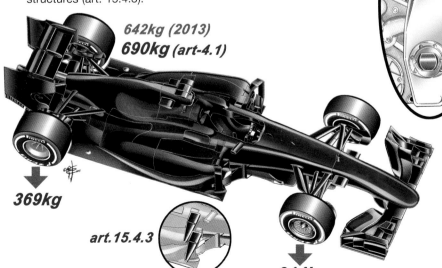

642kg (2013)
690kg (art-4.1)

369kg

art.15.4.3

314kg

KERS 2009

KERS was introduced in 2009 and this drawing shows it connected to the crankshaft at the front of the Ferrari V8, placed in the hollow in the chassis that once housed the oil tank (a configuration already adopted in 1998 by Alan Jenkins on the Stewart and by John Barnard on the Arrows).

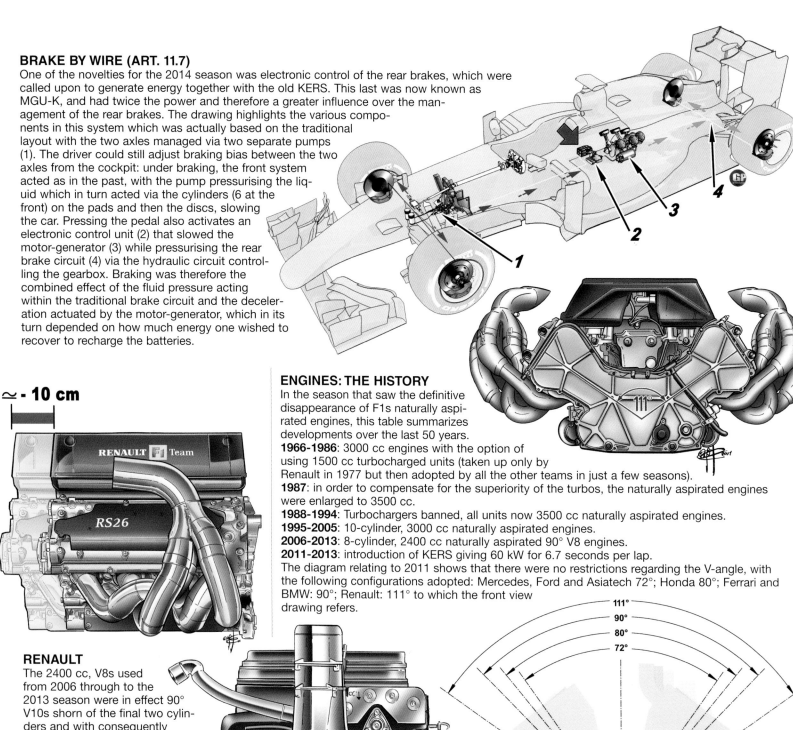

BRAKE BY WIRE (ART. 11.7)

One of the novelties for the 2014 season was electronic control of the rear brakes, which were called upon to generate energy together with the old KERS. This last was now known as MGU-K, and had twice the power and therefore a greater influence over the management of the rear brakes. The drawing highlights the various components in this system which was actually based on the traditional layout with the two axles managed via two separate pumps (1). The driver could still adjust braking bias between the two axles from the cockpit: under braking, the front system acted as in the past, with the pump pressurising the liquid which in turn acted via the cylinders (6 at the front) on the pads and then the discs, slowing the car. Pressing the pedal also activates an electronic control unit (2) that slowed the motor-generator (3) while pressurising the rear brake circuit (4) via the hydraulic circuit controlling the gearbox. Braking was therefore the combined effect of the fluid pressure acting within the traditional brake circuit and the deceleration actuated by the motor-generator, which in its turn depended on how much energy one wished to recover to recharge the batteries.

≃ - 10 cm

ENGINES: THE HISTORY

In the season that saw the definitive disappearance of F1s naturally aspirated engines, this table summarizes developments over the last 50 years.

1966-1986: 3000 cc engines with the option of using 1500 cc turbocharged units (taken up only by Renault in 1977 but then adopted by all the other teams in just a few seasons).

1987: in order to compensate for the superiority of the turbos, the naturally aspirated engines were enlarged to 3500 cc.

1988-1994: Turbochargers banned, all units now 3500 cc naturally aspirated engines.

1995-2005: 10-cylinder, 3000 cc naturally aspirated engines.

2006-2013: 8-cylinder, 2400 cc naturally aspirated 90° V8 engines.

2011-2013: introduction of KERS giving 60 kW for 6.7 seconds per lap.

The diagram relating to 2011 shows that there were no restrictions regarding the V-angle, with the following configurations adopted: Mercedes, Ford and Asiatech 72°; Honda 80°; Ferrari and BMW: 90°; Renault: 111° to which the front view drawing refers.

RENAULT

The 2400 cc, V8s used from 2006 through to the 2013 season were in effect 90° V10s shorn of the final two cylinders and with consequently reduced longitudinal dimensions.

FERRARI

All the engines of the 2013 season had the same 90° V8 architecture and were frozen in development terms to reduce costs, guaranteeing very similar performance levels to the advantage of close racing.

90°

111°
90°
80°
72°

New DEVELOPMENTS

The greatest technical revolution in the history of modern F1 gave rise to a season particularly rich in technical innovations. The F1 cars were radically revised in terms of the various mechanical assemblies in a clear break with the recent past. Obviously, the focus was on the problems associated with the installation and use of the complex Power Units that replaced the old 2400 cc naturally aspirated V8s, and much of the season's development work concentrated on integrating the various systems to bets effect.

However, other areas of the car also boasted brand-new features. The brakes, above all, with the introduction of electronic control of the rear wheels, represented the most important and most complex novelty, closely followed by the integration of the two electric motors with the 1600 cc V6 engine and their complex management. As is always the case when starting out with a blank sheet, new features appeared in other areas too, from aerodynamics to suspension.

Two cars in particular distinguished themselves for the number of their new features, although they enjoyed very different fortunes. From the first winter tests Mercedes stood out as the great protagonist, while the Ferrari only revealed all its secrets in mid-season and unfortunately failed to harvest the results its designers had hoped for. The Maranello-based team effectively fielded a more revolutionary car than Mercedes, but the left-field choices made at Maranello eventually proved to be more of a handicap than an advantage. The W05 was therefore crowned queen of the season, its concentration of innovative features seeing off even the Red Bull of the wizard Adrian Newey that suffered problems with its Renault-supplied Power Unit.

MERCEDES

The GP of China revealed the secret of the Mercedes W05's extremely compact side-pods which relied on the integration of the water/air intercooler inside the chassis (8), highlighted in yellow. This feature could not be copied as it would have required the redesigning of the chassis to create the necessary housing.

1) The internal combustion engine's radiators were practically unchanged with respect to those of the 2013 car.
2) The exhaust manifolds wrapped in insulating material were very compact and short and improved aerodynamic efficiency and heat dispersal even though they cost around 15 hp in maximum power.
3) In order to reduce vibration, two reinforcing rods were added to the cylinder head.
4) The exhaust connection to the turbo.
5) The two additional radiators for the gearbox and the hydraulic circuit with separate cooling ducts.
6) The hot air vent almost at the end of the engine cover in the area of the turbo.
7) The supplementary cooling intakes for the radiators.

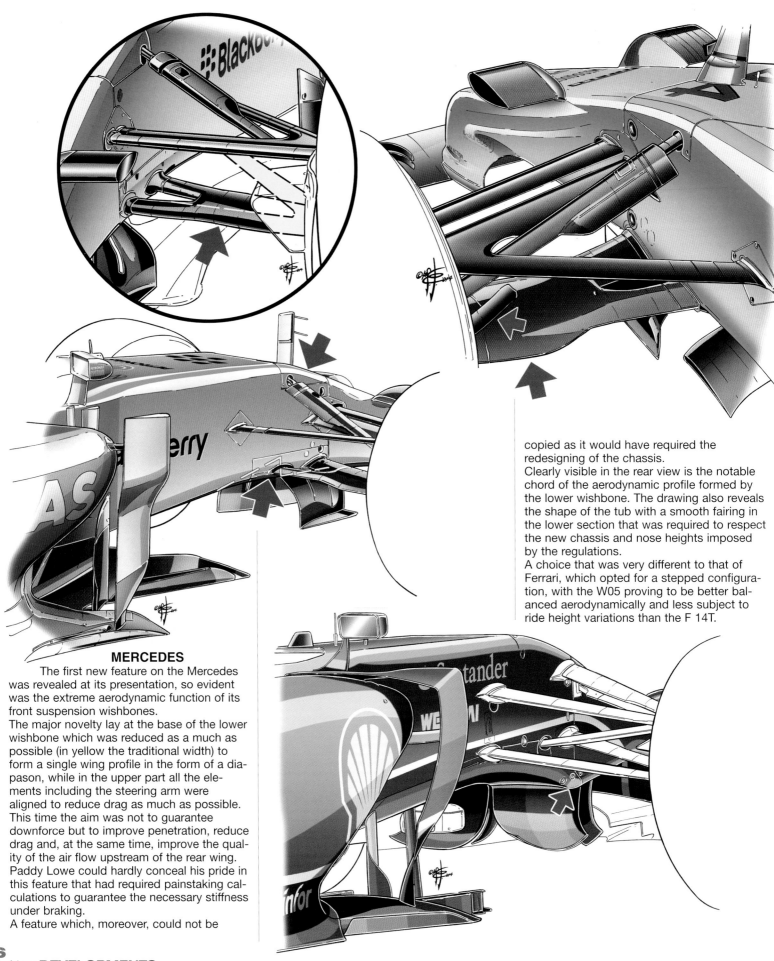

copied as it would have required the redesigning of the chassis.

Clearly visible in the rear view is the notable chord of the aerodynamic profile formed by the lower wishbone. The drawing also reveals the shape of the tub with a smooth fairing in the lower section that was required to respect the new chassis and nose heights imposed by the regulations.

A choice that was very different to that of Ferrari, which opted for a stepped configuration, with the W05 proving to be better balanced aerodynamically and less subject to ride height variations than the F 14T.

MERCEDES

The first new feature on the Mercedes was revealed at its presentation, so evident was the extreme aerodynamic function of its front suspension wishbones.

The major novelty lay at the base of the lower wishbone which was reduced as a much as possible (in yellow the traditional width) to form a single wing profile in the form of a diapason, while in the upper part all the elements including the steering arm were aligned to reduce drag as much as possible. This time the aim was not to guarantee downforce but to improve penetration, reduce drag and, at the same time, improve the quality of the air flow upstream of the rear wing. Paddy Lowe could hardly conceal his pride in this feature that had required painstaking calculations to guarantee the necessary stiffness under braking.

A feature which, moreover, could not be

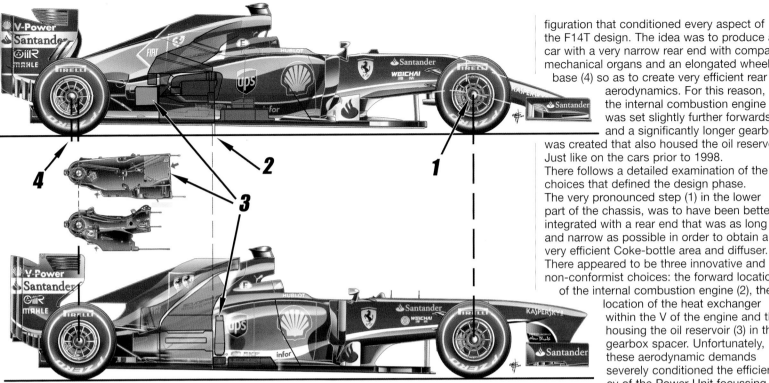

figuration that conditioned every aspect of the F14T design. The idea was to produce a car with a very narrow rear end with compact mechanical organs and an elongated wheelbase (4) so as to create very efficient rear aerodynamics. For this reason, the internal combustion engine was set slightly further forwards and a significantly longer gearbox was created that also housed the oil reservoir. Just like on the cars prior to 1998.

There follows a detailed examination of the choices that defined the design phase. The very pronounced step (1) in the lower part of the chassis, was to have been better integrated with a rear end that was as long and narrow as possible in order to obtain a very efficient Coke-bottle area and diffuser. There appeared to be three innovative and non-conformist choices: the forward location of the internal combustion engine (2), the location of the heat exchanger within the V of the engine and the housing the oil reservoir (3) in the gearbox spacer. Unfortunately, these aerodynamic demands severely conditioned the efficiency of the Power Unit focussing on a united turbine-compressor and MGU-H assembly that was above all much smaller than that of its Mercedes rival.

This was in part so that another innovation could be introduced, the location of the heat exchanger in the V of the engine, which once again helped render the whole more compact. Also dictated by the same demands was the layout of the narrow, high exhausts that freed up the lower area.

FERRARI REVOLUTIONARY LAYOUT

Only in the race that concluded the 2013 edition of this technical analysis, the Hungarian GP in which Alonso's Ferrari finished in 2nd place, did it become clear that the F14T was by no means a traditional car based on fairly conservative technical choices with respect to its bolder rivals such as the Red Bull, as had instead been the case in previous seasons. The F14T project was brave and in many ways non-conformist; as has been the case with other features introduced in recent seasons, it represented a step back in time of no less than 16 years with regard to the con-

figuration of a very important mechanical element. A similar situation to that of the pull-rod rear suspension reintroduced by Adrian Newey on his RB 5 from 2009, after 21 years of the push-rod layout. With the F14T Ferrari went back to locating the oil reservoir in the gearbox, as it did through to 1998, when Stewart and Arrows introduced the revolutionary location in a dedicated niche between engine and chassis. A revolution that immediately caught on and has been adopt through to the present on all the other cars. Behind this choice is an extreme aerodynamic con-

COMPRESSOR

This detail drawing shows that in the case of the Ferrari, the area below the heat exchanger is free while on the Mercedes it is occupied by the classic vertical tank. This because the oil reservoir was moved to the rear of the engine, inside the gearbox casing. This freed up space in the area permitting a very compact and narrow mechanical layout at the rear.

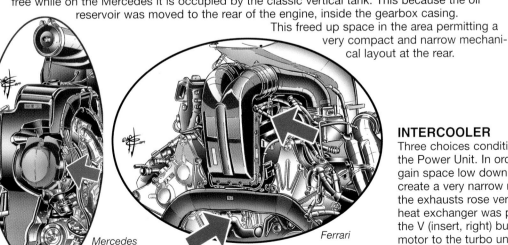

Mercedes   *Ferrari*

INTERCOOLER

Three choices conditioned the Power Unit. In order to gain space low down and create a very narrow rear end, the exhausts rose vertically, the heat exchanger was positioned inside the V (insert, right) but, above all, it was decided to attach the electric motor to the turbo unit (insert, left), which was much more compact than the separate configuration adopted by Mercedes.

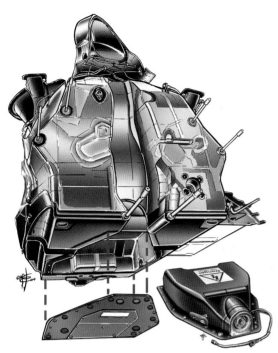

STEWART 1998

One of the most significant revolutions in the field of modern F1 automotive architecture dates back to 1998. In parallel, Alan Jenkins and John Barnard shifted on their respective Stewart and Arrows cars, the oil reservoir from the classic location inside the gearbox casing or spacer to the front of the engine. Two major advantages immediately derived from this layout, the greater concentration of weight around the centre of gravity and ease of installation, with ducting for the radiators reduced to a minimum thus saving weight and space.

EMPTY SPACE

This is the space that was freed up at the rear of the chassis by eliminating the oil reservoir. Clearly, the niche that housed it has been eliminated while the larger battery and CPU assembly is still housed in the lower part of the chassis housing the fuel tank.

MARCH 721

For the record it should be noted that there were sporadic, chronologically distant, examples of cars with centrally located oil reservoirs. For example, the McLaren M28 which proved to be a disaster of a car, the Brabham BT 42 and, above all, the first to adopt the feature, the March 721, another uncompetitive car.

FERRARI 1998

In the era of the technical revolution sparked by Stewart and Arrows, Ferrari boasted a new feature on its car inherited from John Barnard himself, a rear end composed of three pieces: a fabricated titanium transmission unit containing the gears, combined with a carbonfibre spacer containing the oil reservoir and the rear deformable structure, also in carbonfibre.

FERRARI AND RENAULT

The front-mounted oil reservoir had remained a feature of all cars with the exception of Ferrari through to the present. The drawings show the Ferrari 2009 and the Red Bull Renault 2013 engines, highlighting the vertical oil reservoirs and the location of the KERS electric motor.

McLAREN

There was much talk in the winter tests about the novelty introduced by McLaren on the MP4-29 given the generous dimensions of the aerodynamic appendices fitted to the rear suspension arms. In order to compensate for the abolition of the lower profile known as the beam wing imposed by the regulations, the gearbox and the suspension were designed so as to form a kind of shutter via two conspicuous fairings that McLaren called butterflies on the tie-rod and the rear arm of the lower wishbone. Their very overhanging position allowed the extraction effect of the diffuser to be exploited to the full, thus increasing downforce. This feature also remained unique to the team as it would have required the reworking of the entire rear end.

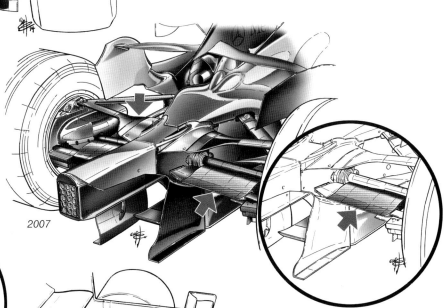

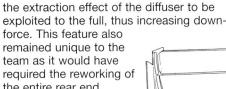

2007

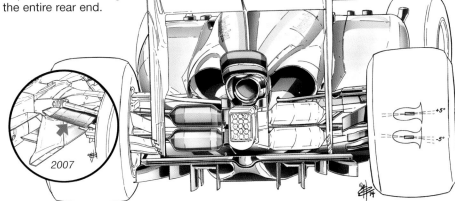

2013

2007

2007

Tyrrell 1996

McLAREN

As early as the 2013 season, McLaren had actuated notable development of the form of the wishbones and brake air intakes in order to draw aerodynamic benefits. Back in 2007 a conspicuous aerodynamic profile had been introduced behind the drive-shaft, a feature subsequently reprised by Adrian Newey on his 2012 Red Bull and then adopted on all the cars (see the New Features 2013 chapter). All were throwbacks to the original feature introduced by Newey himself on the Williams FW16, that of the Senna tragedy in '94, aligning the tie-rod and the lower wishbone so that the sum of the their fairings created a single wide aerodynamic profile, a feature then copied on all of the 2014 season cars. The McLaren Mp4/29 exploited the regulations to the full, eventually giving rise to the excesses of the '96 season (Tyrrell drawing), when the suspension elements were fully faired with wide aerodynamic profiles and the regulations imposed very precise restrictions: the 3.5:1 ratio between the chord and depth of the profile, its perfect symmetry and the tolerance of just 5° plus or minus with respect to the horizontal.

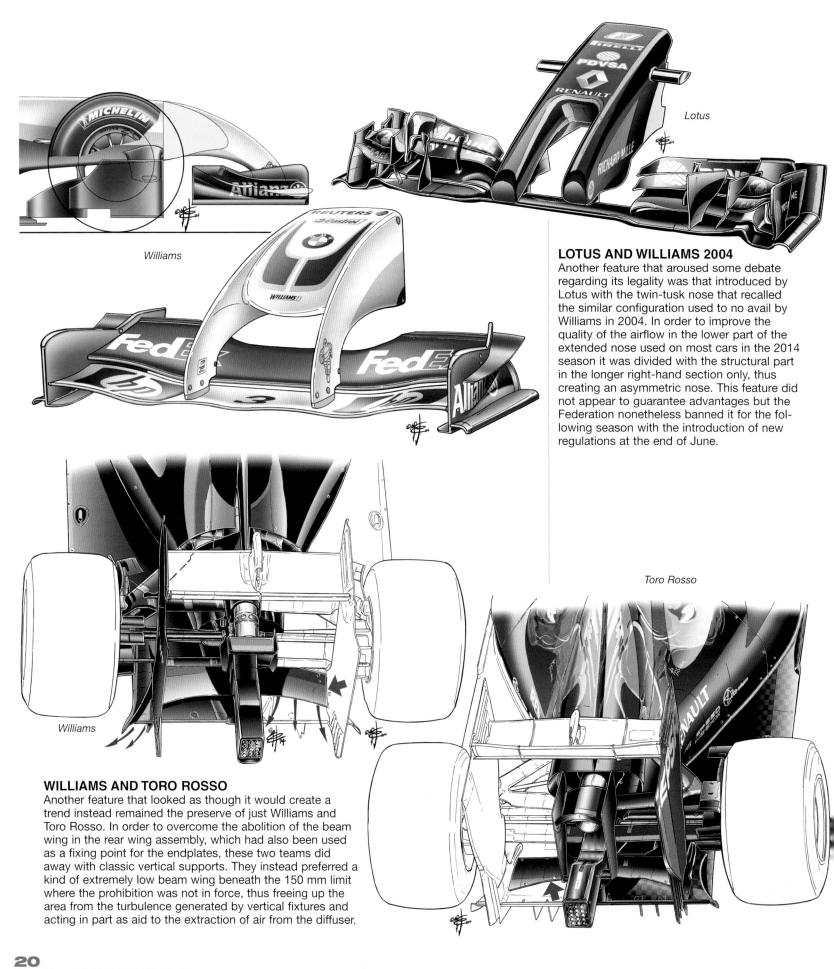

Williams

Lotus

LOTUS AND WILLIAMS 2004
Another feature that aroused some debate regarding its legality was that introduced by Lotus with the twin-tusk nose that recalled the similar configuration used to no avail by Williams in 2004. In order to improve the quality of the airflow in the lower part of the extended nose used on most cars in the 2014 season it was divided with the structural part in the longer right-hand section only, thus creating an asymmetric nose. This feature did not appear to guarantee advantages but the Federation nonetheless banned it for the following season with the introduction of new regulations at the end of June.

Toro Rosso

Williams

WILLIAMS AND TORO ROSSO
Another feature that looked as though it would create a trend instead remained the preserve of just Williams and Toro Rosso. In order to overcome the abolition of the beam wing in the rear wing assembly, which had also been used as a fixing point for the endplates, these two teams did away with classic vertical supports. They instead preferred a kind of extremely low beam wing beneath the 150 mm limit where the prohibition was not in force, thus freeing up the area from the turbulence generated by vertical fixtures and acting in part as aid to the extraction of air from the diffuser.

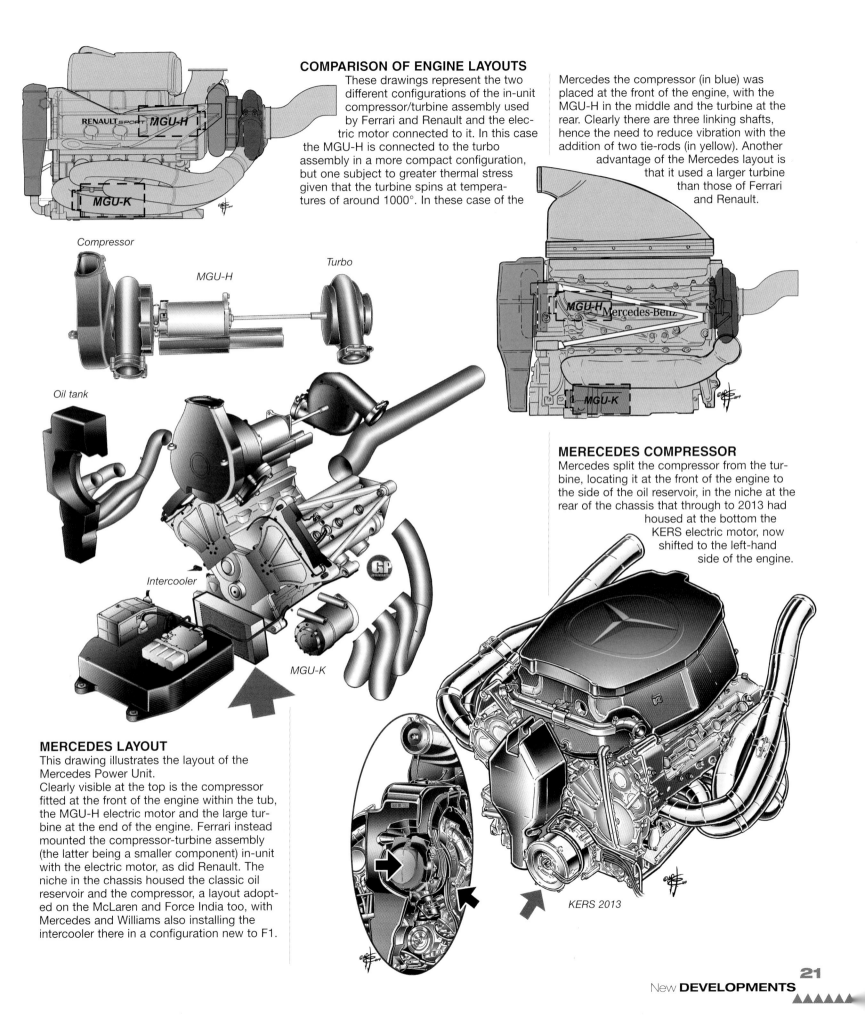

COMPARISON OF ENGINE LAYOUTS

These drawings represent the two different configurations of the in-unit compressor/turbine assembly used by Ferrari and Renault and the electric motor connected to it. In this case the MGU-H is connected to the turbo assembly in a more compact configuration, but one subject to greater thermal stress given that the turbine spins at temperatures of around 1000°. In these case of the Mercedes the compressor (in blue) was placed at the front of the engine, with the MGU-H in the middle and the turbine at the rear. Clearly there are three linking shafts, hence the need to reduce vibration with the addition of two tie-rods (in yellow). Another advantage of the Mercedes layout is that it used a larger turbine than those of Ferrari and Renault.

Compressor

MGU-H

Turbo

Oil tank

Intercooler

MGU-K

MERECEDES COMPRESSOR

Mercedes split the compressor from the turbine, locating it at the front of the engine to the side of the oil reservoir, in the niche at the rear of the chassis that through to 2013 had housed at the bottom the KERS electric motor, now shifted to the left-hand side of the engine.

MERCEDES LAYOUT

This drawing illustrates the layout of the Mercedes Power Unit.
Clearly visible at the top is the compressor fitted at the front of the engine within the tub, the MGU-H electric motor and the large turbine at the end of the engine. Ferrari instead mounted the compressor-turbine assembly (the latter being a smaller component) in-unit with the electric motor, as did Renault. The niche in the chassis housed the classic oil reservoir and the compressor, a layout adopted on the McLaren and Force India too, with Mercedes and Williams also installing the intercooler there in a configuration new to F1.

KERS 2013

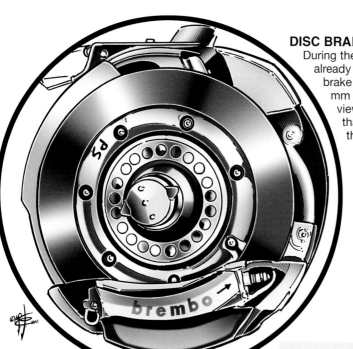

DISC BRAKES

During the 2013 season many teams had already begun testing smaller rear brake discs with respect to the 278 mm permitted by the regulations, in view of the revolution in this area that was to be introduced with the 2014 technical regulations.

BRAKE BY WIRE

The diagram provided by Brembo illustrates the various components of the innovative Brake by Wire system providing electronic control of the rear axle to handle the doubled power and extended use of the old KERS, now known as the MGU-K. The point of departure was the traditional system composed of the brake pedal (1) controlling the two axles via two separate pumps (2 front, 3 rear). The driver could always adjust brake bias between the two axels directly from the cockpit. Under braking the front system worked as usual with, in effect, the pump pressuring the fluid acting via the cylinders (six at the front) on the pads and discs to slow the car. The rear brakes were instead governed electronically with the system featuring a simulator (6) providing the driver with feeling while the work was actually done via an electronic control unit (7) slowing the motor-generator (7) and via an actuator pressurising the rear brake circuit (9).

Braking was thus the combined effect of the fluid pressure acting on the traditional brake circuits and the deceleration of the motor-generator that depends on how much energy needs to be recovered to charge the batteries. While at the front end the classic six-pot callipers remained (10) at the rear the discs were up to 12 mm smaller in diameter with smaller callipers that in some cases had just four cylinders. In the case of anomalies in the electronic management, the system was governed in the traditional manners, albeit with the rear end penalised.

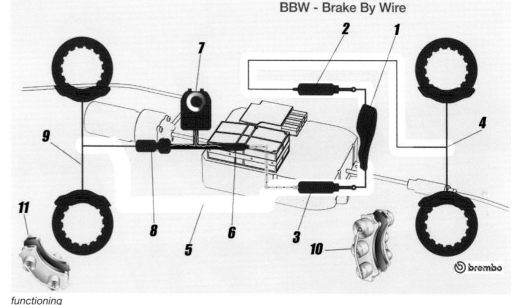

BBW - Brake By Wire

functioning

non-functioning

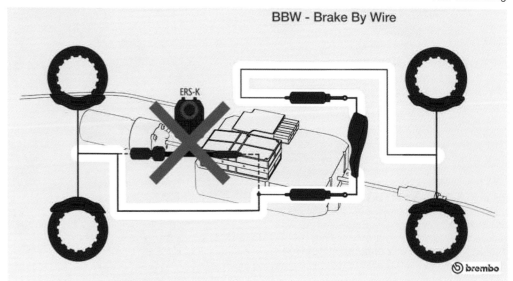

BBW - Brake By Wire

ERS-K

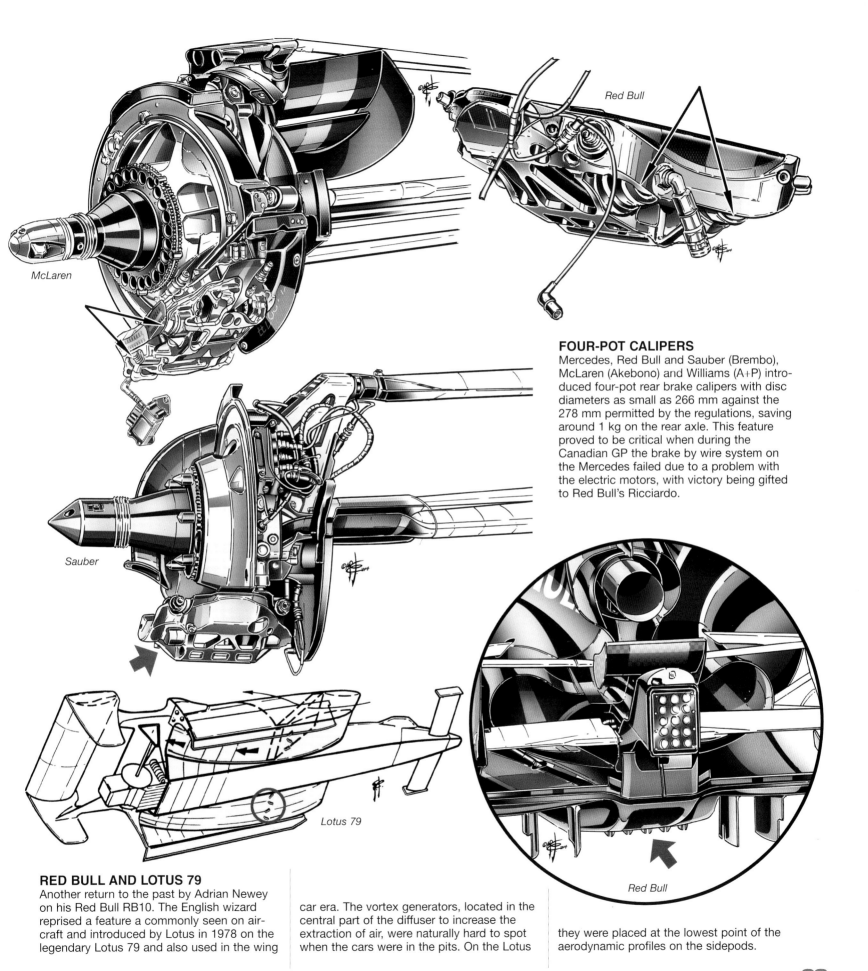

McLaren

Red Bull

Sauber

Lotus 79

FOUR-POT CALIPERS

Mercedes, Red Bull and Sauber (Brembo), McLaren (Akebono) and Williams (A+P) introduced four-pot rear brake calipers with disc diameters as small as 266 mm against the 278 mm permitted by the regulations, saving around 1 kg on the rear axle. This feature proved to be critical when during the Canadian GP the brake by wire system on the Mercedes failed due to a problem with the electric motors, with victory being gifted to Red Bull's Ricciardo.

Red Bull

RED BULL AND LOTUS 79

Another return to the past by Adrian Newey on his Red Bull RB10. The English wizard reprised a feature a commonly seen on aircraft and introduced by Lotus in 1978 on the legendary Lotus 79 and also used in the wing car era. The vortex generators, located in the central part of the diffuser to increase the extraction of air, were naturally hard to spot when the cars were in the pits. On the Lotus they were placed at the lowest point of the aerodynamic profiles on the sidepods.

Controversies **2014**

The outlawing of a technical feature in the most heated part of the season, in mid-summer, has become something of a tradition. As happened in 2006, in 2014 it occurred at Hockenheim on the occasion of the German GP.

In 2006, the dispute centred on the mass damper introduced by Renault the previous year and only judged to be illegal in the July of the following year. In 2014, the feature in question was instead FRIC (Front and Rear Interconnection Control), a further development of that mass damper concept.

This year too the controversy erupted well after FRIC had been introduced (it was being tested back in 2008 and over the last two seasons had been adopted by almost all the teams).

In 2013, Mercedes and Lotus had had the most advanced systems that could connect both between the two axles in line and diagonally and transversally between the wheels on the same axle.

In 2014, alongside the Stuttgart team, Williams proved to be the most active in this area. On the eve of the German GP, five teams (McLaren, Red Bull, Toro Rosso, Marussia and Caterham) asked the FIA for clarification as they felt that FRIC contravened Art. 3.15.1 that bans the use of the suspension elements for aerodynamic purposes.

In effect, this system permitted notable aerodynamic advantages by guaranteeing an optimum stance in all circumstances and permitting more extreme aerodynamic configurations that would otherwise be too sensitive to ride height variations. What emerged was not a ban by the FIA but simply the hypothesis of a possible protest out of which disqualification might originate. This led to the subsequent decision by all teams not to use the system. It is curious to note that in 2006 too, the FIA's delayed ban of mass dampers came about as a result of a request for clarification from McLaren.

FRIC MERCEDES

The drawing shows the front-rear hydraulic suspension interconnection more simply known as FRIC, introduced by Renault in 2008 and illustrated here in the layout employed on the Mercedes in 2013.

The system in itself is fairly simple and features an actuator (1-2) for each suspension corner, linked via hydraulic lines to an accumulator (3) governed by a hydraulic control unit (4) and which operates the actuators on the same axle, on the same side of the two axles and also diagonally. In this way it manages to control the ride height on both axles, above all in relation to the car's decelerations and accelerations, to the benefit of aerodynamic efficiency.

The circle top right illustrates how the system is pressurised prior to being used in much the same way as the braking system.

The diagram of the rear end shows how in 2011 Mercedes had already installed a third hydraulic element that controlled pitch and roll in relation to the loading shifts between the two axles.

This side view shows, indicated by the arrows from left to right, the hydraulic damper, the point where the hydraulic lines from the four suspension corners come together, the hydraulic distributor and the accumulator.

LOTUS 2013

One of the Lotus's strong suits in the 2012 and 2013 seasons was its highly advanced and reliable FRIC. On the Lotuses, the hydraulic actuator governing the balance between the front and rear axles was located in the left-hand side pod. The drawing depicts the bleed operation for pressurising the system.

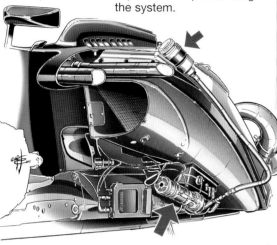

MASS DAMPER FRONT AND REAR

The details above the side views show the front mass damper layout introduced at Monza in 2005 and then the rear unit adopted on the R26 in 2006 with a design integrated with the rear suspension. The system is much clearer in the front unit where the mass (1) of around 7 kg is in effect suspended between two springs (2-3) of different sizes and stiffnesses con-

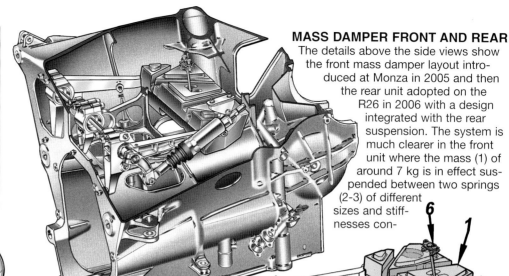

R26 (2006)

tained, along with a damper (5) in a shell (4) with a strut anchoring it in the structure. This supplementary damper governed the variation in ride height, while the mass damper of around 3.5 kg located inside the gearbox and linked to the anti-roll bar reduced the car's skipping.

The front mass damper layout was very simple and hidden away inside the nose.

The ballast (1) of around 7.5 kg is suspended between two springs of different size and stiffness (2-3) coaxial with a small damper (5). The whole assembly is enclosed within a carbonfibre cylinder (4). The more complex rear mass damper is completely concealed within the gearbox casing and had a mass of less than 5 kg. The following list illustrates the various components. (1) Mass of around 3.5 kg. (2) Rocker fixed within the gearbox. (3) Reaction strut for the torsion bar. (4) Rotating dampers. (5) Potentiometer for data recording. (6) Block used in testing.

MASS DAMPER 2005-2006

The 2006 season earned a place in the history of Formula 1 for the mass damper debate that held sway over the summer months and that was resolved with a ban on using the device introduced by Renault in 2005 at the Italian GP (it is no coincidence that it was illustrated in the 2005 volume).

It only came to light on the eve of the Monaco GP, with the controversy exploding at the German GP, as was the case in the 2014 season too.

A "controversy" that had serious repercussions for the 2006 championship. Then too, the mass damper dispute exploded in the pits at Hockenheim.

Despite the fact that it had been banned on the eve of the German GP, Renault arrived at scrutineering with the system fitted to its T-car, while all the other teams that had already raced it (Ferrari, Red Bull, Toro Rosso and Midland), as well as those who had only conducted private tests (such as McLaren and Honda), had removed the device.

The defence put forward at the appeal in Paris by Renault designer Pat Symmonds focussed on the fact that the device should be considered as an integral part of the car's suspension system.

It should be pointed out that while for Ferrari and the other teams that had used the system in 2006 the mass damper had proved to be an adaptation of cars designed earlier, the Renault R26 had actually been designed around the system which was also used on the rear axle, located within the gearbox casting.

The most absurd aspect of this story is that the "controversy" emerged in Germany (the definitive ban only came into effect at the following race in Hungary), after no less than 15 Grands Prix in which the device had been used by many teams. It would have been far better to reject the feature on its first appearance at Monza or to ban it at the end of 2005 so as to prevent any "extreme" developments as has happened in the past with other features introduced by the various teams.

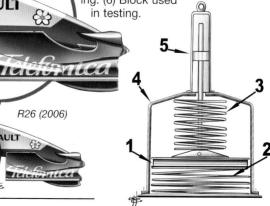

R26 (2006)

100kg ⬇
100kg ⬇

+75 mm
PR
20 mm

795 mm

CONTROVERSIES 2014

Just two objections were made against a team in the 2014 and curiously one occurred in the first and the other in the last race of the championship. On both occasions the culprit was Red Bull.

In Australia the issue actually led to Ricciardo's disqualification after finishing second in the race. The FIA scrutineers had in fact noted that the Red Bull RB10 had a fuel flow rate superior to the 100 kg/h permitted by the regulations. In order to verufy this data, the FIA had obliged all teams to fit a flow meter made by the British company Gill Sensor. This measured instantaneous fuel consumption but was fairly sensitive to variations in temperature and vibration and for this reason criticised by the teams when it was introduced in

winter testing.

In the appeal it presented, the Milton Keynes team claimed that it had respected the parameters requested by the FIA and that it had instead been the flow meter that had provided an erroneous reading. This was why it had not told Ricciardo to slow even when Charlie Whiting had advised the pit wall that the consumption was above the permitted level. The appeal was rejected because the regulations specify that in the case of any controversy the device provided by the FIA and not the teams' telemetry data shall be accepted.

The second case occurred during the final race, an episode that left no room for doubt as to Red Bull's guilt as it was caught with the front wing flaps too flexible. The element that nailed the RB10s was the manual adjustment system for the flap incidence used by the mechanics which incorporated a rubbery material and a small spring. This detail allowed precise and by no means accidental control over flexion and above all become in its turn an element of variable deformation, thus contravening the regulations.

In the two photos taken on the Saturday morning and on the start line the difference in the material used on the two occasions can be seen: for the Saturday session a matte black colour can be seen while on the Sunday it is a light titanium grey.

That something was in the air could be intuited on the Saturday morning when in a surprise move Joe Bauer went personally to check the flexibility of the latest Williams, Red Bull and McLaren flaps after TV images had shown suspect flexing with the incidence of the flaps decreasing drastically mid-straight, thus ensuring higher top speeds. Art. 3.15 of the regulations prohibits flexing of those parts having an aerodynamic influence and for this reason the test regarding the flexion of the front wing assembly has become stricter in recent years. We should however provide clarification: the method whereby the test was conducted (scrutineering drawing) did not involve the flap in question and the component was flexible to a greater or lesser degree on all cars. The question has to be asked, given that Ricciardo, who started from the pit lane (with the worst exit in the championship) managed to finish fourth, was it worth risking disqualification for a similar detail?

saturday

sunday

Engines **2014**

In 2014 Formula 1 introduced the greatest ever revolution in its engine regulations: the naturally aspirated, 2.4-litre V8 engines producing 850 hp were replaced with new Power Units. What was new? Small, 1.6-litre 90° V6 turbocharged engines with direct ignition, a maximum crankshaft speed of 15,000 rpm and a hybrid ERS (Energy Recovery System) featuring two electric motors: the MGU-K that recovers kinetic energy under braking and the MGU-H that instead transforms the heat produced by the turbo into electrical energy. Completing the unit was the battery pack storing the electrical energy and the control electronics essential for governing the hybrid section. Not just an engine, therefore, but rather six different elements combined in the interests of downsizing.

The MGU-K is an electric motor that acts as a flywheel when the turbocharged V6's throttle is released, storing electrical energy in the battery, while under acceleration it can deliver up to 120 kW (164 hp) for 33 seconds per lap. In comparison, the old KERS from 2013 could deliver a maximum of 60 kW for 6.6 seconds per lap. The second electric motor is the MGU-H, linked to the turbo via a shaft and which draws energy from the hot exhaust gases that would otherwise be lost. While it is capable of spinning to a permitted 120,000 rpm, in 2014 no constructor took it to the limit of the regulations, with Mercedes only rarely breaking the 100,000 rpm threshold. The energy recovered may be directed to the battery for a maximum of 90 kW, or it may go directly to the MGU-K with no restrictions imposed by the regulations. The MGU-H is also used to control of the turbo rotation speed and reduce its reaction time. The lithium battery, which the regulations required to be located between chassis and engine, in the area below the fuel tank, the most well protected point of the car, may be changed by the MGU-K for a maximum of 2 MJ per lap and may release up to 4 MJ a lap.

The intent of the International Federation was to significantly improve the efficiency of the engines so as to ensure that the search for performance also focused on reducing fuel consumption and pollution, thus permitting real trickle down benefits for automotive production. The objective was to cover the distance of a Grand Prix, around 305 km, with a limit of 100 kg of fuel, a reduction of 30% with respect to the past. The fuel savings have been surprising given that races such as Monte Carlo were disputed with no more than 84 kg of fuel, 14% less that the pre-established limit, while only the Grands Prix at Abu Dhabi, Austin and Montreal required full tanks with the drivers lifting off and coasting before the end of the straight in order to stay within the limits. These fuel savings themselves became important factors in performance as starting a race with 10 kg less on average meant a saving of 0.3 seconds per lap.

Making what was already a difficult technical issue even more complicated was the regulation that restricted the fuel flow to 100/kg above 10,500 rpm. It is therefore clear why the engineers restricted the crankshaft speeds of the V6 turbo to no more than 12,000 rpm per gear change given that the power units were tuned to deliver optimum performance between 7,500 and 10,000 rpm. This drastic lowering of the engine speed from the 18,000 of the naturally aspirated V8s, together with the single exhaust led to a significant reduction in noise levels that provoked outrage, especially at the start of the season, among those nostalgic enthusiasts who consider the sound of the engines to be an integral part of the Formula 1 spectacle. In order to check fuel consumption the FIA adopted the Gill Sensors ultrasound flow meter. The less than perfect fine-tuning of the system led to a heated dispute between the FIA technicians and Red Bull Racing. At the Australian Grand Prix, the reigning world champion team suffered the annulation of the second place obtained by Daniel Ricciardo in Melbourne, on the RB10's debut, because the Energy Renault engine had consumption peaks well over 100 kg/h.

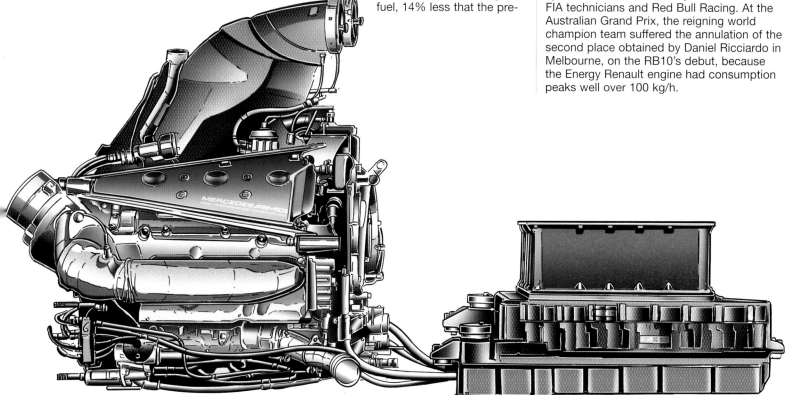

Three constructors, Mercedes, Ferrari and Renault, signed up to the 2014 regulations. The German firm supplied its Power Units to Williams and Force India as well as, naturally, the Silver Arrows, while Ferrari collaborated with Sauber and Marussia. Renault for its part supported Red Bull Racing, Toro Rosso, Lotus and Caterham. It is interesting to note how each constructor developed its own very different layout despite having to interpret stringent regulations. Each driver was allowed five engines over the course of the season. Development of the units was frozen at the end of February, ahead of the first race of the season in Oceania. FIA only permitted interventions that improved the reliability of the Power Units on the condition that they had no effect on performance. The teams supplied by Mercedes and Ferrari were not subject to penalties, while those powered by Renault went over the limit: Daniil Kvyat (Toro Rosso) seven Power Units, one more than Sebastian Vettel (Red Bull Ring), Pastor Maldonado (Lotus) and Jean-Eric Vergne (Toro Rosso).

Mercedes led the way with the PU106A in that the Brixworth engineers had the bright idea of separating the turbo from the compressor. The former was fitted behind the engine, towards the gearbox as was the norm, while the second was isolated from the hottest area and was placed at the front of the engine with the MGU-H in the middle and linked to the two elements via a shaft. Installing the compressor overhanging the 90° V, the engineers directed by Andy Cowell were able to homologate a bigger unit than Ferrari and Renault were able to do, obtaining a greater flow of cool air to the intake manifold of the six-cylinder engine. Moreover, the fact that the air/water intercooler was buried in the chassis of the W05 Hybrid permitted the creation of very short and light ducts and allowed for narrower sidepods to the advantage of aerodynamics. This feature was exclusive to the Silver Arrows, while the client teams Williams and Force India had a more conventional air/air intercooler mounted in one of the sidepods. It should be pointed out that Mercedes constructed its own turbocharging system after having recruited highly specialised staff from IHI for a dedicated research centre in Germany. Mercedes also paid great attention to the extremely short and well-insulated exhausts so as to lose as little heat as possible, favouring tur-

bine efficiency at the expense of a slight loss of power (around 10 hp) from the internal combustion engine. The Mercedes AMG High Performance Powertrains Power Unit proved to be the only one capable of recharging the maximum electrical energy every lap thanks to well-calibrated electronic management of the hybrid systems. A great contribution to performance was provided by the Petronas fuel in that it was estimated that the fuel produced at Villastellone near Turin was worth 3 tenths of a second per lap, despite the 500 bar Bosch direct injection not yet being available.

In contrast with Mercedes which concentrated on the utmost functionality if its Power Unit, Ferrari instead decided to privilege the chassis engineering and aerodynamics. For example, on the F14 T the oil reservoir, usually located between the chassis and the engine was located in the gearbox spacer along with the MGU-K which was cantilevered from the 6-cylinder engine. This was not the only feature characterising the 059/3 given that, in order to obtain narrow sidepods with very compact radiator packs the Rosse boasted a new water/air intercooler location inside the V between the banks of cylinders where space was also found for the turbocharger and the MGU in contact with the hottest parts of the car. In order to support the decisions of the chief designer Nicholas Tombazis, Luca Marmorini

stepped down from his position as engineer designer. The Honeywell turbine that had been homologated proved to be too small to satisfy the demands for recharging the ERS and at the start of the 2014 season at least, the Ferrari Power Unit was around 80 hp down on its Mercedes rival. The Prancing Horse's engineers were also some way behind in terms of the management strategies for the electric motors and while the 6-cylinder turbo was by no means a bad engine it did consume more fuel than the Mercedes. Due to an error in interpreting the regulations the exhausts were not insulated with a material similar to that which Mercedes had been using on the W05 Hybrid from the start of the season. The modification was worth 12 kW of extra energy, that is to say around 15 hp. Too little to make up the gap on the Mercedes...

While things went badly at Maranello, at Viry Chatillon, home of Renault Sport F1, the season started even worse. In winter testing the French company had discovered just how tricky the new Power Unit regulations were. Red Bull Racing was virtually unable to complete a lap due to the continual and ever different problems afflicting every component of the Power Units. Moreover, they contributed to increasing the problems with the extreme aerodynamic design of the RB10 designed by Adrian Newey, little inclined to open slots in the coachwork to improve cooling of the 6-cylinder Energy Hybrid. The technical director, Rob White, had launched an ambitious project with the French engineers committed to the development of the many elements of the Power Units the other constructors had farmed out to exclusive suppliers. The batteries were developed in collaboration with Red Bull Technology and turbocharging system with Pankl APC Turbosystems GmbH, the former KKK queen of the 1980s. After a tumultuous and difficult apprenticeship, enriched by violent arguments picked by the Red Bull Racing men, the 6-cylinder Renault managed to win three races with Daniel Ricciardo. The fortunate victory in Canada was followed by those in Hungary and at Spa which instead revealed the progress made with the French engine over the course of the season once a certain stability had been achieved with the energy recharging systems. At Viry Chatillon they developed the Power Unit with the most... basic layout, in practice a turbine and compressor mated to the MGU-H. The French company suffered serious electrical and electronic problems that significantly delayed development of the 6-cylinder engine that, from a mechanical point of few was not at all bad once the initial crankshaft problems had been resolved. Once the strategies to get the best out of the electrical energy, including the management of the pop-off valve, had been fine tuned, the potential of the Renault Power Unit began to be realised and Daniel Ricciardo eventually finished third in the Drivers' World Championship.

Eng. Franco Nugnes

MERCEDES

The Mercedes Power Unit was the leading player in the 2014 season, the strong suit of the dominant W05 and difference behind the competitiveness of the Williams. Great interest was aroused by the location at the front of the engine of the large compressor (1), generally semi-concealed by the traditional oil reservoir (2). The turbine (3), which was also notably large, was instead installed at the other end of the engine, with the MGU-H electric motor inside the V. The exhausts (4) were grouped in a form of niche and had very short tail pipes so as not to disperse heat.

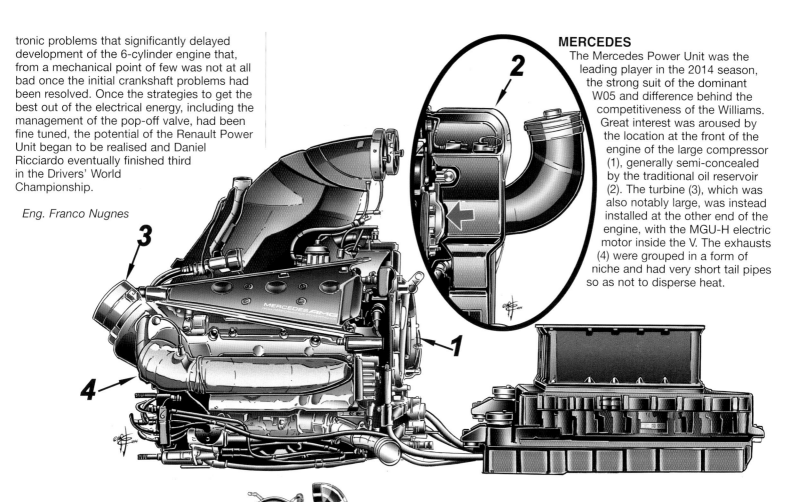

FERRARI

The layout of the Ferrari Power Unit was completely different, with the compressor close to the turbine in a very low position, both components being smaller than their Mercedes counterparts so as to privilege the aerodynamics of the rear end. Both the MGU-H electric motor and the heat exchanger were set in the V of the 1600 cc engine. A great deal of work was done on the exhausts so as not to disperse the heat required for the optimal functioning of the MGU-H. They were bound with a special tape firstly on the Marussia before being fitted with a Mercedes-style casing at the Belgian GP.

Spa

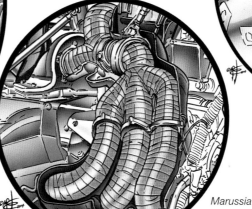

Marussia

RENAULT

The Renault engine used the same compressor and turbine configuration as the Ferrari, in a single unit at the end of the engine. The same was true of the location of the MGU-H in the V of the engine.

The diagram supplied by Renault clearly shows the location of the battery pack within the fuel tank area: a regulation imposed by the FIA.

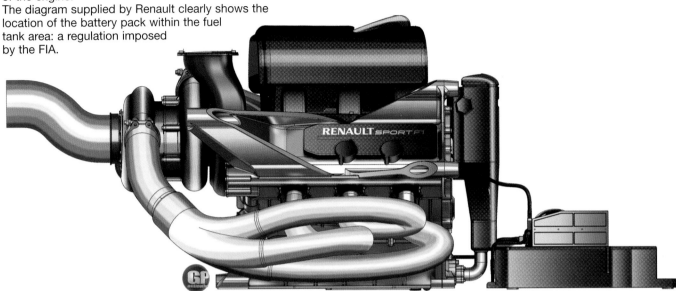

Gear RATIONS 2014

Alongside the innovative Power Units, the 2014 season also saw the adoption of new regulations regarding the transmission system and in particular the gearbox. Eight gears plus reverse were permitted with the ratios to be defined at the beginning of the season and communicated by the teams to the FIA delegate ahead of the first race of the year. For 2014 only, each competitor had the opportunity, taken up by many, to change one or more of the ratios initially chosen for the season and inform the FIA of the new set chosen. The regulation also specified that each driver should use no more than one gearbox for six consecutive events; in the case of replacement before the sixth race, the driver was to be penalised five grid positions, unless the race had been completed in which case a new unit could be fitted for the next Grand Prix.

This innovation changed the approach of the teams' engineers who would previously choose the ratios circuit by circuit, taking into account the torque curve of the engine, cornering speeds and therefore the aerodynamic configuration loading adopted, and the maximum speed, all values deduced from data harvested over previous years and from simulations. The choice was made with painstaking precision in order to have gears and engine speeds suitable for every corner and to exploit to the full the drop in revs between one ratio and the next so as to keep close to the peak max torque of the engine speed. Having to define ratios that were the same for Monza, where the maximum speed is over

340 kph, and Monaco where the top speed is under 300 kph, inevitably means having to compromise while providing acceleration suited to with the aerodynamic load and the torque output delivery of the engine. This without ignoring the presence of DRS which on certain circuits, thanks to reduced drag improved aerodynamic penetration, allows speed increments of up to 15 kph.

It was actually the torque delivery of the turbo engine, with its restricted fuel flow over 10,500 rpm, combined with that of the MGU-K kinetic motor-generator, that conditioned the choice of ratios.

The graphs show the fuel flow and torque curves in relation to the engine speed; the restricted fuel flow meant that the peak power of the internal combustion engine was achieved at around 11,500-11,800 rpm; taking into account mechanical inertia and friction, the choice of ratios was thus made on the basis of a hypothetical maximum rpm no higher than 12,200÷12,500.

Thanks to turbocharging and the electronic engine management available today, the internal combustion engine's torque output delivery is fairly consistent over a broad range, similar to the delivery of the electric motor. In order to overcome the delay in the turbo's response to throttle release, ALS anti-lag systems have been developed, generally electronically governed, along with others acting on the MGU-H that control the turbine's minimum rotational speed. These systems, together with electronic management of

the electric motor's torque, permitted a very flexible delivery of the combined, internal combustion and electric, torque from relatively low engine speeds – 6,500/7,000 rpm in extreme cases such as Monaco – which made a major contribution to reducing the consequences associated with a poor choice of ratios.

Given the availability of these systems having eight ratios actually appeared excessive in view of the great flexibility of the torque delivery and the absence of lag. The eight-cylinder naturally aspirated engine used previously had a much narrower rpm range with high torque. Certain problems were perhaps encountered with the high gears, due to overly optimistic calculations regarding aerodynamics and the power of the internal combustion engine; however, the nature of the tracks from a certain point of the season onwards also has to be considered, with long straights and higher top speeds as well as the fuel flow restriction which suggested specific configurations. For the sake of clarity we have hypothesized a maximum engine speed of 12,500 rpm, a level reached frequently, rather than the 15,000 rpm permitted by the regulations. From the diagrams below we can see that various teams made modifications during the season.

This was the case with Mercedes, which in the finale to the championship very clearly shortened its top three gears.

Ferrari was instead obliged to lengthen all its ratios which, compared with the other teams, had appeared to be rather short. Even after

POWER UNIT TORQUE

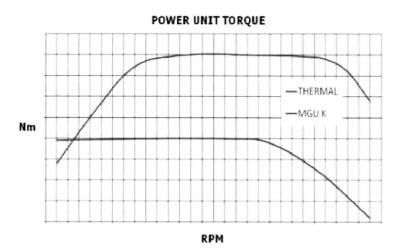

FUEL MASS FLOW

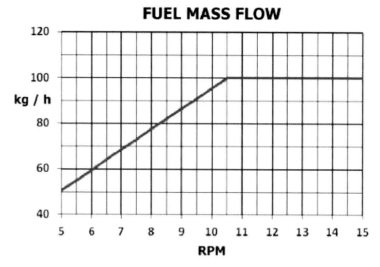

MERCEDES

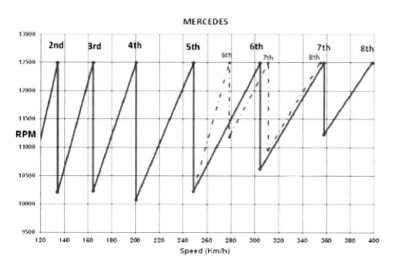

FERRARI

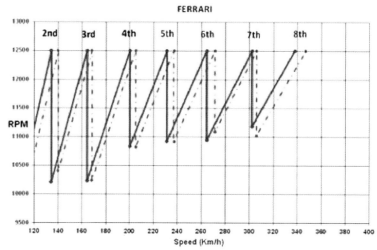

RED BULL

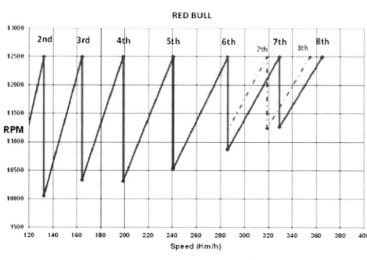

WILLIAMS

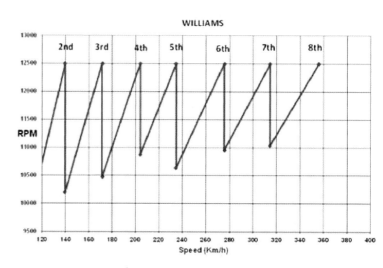

this modification, the theoretical maximum speed in 8th was still lower than that of the teams Mercedes and Renault rivals.
Red Bull instead changed only its 7th and 8th ratios, introducing shorter gears like Mercedes. A comparison of the top speeds of these three teams shows values of around 350 kph and fairly similar rpm drops between gears.
Only Ferrari adopted a different approach with elevated rpm drops between 2nd and 3rd and between 3rd and 4th (2,300/2,500 rpm) but reduced in the successive gears (1,500/1,700 rpm).
Williams took a different path, selecting longer 2nd, 3rd and 4th ratios than its rivals which it retained throughout the season.

Eng. Giancarlo Bruno

Talking about **BRAKES**

The great technical revolution that shook up the Formula 1 cars for the 2014 season affected another sector as well as that of the engines. This was the braking system, with the introduction of electronic control of the rear callipers, those involved in the recovery of energy via the "old" KERS in a further uprated form. The Brake by Wire system represents another conquest in the filed of electronics following the introduction by McLaren on the MP4/7, back in 1993, of the Fly by Wire electronic throttle in place of the traditional cable control. This was eventually adopted on all cars after having been copied by just two teams in the 1994 season, Williams and Benetton.

Brake by Wire is in effect a concession by the FIA to allow the teams to better manage braking in the light of the inevitable interactions with the redoubled power output of the new KERS, now known as MGU-K and receiving the support of another electric motor introduced in 2014, the MGU-H, associated with the recovery of energy from the heat of the turbine. The Brake by Wire system

created numerous problems and no little cause for concern during the 2014 cars' first track tests, but during the course of the season only suffered reliability issues on one occasion, during the Canadian GP on the two Mercedes. In particular, the electronic control of the braking system when actuated actually subtracted braking force from the rear axle. Mercedes, which on that occasion had opted for an extreme rear axle configuration with four-pot callipers (like Red Bull Sauber and McLaren) in place of the usual six-pot components and smaller discs, was the victim of a form of electronic black out. During the race, in fact, the German cars, as well as having lost the 160 hp of the electric motors suffered severe loss of braking efficiency on a track where the brakes were in action for 13% of the lap time. With the electronic control of the rear brakes out of action, the "traditional" control immediately rendered the rear axle braking system under-sized and critical. The general trend in this area had been that of "lightening" and revising the rear braking system. Firstly, discs were chosen with a

diameter smaller than the 278 mm permitted by the regulations (specifically 272 or even 268 mm) with reduced friction surfaces in contact with the pads. The width of the friction surface in fact decreased from 38 to 36 mm. Consequently, the friction surfaces of the rear brake pads were also smaller. What derived was a slightly smaller, lighter calliper. Some teams (Red Bull, Mercedes and Sauber) actually chose a four-pot caliper for the rear axle that was very small and light with pads that were in turn smaller. It should be remember that the four-pot caliper on the rear axle had been introduced by Brembo in 2009 and fitted to the Brawn GP and Red Bull cars only, before being abandoned from 2010.

The introduction of the Brake by Wire system affected neither the driver's ability to adjust the brake bias between the two axles nor the configuration of the front brakes. With regard to the front axle, two paths were followed in terms of the brake calipers: "heavy" calipers so as to retain stiffness and enhance cooling (Ferrari), obviously with six pistons and

BRAKE BY WIRE DIAGRAM

The diagram supplied by Brembo highlights the various components of the innovative Brake by Wire system involving electronic control of the rear axle to manage the redoubled power and prolonged use of the old KERS (now known as MGU-K).

The starting point was the traditional system composed of the brake pedal (1) which controls the two axles via two separate pumps (two front and three rear).

The driver can always adjust the brake bias between the axles from the cockpit. Under braking, the front system works as in the past: the pump pressurises the fluid acting on the pistons (6 at the front), the pads and the discs, slowing the car.

The rear brakes are managed electronically with the system comprising a "compliance chamber" made by Brembo for its teams (6)

that provides the driver with more feel; the system is governed by an electronic control unit (7) that slows the motor generator (7) and, via an actuator (8), pressurises the rear brake circuit (9).

Braking is therefore the combined effect of the pressure of the fluid acting on the traditional brake circuit and the deceleration effected by the motor generator that, in its turn, depends on how much energy one wishes to recover to recharge the batteries. While at the front end the classic six-pot calipers were retained (10), at the rear there are smaller discs (up to 12 mm less in diameter) and smaller calipers, some with just four pistons.

In the case of problems with the electronic management, the system works in the traditional fashion, although naturally the rear brakes are penalised.

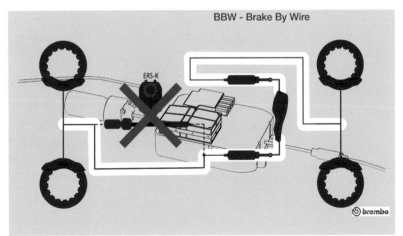

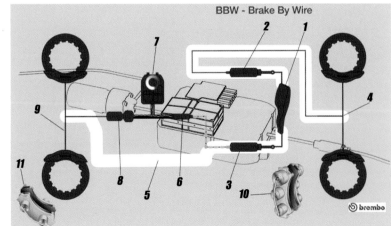

MERCEDES

Mercedes was one of the four teams that adopted four-pot calipers at the rear in the se 2014 season, combined with discs that were smaller than the maximum permitted by the regulations (278 mm). This feature, together with the Brake by Wire system that failed in Canada, compromised the performance of the two W05's, gifting victory to Red Bull, which while having a similar brake system configuration did not suffer the electronic failure.

specifically designed for each of the cars supplied by Brembo, and lighter components (Mercedes and Red Bull) to the detriment of stiffness. In this case too, the engineers attempted to optimising cooling of the callipers so as to keep them at as low a working temperature as possible (<180°C) and therefore guaranteeing a constant level of stiffness over the course of the race.

With regard to the brake discs, all the teams used front discs of the largest permitted diameter (278 mm) and thickness (28 mm), with significant progress in terms of ventilation (over 1,000 holes per disc) thanks to CFD (Computational Fluid Dynamics) and FEM (Finite Element Method) analyses.

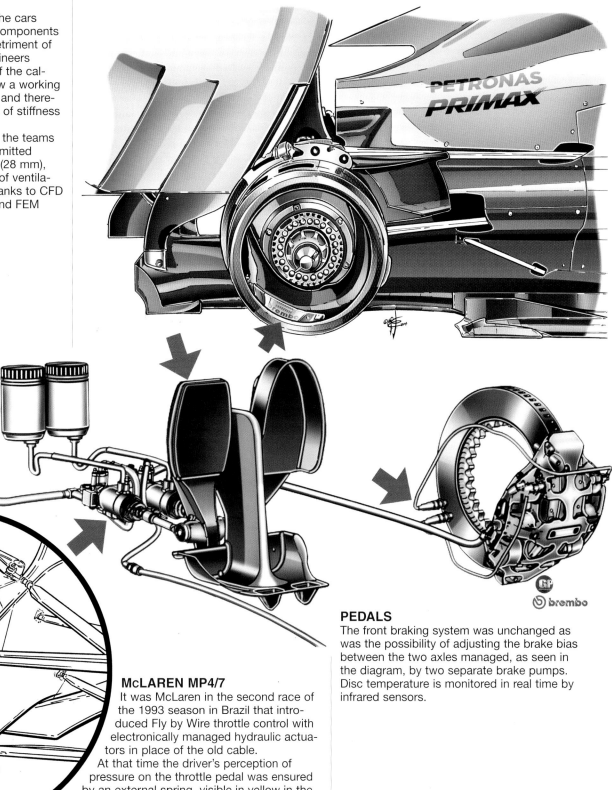

MP4/7 1992

McLAREN MP4/7

It was McLaren in the second race of the 1993 season in Brazil that introduced Fly by Wire throttle control with electronically managed hydraulic actuators in place of the old cable.

At that time the driver's perception of pressure on the throttle pedal was ensured by an external spring, visible in yellow in the detail.

PEDALS

The front braking system was unchanged as was the possibility of adjusting the brake bias between the two axles managed, as seen in the diagram, by two separate brake pumps. Disc temperature is monitored in real time by infrared sensors.

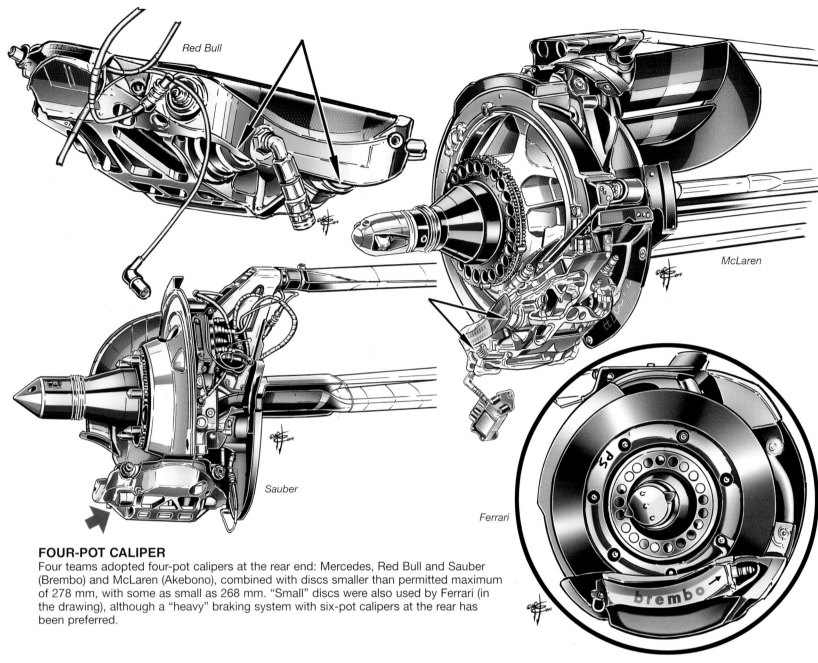

Red Bull

McLaren

Sauber

Ferrari

FOUR-POT CALIPER

Four teams adopted four-pot calipers at the rear end: Mercedes, Red Bull and Sauber (Brembo) and McLaren (Akebono), combined with discs smaller than permitted maximum of 278 mm, with some as small as 268 mm. "Small" discs were also used by Ferrari (in the drawing), although a "heavy" braking system with six-pot calipers at the rear has been preferred.

BREMBO 2009 FOUR-POT CALIPER

Brawn GP and Red Bull were the first to introduced four-pot calipers made by Brembo in the 2009 season when the title was won by Jenson Button. This feature was abandoned in 2010 before being reprised in the 2014 season by Mercedes, Red Bull, Sauber (Brembo) and McLaren (Akebono).

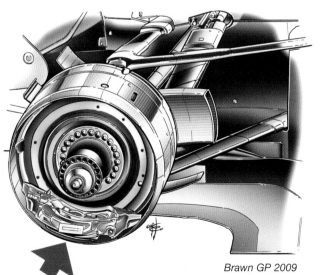

Brawn GP 2009

Red Bull 2009

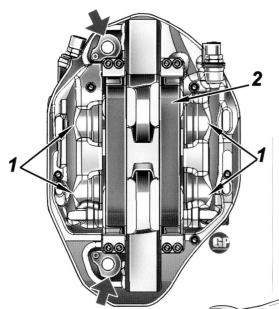

FOUR-POT CALIPER (2009)

This drawing shows the Brembo four-pot caliper from 2009 with the pistons (1) highlighted and the two pads (2), which at that time were not lightened like the current versions.

SIX-POT CALIPER

For the 2014 season, the customization of callipers for each team was taken even further with more or less lightening (highlighted in yellow) depending on the demands of the various teams. The general view highlights the lightening holes in the pads.

BRAKES REGUALTION 1998

In the 1998 season the FIA had introduced strict restrictions on the braking system: calipers with a maximum of six pistons, no more than two pads, maximum disc diameters and thickness of of 278 mm and 28 mm respectively.

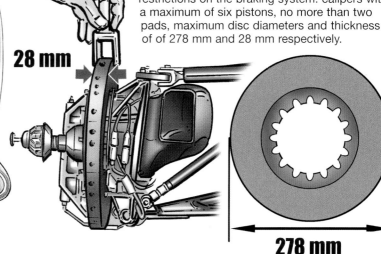

28 mm

278 mm

RED BULL

Red Bull is always at the forefront in the lightening of unsprung weight: this is the case with this bell housing that has been notably lightened and was used both in Belgium (a track relatively gentle on brakes) and at Monza.

DISC EVOLUTION

Major progress has been made in the area of braking above all in terms in of the materials used for the discs: Brembo has replaced its CR that guaranteed maximum wear of 4/5 mm at the end of a race on the hardest tracks with its CER 100 and wear reduced to 1 mm.
Much attention has been paid to ventilation, with the number of holes increasing over the years, as documented in this sequence provided by Brembo. The drawing shows the 100-hole disc (five holes on each row) and the large caliper supplied to Ferrari that for some time has opted for reliability and stiffness in its braking systems.

2005	2006/7	2008	2012	2014
100	100	200	600	1000

Talking about TYRES

The in-depth changes to the F1 technical regulations that came into force in 2014 obliged the Pirelli engineers to develop a product that while meeting the safety standards demanded by the FIA could satisfy and facilitate the different output delivery of the Power Unit. The combination of a turbocharged internal combustion engine and two electrical motor-generators, one dedicated to traction, the MGU-K MHU-K, significantly changed the torque output delivery characteristics and therefore the nature of the stresses on the tyres. The Pirelli engineers' job was made even more complicated by the addition of certain restrictions on the wing profiles and the geometry of the cars' nose that determined a reduction in overall aerodynamic downforce loading.

The result was an increase in longitudinal stress on the tyres due to the greater torque to be transmitted to the road surface and a slight reduction in lateral stress.

The increase in torque was significant; to that provided by the internal combustion engine, presumably 400 Nm, should be added the 200 Nm of the electric motor, restricted by the regulations and featuring a very flat, constant delivery through to a certain rpm.

Via the CPU, actuated by the throttle accelerator pedal, and via controls on the steering wheel, the torque may be modulated (dashed red lines); the same is true of the internal combustion engine, again via the throttle accelerator pedal (dashed black lines).

The combined torque is therefore the sum of the two and may be higher or lower (dashed green lines) in relation the position of the accelerator pedal, modulated by the driver in relation to available grip.

The effects of this variation in torque and the very flat delivery curve across a very wide rev band translate into the possibility of longitudinal wheelspin when accelerating out of corners. It was on this aspect that the Pirelli engineers focussed their studies and development at the start of the 2014 season that opened the second three-year F1 supply contract. In order to produce a reliable, high performance product, virtual models and test bench simulations were used along with data acquired by the various teams during the course of the previous season to create a completely new generation of tyres.

The carcass and the compounds were in fact changed. The structural modifications were required to cope with the 50 kg increase in the minimum weight of the cars, particularly noticeable in qualifying trim; the new carcass permitted a larger contact patch and allowed the temperature distribution to be improved, a factor that enhanced the cars' grip and handling.

While Pirelli has not confirmed as much, it may be presumed that there was also a slight increase in the vertical stiffness of the tyre to cope with the increased weight and torque. In race condition trim, the differences on the cars were less than in 2013 because the increase in minimum weight was partially compensated by the 100 kg maximum fuel load, against the 130/140 kg carried on average the previous season.

The compounds were also slightly harder than their equivalents in 2013, without however compromising or penalising grip and performance. The objective was that of enhancing tyre stability and reducing degradation during the race in race trim.

The modifications to the engine and aerodynamics imposed by the regulations also led to a variation in the profile of the front tyre to improve handling. The modifications to the rear tyre were less significant.

The tread pattern of the full wets was modified, with new grooving that reduced the risk of aquaplaning and increased by increasing the quantity of water drained from 60 l/s to 65 l/s at 300 kph. The wet compound was also modified to allow the tyre to work better in damp conditions, shifting the crossover point with respect to the intermediates.

These last were instead unchanged in terms of tread and compounds, retaining a drainage capacity of 25 l/s at 300 kph.

With regards to the dry tyres, the working ranges of the various compounds were closer, so as to obtain reduced steps between the low working range and the high working range compounds. This was in part to ensure an average difference of around a second between one compound and the next, permitting the teams to explore diversified race strategies.

The designations and the coloured bands were unvaried for each compound.
Red super soft – Low Working Range
Yellow soft – High Working Range
White medium – Low Working Range
Orange hard – High Working Range
Green intermediates
Blue full wets

Along with the technical changes, 2014 also saw a modification in the supply of sets of slicks over the race weekend, with teams now receiving 13 instead of 11, of these seven were of the hardest compound and six of the softest; a set of the hardest compound could be used only in the first 30 minutes of free practice to favour the increase of track action, compatibly with the number of Power Units available for the season. However, this set had to be returned prior to the start of the second free practice session.

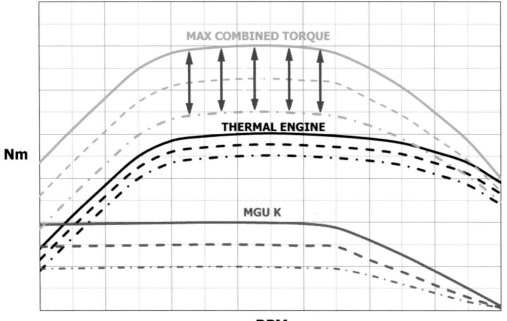

POWER UNIT TORQUE

MAX COMBINED TORQUE

THERMAL ENGINE

MGU K

Nm

RPM

Season 2013

	SS	S	M	H
Australia	■		□	
Malaysia			□	▨
Bahrain			□	▨
China		▨	□	
Spain			□	▨
Monaco	■	▨		
Canada	■		□	
India		▨	□	
Great Britain			□	▨
Germany		▨	□	
Hungary		▨	□	
Belgium			□	▨
Italy			□	▨
Singapore	■		□	
Japan			□	▨
Korea	■		□	
USA			□	▨
Brazil			□	▨
Abu Dhabi		▨	□	
	5	6	18	9

Season 2014

	SS	S	M	H
Australia		▨	□	
Malaysia			□	▨
Bahrain		▨	□	
China		▨	□	
Spain			□	▨
Monaco	■	▨		
Canada	■	▨		
Austria	■	▨		
Great Britain			□	▨
Germany	■	▨		
Hungary		▨	□	
Belgium		▨	□	
Italy			□	▨
Singapore	■	▨		
Japan			□	▨
Russia		▨	□	
USA		▨	□	
Brazil		▨	□	
Abu Dhabi	■	▨		
	6	14	13	5
	85-110	105-125	90-115	110-135

	2013	2014
Hard	Austin 259	Monza 202
Medium	India 261	Russia 304
Soft	Abu Dhabi 150	Austria 237
Super Soft	Monaco 150	Monaco 203

In qualifying, each team had seven sets per driver, four with the hard compound – Prime - and three four with the soft – Option - ; those drivers reaching Q3, with the standings defining the grid positions, could use the extra set in this session only and were required to return it at the end of qualifying. In this way, the first 10 drivers were obliged to start the race with the tyres they had used to set the fastest times in Q2. The other drivers who had not participated in Q3 could choose the compound with which they started the race and could also use this additional set of soft compound tyres. The supply of wet tyres was unchanged, four sets of intermediates and three full wets.

Comparing the use of the various compounds in 2013 and 2014 a number of conclusions can be drawn.

- The Softs were the most widely used (74% of the Grands Prix), 463 sets against the 135 of 2013, almost doubling the average distance covered by each set from 47 to 93 km. This increase in kilometrage generated highly diversified race strategies.
- The Mediums were less used (68% of the Grands Prix), 378 sets against the 720 of 2013 for an average distance covered per set of 96 km.
- There was a sharp drop in the use of the Hard compound, 83 sets instead of 316, with the average kilometrage increasing from 96 to 110 km.

It should also be pointed out that there was an increase in the maximum distances covered with the individual compounds compared with 2013, with the exception of the Hard compound.

The dry race with the greatest number of pit stops was Bahrain with 58.

In order to guarantee maximum safety and avoid failures, excessive degradation or the possibility of bead slippage, Pirelli suggested minimum tyre pressures for each circuit to be respected from the moment the cars left the pits, along with maximum EOS Camber values.

	Minimum Dry Tyre Pressure (psi)		Maximum Camber (degrees)	
	front	rear	front	rear
Australia	17	17	-4,25	-2,75
Malaysia	17	17	-4,50	-3,00
Bahrain	17	17	-4,00	-2,50
China	18	17	-3,75	-2,50
Spain	18	17	-3,75	-2,50
Monaco	16	16	-4,50	-3,00
Canada	17	17	-4,00	-2,50
Austria	17	17	-4,00	-2,50
Great Britain	18	18	-3,50	-2,50
Germany	18	18	-3,50	-2,50
Hungary	16	18	-4,50	-3,00
Belgium	18	18	-3,50	-2,50
Italy	18	18	-3,50	-2,50
Singapore	16	16	-4,50	-3,00
Japan	18	18	-3,50	-2,50
Russia	19	17	-3,75	-2,50
USA	18	17	-3,50	-2,50
Brazil	18	18	-3,50	-2,50
Abu Dhabi	18	18	-3,75	-2,50

This last value refers to the moment immediately preceding braking on the fastest straight, a moment at which the aerodynamic loading and the compression of the suspension are at their highest and the maximum camber value is presumably reached.

Over the course of the season, however, the camber values adopted by the teams proved to be lower; depending on the track, at the rear values close to zero were even observed in order to increase the contact patch and favour traction, while at the front they were lower to improve braking and reduce degradation without excessively penalising cornering performance.

Over the course of the season Pirelli also conducted a test at Silverstone with Concept tyres fitted to 18" rims and therefore with an ultra-low profile.

As the volume of air was much lower than with the tyres fitted to 13" rims, the engineers had to work on the construction and the carcass to obtain vertical stiffness comparable to that achieved with the current tyres and therefore suitable for the suspension geometries and stiffness currently in use on the cars. The flexibility of the sidewalls, in fact, combined with the vertical rigidity of the suspension makes a fundamental contribution to the movement of the car with consequent aerodynamic and performance implications. The experiment was a prelude to the introduction to F1 of tyres closer to those used in mass production in view of a transfer of technology from racing to production.

Eng. Giancarlo Bruno

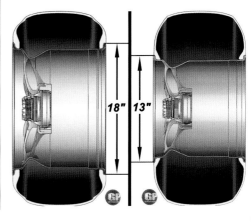

Talking about **COCKPITS**

The epochal revolution that has swept through Formula 1 has had a significant effect on driving styles and the drivers' workplace, the cockpit, and all the more so on the command centre at their disposition, the steering wheel.

Nonetheless, in recent seasons there has been a trend towards simplification due in part to the difficulties encountered by, for example, Giancarlo Fisichella when, in 2009, after just missing out on victory in Belgium with the less sophisticated Force India, only

FERRARI F14 T: STEERING WHEEL

The most obvious difference between the F138 steering wheel and that of the F14T is the larger screen (5.4 x 9.5 cm) in place of the MES-supplied component made obligatory in 2008 as part of the drive to reduce costs in F1. Retained at the top are the sequential lights telling the driver when to make a gear change, along with a signal audible through his earphones.

1) Yellow, blue and red lights that reproduce the flags shown by the track-side marshals.
2) Pit lane speed limiter.
3) KERS control behind the rim.
4) BB brake bias control.
5) KERS management.
6) SIOC State of Charge, allowing the status of the electric motors to be checked.
7) Change screen display.
8) Air/fuel mixture.
9) Confirmation of settings changes.
10) Switches adjusting mapping for slow running (e.g. safety car) and wet tyres
11) Start setting
12) BO "burn out" for warming up tyres and safe burn outs.
13) Mapping adjustment for various strategies
14) Recovery for adjustable flap
15) Supplementary oil pump
16) Drink button
17) Torque management
18) Radio
19) Multi-functional dial
20) Corner entry differential
21) Rear flap button indicator
22) Neutral

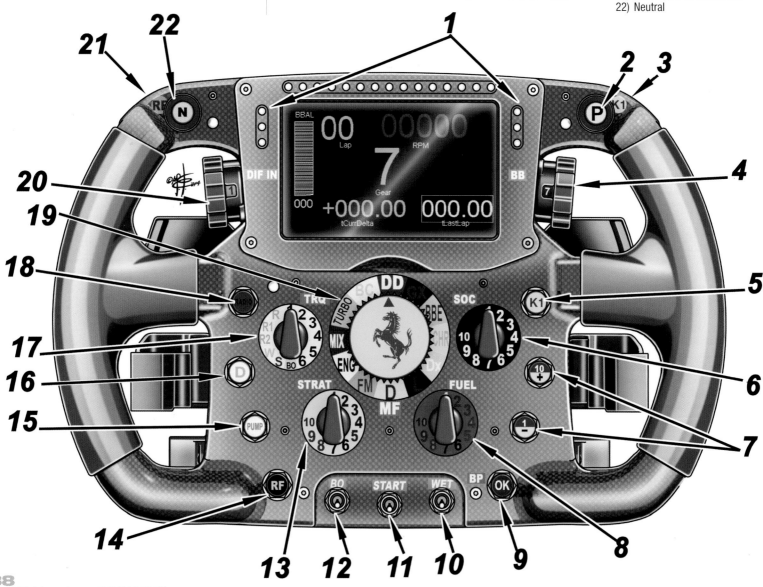

15 days later, driving the Ferrari, he failed in qualifying in part due to the greater difficulty in dealing with the range of steering wheel controls that characterised the F60.

In recent years, Alonso obtained a simpler steering wheel from Ferrari: to take just one example, the differential selectors previously involving three separate control and then unified in a single knob.

Another innovation for 2013 had been the option of a new display with a maxi-screen to be fitted in place of the "economical" version imposed by the Federation through to the previous season. In fact, with the technical revolution introduced by the Federation requiring management of the complex Power Units, there had been an absolute necessity to provide the drivers with more information. Hence the possibility of using a new, larger display, again supplied by MES, that allowed much more information to be displayed at the same time. This display not only had notable dimensions (54 x 95 mm) but also boasts better quality and modes of reading with a variety of around 100 different screens.

At the top is the usual sequence of lights, outside the screen, which together with a audible signal, indicate the correct moment for gear changing. Five teams did not adopt the new screen, preferring the lighter but less capable 2013 version: Red Bull, Williams, Lotus, Force India and Caterham.

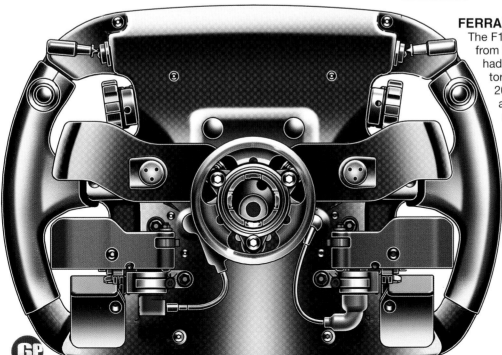

FERRARI: FLAP AND KERS CONTROL

The F14T'0s steering wheel retained the flap and KERS controls at the top of the rear of the rim so they can be actuated with the forefinger without taking the hands off the grips. The position of these two controls (2-21) is indicated on the front of the steering wheel.

FERRARI F138

The F14T's steering wheel was derived from that of the F138 that naturally had the small MES display, obligatory for all cars in the period 2009-2013. It also had a an additional adjustment dial (5 instead of 4) as well as the large, central multi-function dial.

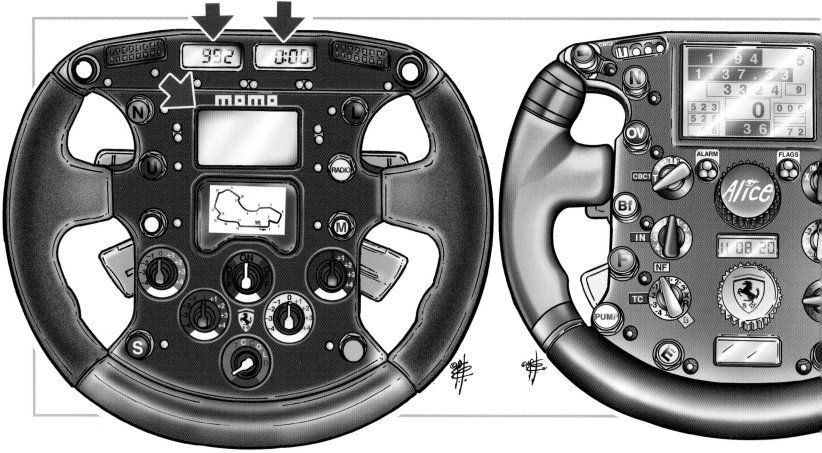

LARGER DISPLAY

With the introduction of the complex Power Unit, a larger, more powerful and therefore more expensive display was required. The Federation again commissioned MES, but this time allowed the teams to choose between two different displays. The difference in size is clear, but the most important factor is the possibility of having more information much more quickly. Five teams opted to continue to use the old display: Red Bull, Williams, Lotus, Force India and Caterham; the first two for technical motives associated with weight saving, the other three for simple budget questions.

Red Bull

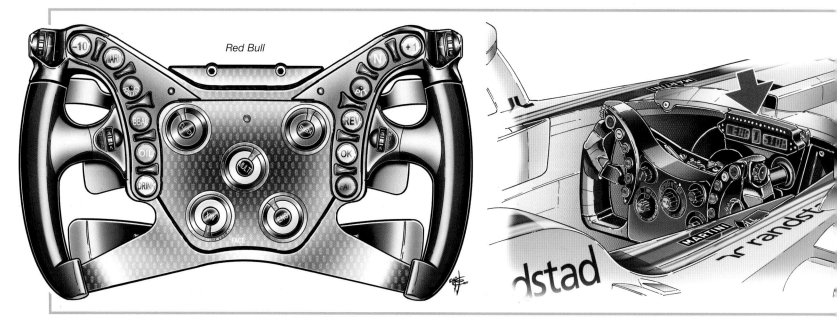

FERRARI STEERING WHEEL COMPARISON

Ferrari played a crucial role in the evolution of F1 steering wheels not only because it introduced steering wheel gear changing with the 640 in 1989, but also because it contribution to important phases in the technological evolution of the computerised wheel.

The most important phases are reviewed here.

The steering wheel of the F2000 had a fairly large central display and two smaller one in the upper section. The lights signalling gear change points were set either side of it. The wheel was square-cut at the top but rounded below, a shape that remained virtually unchanged through to the 2007 season, with the wheel also retaining a very large central display and small lights.

There was a major revolution with the F2008 following the Federation's decision to impose a "more economical" made by MES for all teams. This featured two displays in a single block and the gear change lights set at the top. The Ferrari wheel took on a new shape and was much smaller. The display then remained unchanged through to the 2013 season.

TORO ROSSO

Red Bull's "poor" cousin instead opted for a new rectangular wheel equipped with the larger MES display and no less than seven dials handling the various functions. A Ferrari-style large multi-function dial was not included. There is also an unusual position for the neutral button, different to all the other teams, bottom left marked with an "N".

WILLIAMS AND RED BULL

Both Red Bull and Williams preferred to continue to use the old display, attached not to the steering wheel but rather the dashboard, creating additional difficulty in reading the information with the wheel turned slightly. Both teams chose the lightest and most direct steering wheel possible.

FRONT VIEW COMPARISON 2013

The 2014 Mercedes steering wheels were very different to those used in 2013, due in part to a slightly different driving position. The lower part of the rim was cut away to reduce the component's height and enhance driver comfort.

HAMILTON'S SWITCHGEAR

1) PL = Pit lane speed limiter
2) +1 = To change information on the display
3) PC = Pits re-entry confirmation alerting mechanics
4) EXIT = Corner exit differential
5) BBAL = Brake balance
6) TALK = Radio
7) HI SPEED = High speed differential
8) RACE START = Engine mapping
9) MARK = Select important data
10) HPP KNOB = Controls various Power Unit settings and MGU-K management
11) CENTRAL KNOB = Controls 15 different settings including Brake by Wire, tyres and others
12) STRATEGY KNOB = Controls various settings for practice (for example, energy storage)
13) RADIO RESET = Resets the radio in the case of malfunctioning
14) Spare
15) MID = Mid-corner differential
16) X = Button for resetting any anomalies
17) BB+ BMIG = Engine braking, brake bias, brake pedal travel
18) ENTRY = Corner entry differential
19) DRS = Adjustable flap control
20) +10 = Scroll up to visualise data
21) N = Neutral button

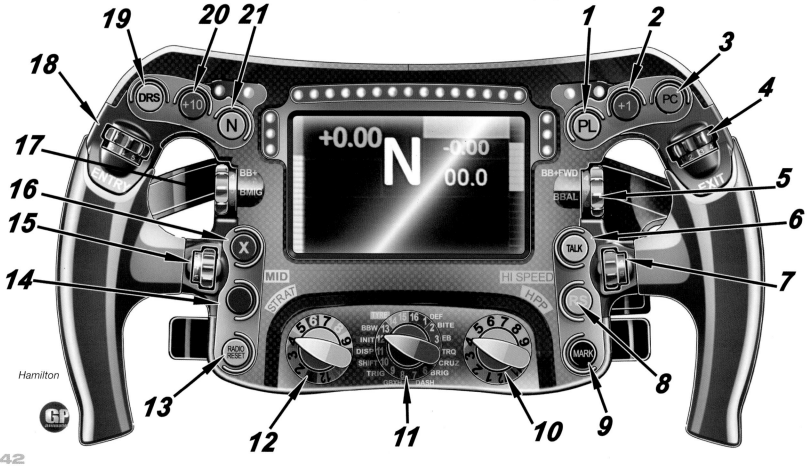

Hamilton

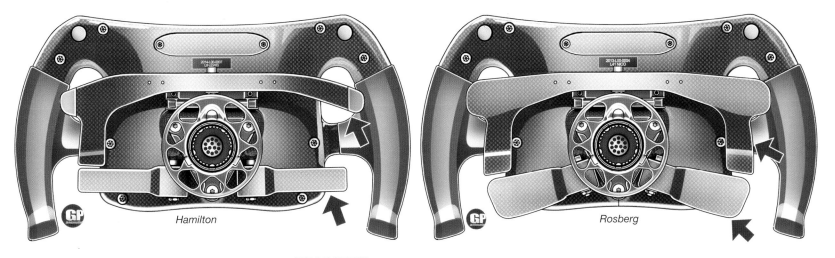

Hamilton

Rosberg

REAR VIEW

At the rear the two steering wheels have levers of slightly different shapes. As in 2013, Rosberg had gear change rockers extending downwards on both sides, with two larger clutch paddles. In the 2013 season there were six levers at the rear.

ROSBERG'S SWITCHGEAR

1) RADIO = Radio controls
2) BB+ = Brake by Wire management
3) DRS = Adjustable flap control
4) MID = Mid-corner differential
5) ENTRY = Corner entry differential
6) +1 = To change information on the display
7) EXIT = Corner exit differential
8) LIMITER = Pit lane speed limiter

9) PV R = Pits re-entry confirmation alerting mechanics
10) HPP KNOB = Controls various Power Unit settings and MGU-K management
11) CENTRAL KNOB = Controls 15 different settings including Brake by Wire, tyres and others
12) STRATEGY KNOB = Controls various settings for practice (for example, energy storage)
13) MARK BPF = Highlights data of interest to the driver

14) ON-OFF = To be used together with the levers
15) EB = Engine braking
16) +10 = To change information on the display
17) BB+ BMIG = Engine braking, brake bias, brake pedal travel
18) FINE = High speed differential
19) OT = Overtaking button
20) BB- = Brake balance
21) N = Neutral button

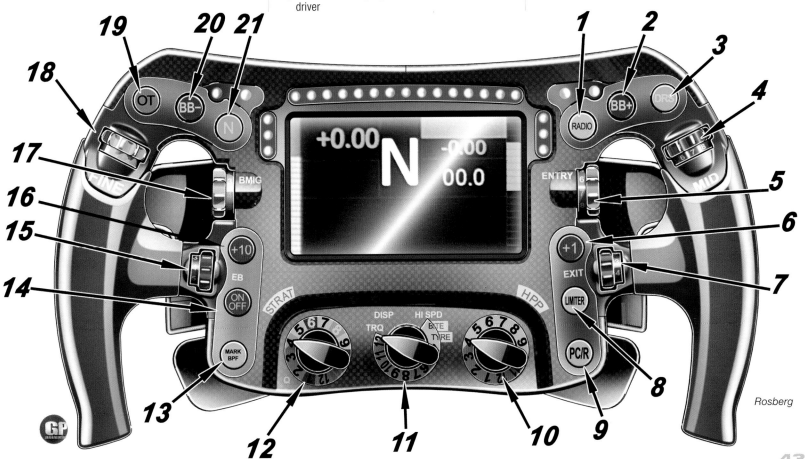

Rosberg

MERCEDES

Mercedes W04
Sao Paolo

Mercedes W05
Launch

Ross Brawn was right when, at the end of the 2013 season in the customary analysis of the year's technical developments, he predicted the dominion of the future W05, the gestation of which had begun much earlier that all its rivals.

The original project had actually been discarded in favour of an all-new car rich in innovative features, not all of which were associated with the Power Unit and its installation. This was confirmed by the team's technical director Paddy Lowe who had joined Mercedes in the June of 2013. On the car's debut at Jerez they were on the 27th layout of the cooling system, while the first bench testing of the complete

car had begun around Christmas, and they reached 32 at Suzuka with the last major evolution of the car. This was confirmation of the extent to which the installation of the complex Power Unit and above all its cooling system monopolised the project. However, the most extraordinary aspect was that while the other cars had to be subjected to significant compromises in terms of both dimensions and shape, the W05 closely resembled the previous season's car. A concentrate of new features with

the most obvious identified just a few minutes after the presentation. We are referring to the front suspension and specifically the lower wishbone. Its anchorage to the chassis was unusually narrow but above all it became a kind of single element with the shape of a broad aerody-

namic profile. A feature that had never previously been seen and which, obviously, had the objective of improving the quality of the air flow in this delicate area of the car. This choice involved intensive design work given that the component is subject to notable structural stresses. Another brand new feature, at least in terms of the result obtained, was the complete fairing in a kind of second skin of all the accessories within the sidepods and the diverse radiator packs. This resulted in notable cooling efficiency and smoother aerodynamics. This factor contributed to creation of sidepods and a wheelbase that were very similar to those of the 2013 car. A contribution because the other major innovation of the W05 was the unusual location of the intercooler within the chassis, as we discovered during practice for the Chinese GP. The incredible competitiveness of the Mercedes was perfected by the arrival at the fourth race of the season of the short nose, destine for the W05 from the design phase, but which until then had not passed the crash tests. Very short, at the limit of the 750 mm permitted by

WE05

The strong suit of the Mercedes WE05 was without doubt the new PU106A and its unique architecture. The large compressor is in fact located at the front of the engine (1) partially hidden by the oil reservoir (2), while the turbine is placed at the back of the engine (3) with the MGU-HJ at the centre of the V. The exhausts were also new with very short terminals (4) enclosed in a kind of fairing to retain as much heat as possible to be transferred to the MGU-H.

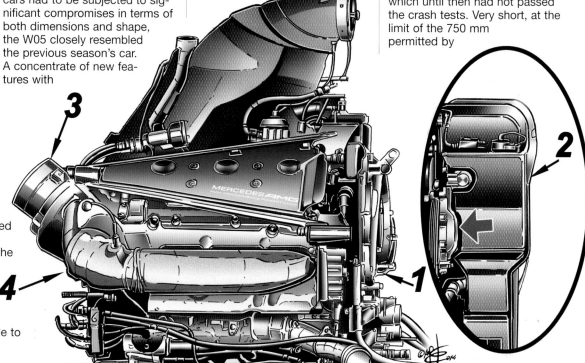

the regulations, this nose design allowed more effective use of the central portion of the wing.

All the various pieces that composed the perfect mosaic of the rational installation of the Power Unit and its accessories then came into focus and permitted an extremely compact and efficient aerodynamic package. The idea of locating the water/air intercooler inside the tub offers two advantages: firstly it saved space upstream of the radiators, while secondly and above all no one would be able to copy the configuration that season without completely redesigning their chassis. Another piece in the puzzle, the compactness of the exhausts; they were so short and well packaged as to be almost hidden and furthermore they avoided creating any obstruction to the dispersal of heat from the sidepods which were almost identical to those of the W04 from 2013. The exhausts cost around 15 hp in terms of maximum power, but the advantages compensated for this reduction. Another very important aspect of the Silver Arrows' success was better tyre conservation, generally the Mercedes Achilles heel in past seasons. This result was achieved in the design phase and refined on track with optimal set-ups. The only weak point of the W05 came to light at the Canadian GP when a problem

with the ERS compromised the brake by wire system.

For the 2015 season, in fact, thanks to the greater contribution of KERS and the electronic management of the rear brakes, Mercedes, like Red Bull, McLaren and Sauber has adopted four-pot calipers instead of the usual six-pot components and has them acting on 262 mm discs rather than the maximum 278 mm permitted by the regulations.

This configuration is perfectly adequate when the car was working efficiently but critical in the case of any problems with the electrical system.

Intensive work was conducted to adapt to the demands of the various tracks the front wing and the monkey seat which we have illustrated in no less than four different versions.

FRONT SUSPENSION

The great novelty, clearly evident from the presentation at Jerez, was the major role played by aerodynamics in the configuration of the front suspension. The lower wishbone was very narrow, as highlighted in the drawing with a dashed line indicating the traditional base. In this way a kind of tuning fork shape was created with a broad aerodynamic profile. The steering arm was aligned and faired with the wishbone so as to improve aerodynamic penetration. This feature required intensive structural calculations.

GEARBOX

Mercedes retained the dual gearbox casing introduced in 2013 in order to allow the rear suspension to be changed and adapted to the demands of the Pirelli tyres without having to modify the gearbox, an operation that would have led to a five-position penalty. One feature that Aldo Costa brought with was an extreme version of the carbonfibre skin introduced on the Ferrari F2004 to strengthen the titanium casting. On the W05 instead, a second structure in carbonfibre acted as a suspension mount. The drawing also shows the damper assembly and the various components of the FRIC system for balancing the front and rear axles, a feature banned from the Hungarian GP.

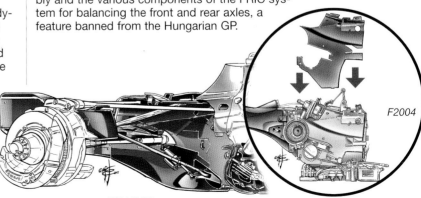

F2004

W04-W05

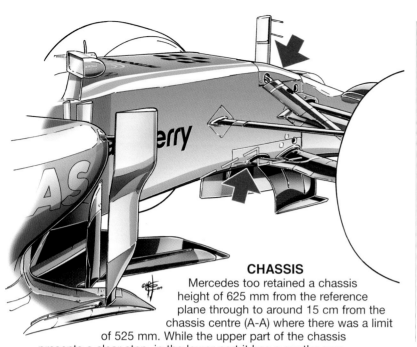

In testing in Bahrain ahead of the championship season, Mercedes used two different engine covers as seen in this comparison. The central section ends with a conspicuous Red Bull-style oval vent (1), while either side of the cockpit were rectangular vents (2) that were much larger than those of the debut. Also of note was the presence of a radiator for the gearbox at the end of the engine cover. For the 2014 season there was a ban on providing a hole for a starter but Mercedes got round this regulation my creating a mini-channel in the centre (4). The engine cover with the larger vent was used at Sepang.

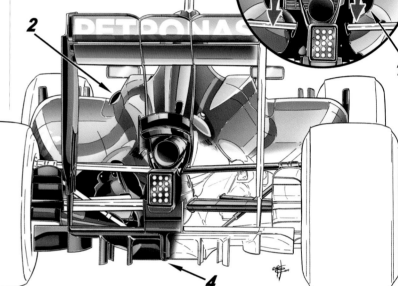

CHASSIS

Mercedes too retained a chassis height of 625 mm from the reference plane through to around 15 cm from the chassis centre (A-A) where there was a limit of 525 mm. While the upper part of the chassis presents a clear step, in the lower part it has a gentler configuration than that of the Ferrari. The yellow dashed line in fact shows the line of symmetry with the upper step allowing the minimum chassis dimensions to be respected.

Melbourne

CENTRAL CHANNEL

This additional mini channel (1) aroused some curiosity, as wide as the deformable structure, it is formed in the central area with no dimensional restrictions. In the area close to the wheels there was a kind of finger (2) pointing forwards. This served to create mini vortices that interfere with those generated by the tyres in movement.

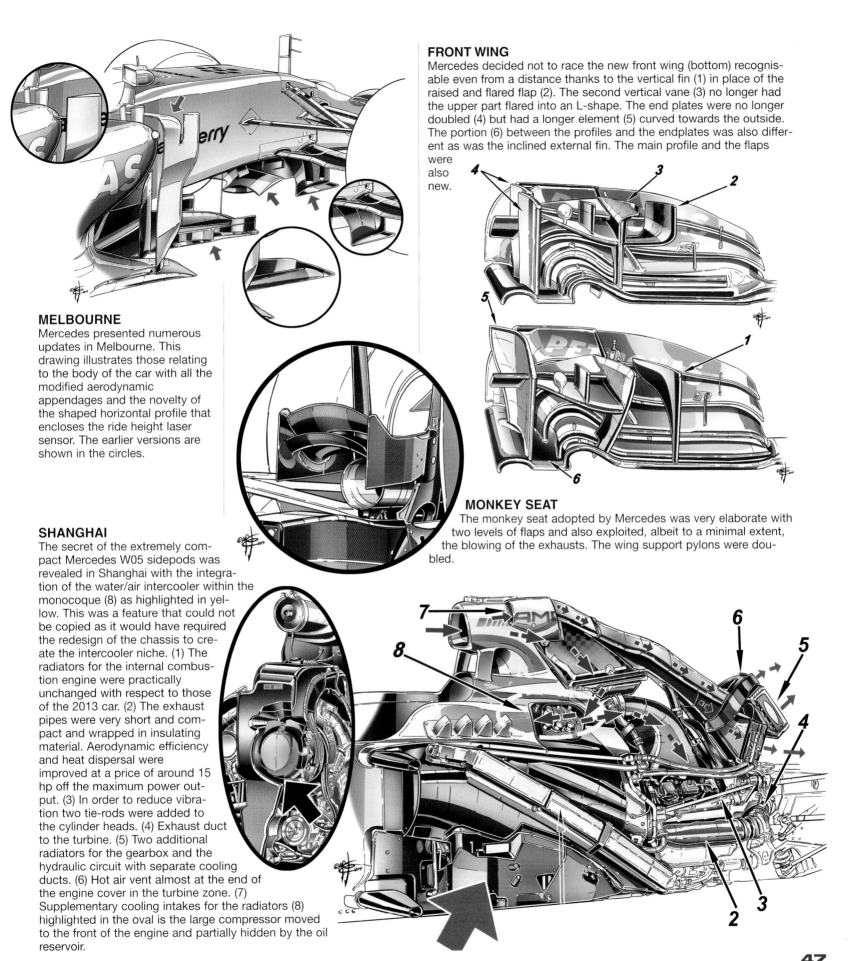

FRONT WING

Mercedes decided not to race the new front wing (bottom) recognisable even from a distance thanks to the vertical fin (1) in place of the raised and flared flap (2). The second vertical vane (3) no longer had the upper part flared into an L-shape. The end plates were no longer doubled (4) but had a longer element (5) curved towards the outside. The portion (6) between the profiles and the endplates was also different as was the inclined external fin. The main profile and the flaps were also new.

MELBOURNE

Mercedes presented numerous updates in Melbourne. This drawing illustrates those relating to the body of the car with all the modified aerodynamic appendages and the novelty of the shaped horizontal profile that encloses the ride height laser sensor. The earlier versions are shown in the circles.

SHANGHAI

The secret of the extremely compact Mercedes W05 sidepods was revealed in Shanghai with the integration of the water/air intercooler within the monocoque (8) as highlighted in yellow. This was a feature that could not be copied as it would have required the redesign of the chassis to create the intercooler niche. (1) The radiators for the internal combustion engine were practically unchanged with respect to those of the 2013 car. (2) The exhaust pipes were very short and compact and wrapped in insulating material. Aerodynamic efficiency and heat dispersal were improved at a price of around 15 hp off the maximum power output. (3) In order to reduce vibration two tie-rods were added to the cylinder heads. (4) Exhaust duct to the turbine. (5) Two additional radiators for the gearbox and the hydraulic circuit with separate cooling ducts. (6) Hot air vent almost at the end of the engine cover in the turbine zone. (7) Supplementary cooling intakes for the radiators (8) highlighted in the oval is the large compressor moved to the front of the engine and partially hidden by the oil reservoir.

MONKEY SEAT

The monkey seat adopted by Mercedes was very elaborate with two levels of flaps and also exploited, albeit to a minimal extent, the blowing of the exhausts. The wing support pylons were doubled.

SHORT NOSE SHANGHAI

Finally making its debut in the fourth race of the season, was the W05's original nose, 7/8 cm shorter than the one prepared at the last minute for the first races. The short nose was at the limit imposed by the regulations of 750 mm and this led to some difficulty in passing the crash test, with the all clear only coming after the Grand Prix of China, following four unsuccessful attempts. The short nose permitted greater efficiency in the central area of the wing and improved air flow quality towards the rear of the car.

BARCELONA

In Spain the front wing was modified slightly with the addition of a mini-fin on the inside part of the endplates.

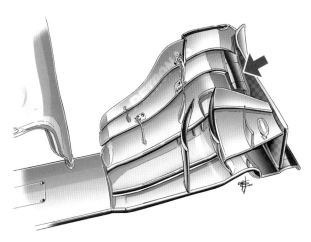

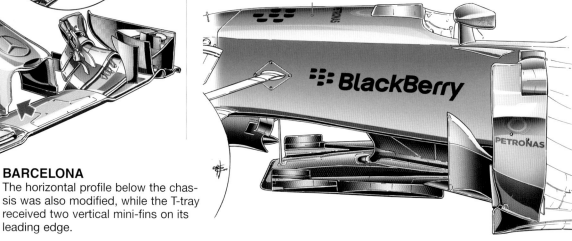

BARCELONA

The horizontal profile below the chassis was also modified, while the T-tray received two vertical mini-fins on its leading edge.

MONACO

A new monkey seat for the Mercedes, derived from the version seen in testing after the Spanish GP, along with modified curved endplates. The novelty lay in an additional profile set in the upper part and indicated by the arrow.

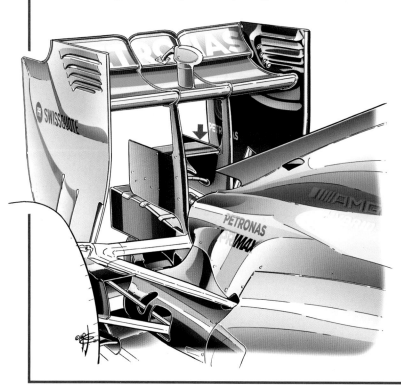

MONACO FRONT WING

Mercedes tried two different front wings. The one at the bottom is the last to be introduced in Spain and characterised by a different end-plate shape (1) and a small turning vane with a greater flare (2). The support pylon for the raised flaps (3) was also modified, effectively being trimmed. The view from the inside shows the two slots on the horizontal plane close to the vertical vane.

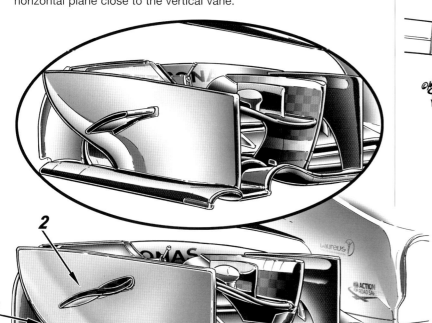

MONTREAL

On the Montreal track that is particularly hard on brakes, Mercedes retained the Monte Carlo brake intakes but opened a window at the top of the right-hand front duct to allow the brake to reach operating temperature more quickly.

LOWER WISHBONE

Refinements in Montreal for Mercedes with the fairing of the lower wishbone slightly modified and the addition of this small fin immediately below the strut.

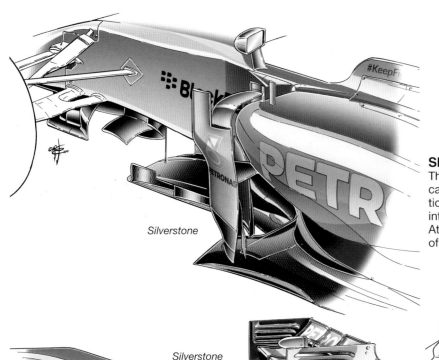

Silverstone

SILVERSTONE

The third evolutionary package for Mercedes in the area of the vertical turning vanes at the sides of the sidepod mouths. In the rear section the sidepods were slightly lower and tighter than the version introduced in Spain.

At the front, the leading edges of the turning vanes in the lower part of the chassis were modified with a slight flick.

Silverstone

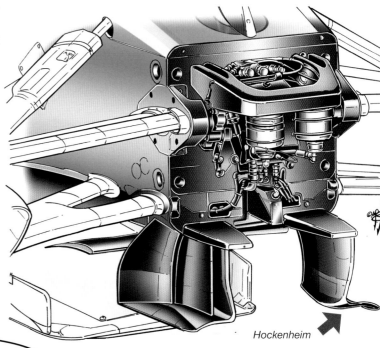

Hockenheim

SPA REAR WING

A new rear wing with the trailing edge divided into three arches; for qualifying and the race it was used without the Gurney flaps given the forecasts for a dry race. There was also a new monkey seat that had appeared in the post-Silverstone tests, equipped with a single profile. The inset shows the previous configuration.

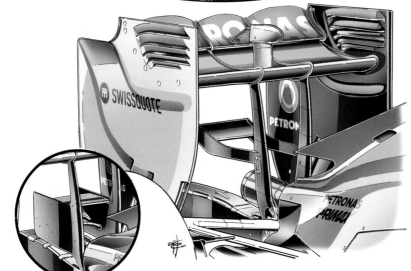

SPA NOSE

A new nose slightly that was more cut-away in the lower section but above all lighter and subjected to a new crash test. From the beginning of the year the weight-loss programme on the bodywork alone saved no less than 8 kilos which has been evaluated as the equivalent of two tenths per lap.

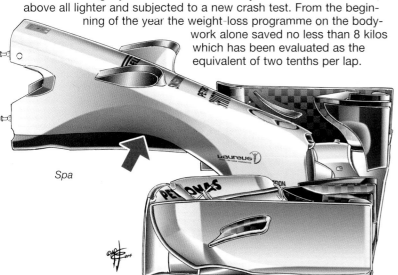

Spa

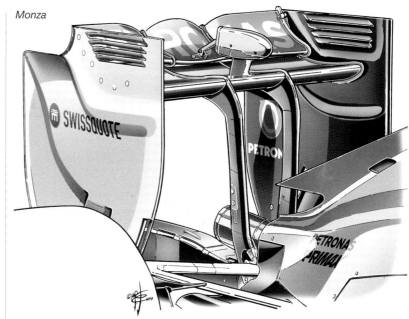

MONZA

Mercedes raced with a new front wing with modifications to both the cascades, with just three slots and the main profile. The Spa flaps without Gurney flaps were retained while the monkey seat was eliminated.

SINGAPORE MONKEY SEAT

At Singapore, the higher downforce monkey seat introduced at Monaco and used again in Budapest, was fitted with double mini-flaps at the top (arrow) to guarantee even great downforce.

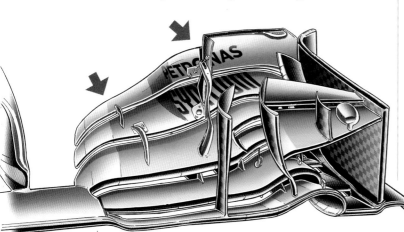

Spa

MONZA FRONT WING

Monza is the fastest circuit of the season requiring even lower downforce aerodynamic set-ups than Spa. Mercedes reduced the chord and incidence of the last flap on the wing used in Belgium.

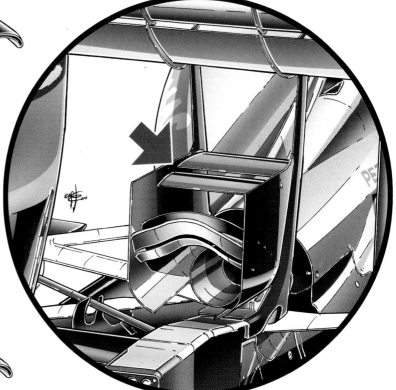

SUZUKA

At Suzuka, Mercedes introduced the most comprehensive evolution of the season, made possible thanks in part to the space in the sidepods freed up by the abolition of FRIC which permitted a drastic reduction in the sections. New vertical turning vanes (1) were attached to the stepped bottom differently (2) as seen in the comparison with the old version (without numbers). There was a new Red Bull-style horizontal slot (3) and new fins (4) either side of the cockpit. At the rear, all the lower area (1) was cut-away more and narrower, there was a new L-shaped cut ahead of the wheels (2), again of Red Bull derivation.

SUZUKA DIFFUSER

The last component in the comprehensive aerodynamic evolution introduced by Mercedes at Suzuka concerned the diffuser which was modified above all in the central section. The very narrow U-shaped central mini-channel was eliminated in favour of a more traditional configuration but equipped in the lower part with vortex generators to improve the efficiency of the central channel. This feature was introduced at the start of the season by Red Bull.

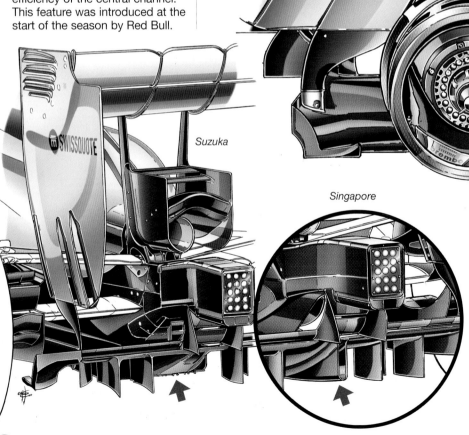

Suzuka

Singapore

SUZUKA

The new rear aerodynamics introduced by Mercedes at Suzuka with the Coke bottle area even more sharply tapered and low. Note the smaller brake discs, supplied by two different manufacturers, Brembo at the rear and Carbon Industrie at the front.

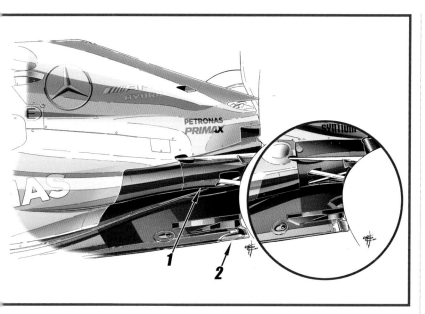

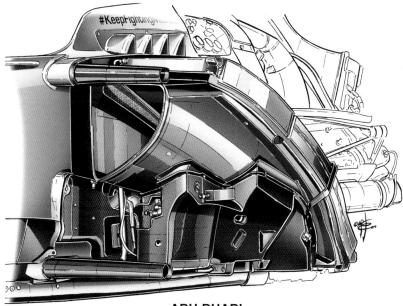

ABU DHABI

It was not new but still one of the features that no other Formula 1 car was then running: the complete fairing of the internal part of the side-pods, adopted to reduce as far as possible the toxic internal turbulence, while on all the other cars this area was very dirty with exposed electronic components and accessories.

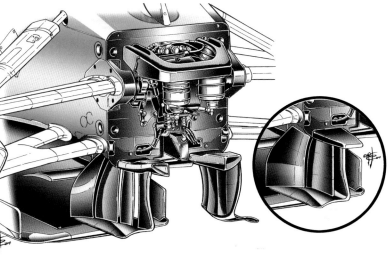

TURNING VANES

For qualifying and the race both Mercedes used the new turning vanes below the monocoque tested only on the Friday in Brazil. They were composed of four elements rather than the usual three.

NOSE COMPARISON

In a tribute to the work done with the animations, here is the comparison between the early season nose and the short version introduced in China after having failed four crash tests. Note how the new configuration permits a greater passage of air towards the rear of the car.

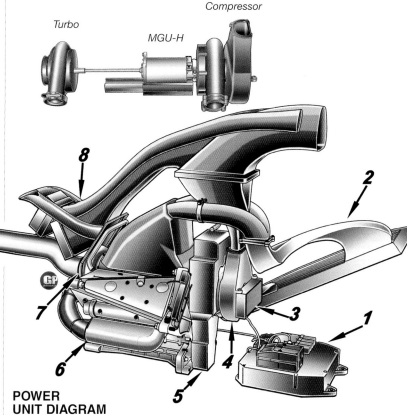

POWER
UNIT DIAGRAM

This diagram of the Mercedes Power Unit also comes from an animation. (1) Battery pack and control units inside the fuel tank as provided for by the regulations. (2) Radiators in the sidepods. (3) Intercooler set within the chassis, a unique to Mercedes feature. 4) Another unique feature was the large compressor (4) set at the front of the engine, partially concealed by the oil reservoir (5). (6) Characteristic very short exhausts insulated to retain heat and feed the MGU-H. (7) Hydraulic system radiator.

RED BULL

A true miracle was performed by Red Bull in the 2014 with its 2nd place finish in the opening race of the World Championship in Australia (subsequently scrubbed due to a disqualification over and irregularity with the flowmeter), an unexpected result after the catastrophic debut of the new RB10 and the reliability problems suffered throughout pre-season testing. However, the most significant result of the season was the second overall in the Constructors' Championship and the merit for having been the only team to interrupt the hegemony of Mercedes with three wins in Montreal, Budapest and Spa. The series of incidents that struck the RB10 during pre-season testing was virtually unprecedented: just 1609 kilometres were covered over the course of the 12 days available to all teams. The delays in the preparation of the Renault Power Unit and above all an extreme installation in the car were factors that risked seeing the new car blocked in the pits. However, it eventually made it to Melbourne thanks to modifications that allowed the situation to be overturned.

The fil rouge of the 2014 season, in the opening races at least, was that of focussing on reliability at the expense of competitiveness, something that hardly filled with joy Adrian Newey who had always been a lover of pure performance to the point at which over the last four years his cars had dominated despite a KERS installation that frequently caused problems with reliability.

It has to be said that in this respect the FIA had in a sense helped Red Bull by banning the daring KERS battery location alongside the exhausts and imposing a single large battery weighing 25 kg and location within the fuel tank area; a kind of hatch in the lower part of the monocoque to house the battery pack and the various associated accessories. However, this time

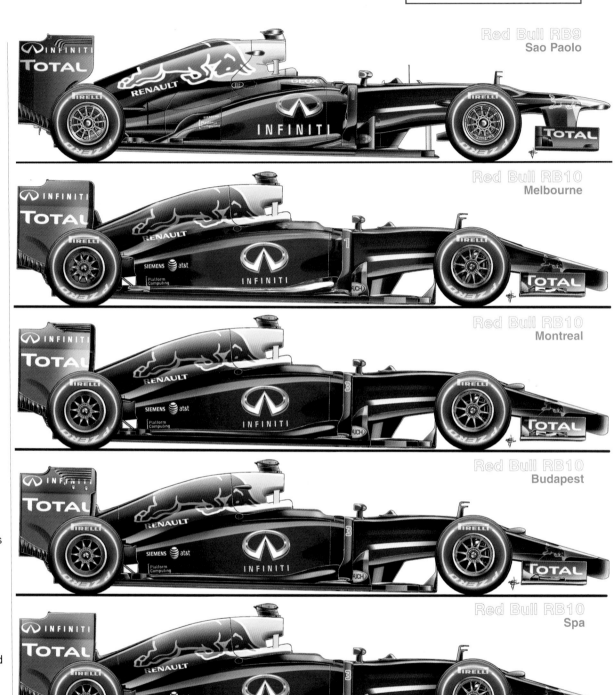

Red Bull RB9
Sao Paolo

Red Bull RB10
Melbourne

Red Bull RB10
Montreal

Red Bull RB10
Budapest

Red Bull RB10
Spa

too Newey distinguished himself by removing the ERS control units from this area and placing them ahead of the exhausts, in a position similar to that of the twin batteries of the RB09. This was with a view of creating a shorter fuel tank, shifting the engine forwards and having a very narrow, long gearbox.

Despite having to cope with 50% more heat dispersal from the Power Unit than in the past, the sidepods of the new RB10 were no bulkier than those of the RB09 with the exception of the end section that no longer descended as a ramp but presented conspicuous vents as well as the central oval one that had already featured on the previous Red Bulls. It was no coincidence that it was in the cabling and plumbing of the cooling system that Newey sought extreme solutions, as he himself admitted. What delivered a KO to the Red Bulls in the first day's testing in Bahrain was another of the major novelties of the 2014 season: electronic brake control, the development of which was by no means simple and proved problematic for more than one team in the first track session at Jerez. Then, however, came the almost miraculous recovery seen in Melbourne, with components even being fitted to the car for the first time and never having previously been tested. Newey then confirmed himself as a "miracle man" by finding a loophole in the 2014 technical regulations: the FIA had in fact codified the position of the video cameras which could no longer be placed strategically on the top of the nose or in correspondence with the front wing, thus becoming devices capable of improving aerodynamic efficiency. According to the regulations their position was now to be fixed both longitudinally and vertically, but there was no mention of the transverse axis; hence, on the RB10 the two video cameras initially appeared to have disappeared whereas they were actually set into the vanity panel: the one on the left functioned with a small hole for the lens, the one on the right was instead completely hidden under the bodywork.

The FIA then introduced a restriction on the transverse positioning and at Monte Carlo Red Bull presented itself with a classic positioning.

The aerodynamic qualities of the chassis and the braking system proved to be another strength of the RB10. Newey kept faith with the underslung callipers on the front axle and introduced four-pot versions at the rear.

The system was realised ad hoc by Brembo, with even the discs being exclusive (used for example in Canada). Again in this sector, the team proceeded with extreme solutions to the assembly of the system, as in the case

of the lightened flanges saving unsprung weight. A great deal of work was conducted on the brake intakes which became true aerodynamic devices. Also of note was an inversion of the trend in aerodynamic set-ups: from the higher loadings seen in previous seasons there was a shift to lower loadings on the RB10. This was made necessary to overcome the lower power output of the Renault Power Unit, a factor that remained the RB10's Achilles' heel throughout the season.

RB9-RB10: OVERHEAD COMPARISON

Red Bull interpreted in a wholly original manner the low nose imposed by the FIA, introducing a kind of bulb (1). There was a new alignment (2) of the endplates with respect to the front wheels. (3) Through to the Monaco GP the video cameras (3) were concealed (as shown in the circle) inside the nose, exploiting a loophole in the FIA's regulations regarding their positioning. (4) The front suspension had a different geometry. (5) At the front the sidepods are more swollen and equipped with large hot air vents near in the area close to the cockpit (6) but then they narrow considerably in the so-called Coke bottle area. On the RB9 they formed a kind of chute with the exit of the exhausts exploiting the Coanda effect to blow into the diffuser. On the RB10 all the hot air from the sidepods is evacuated towards the end section via the large oval aperture in the engine cover.

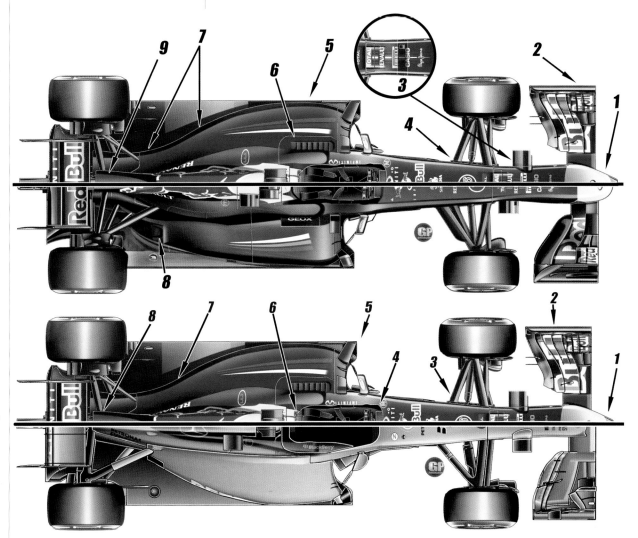

RED BULL – MERCEDES COMPARISON

In the overhead view, the differences between the Red Bull and the Mercedes are even clearer. On the RB10 the nose is very long (1) while on the W05 it is the shortest in the field, at the minimum permitted by the regulations. (2) The front wing and endplate assembly is completely different. (3) Mercedes introduced a new, very narrow lower wishbone, but the upper wishbone is instead very wide. On the RB10 the cockpit is shifted forwards along with the engine (6). On the W05 the front axle is further ahead of the sidepod mouths. On the RB10, the narrowing (7) of the bodywork ahead of the rear wheels is much more severe. The hot air venting on the RB10 is concentrated in the end part of the sidepods (8) and the large, oval central vent.

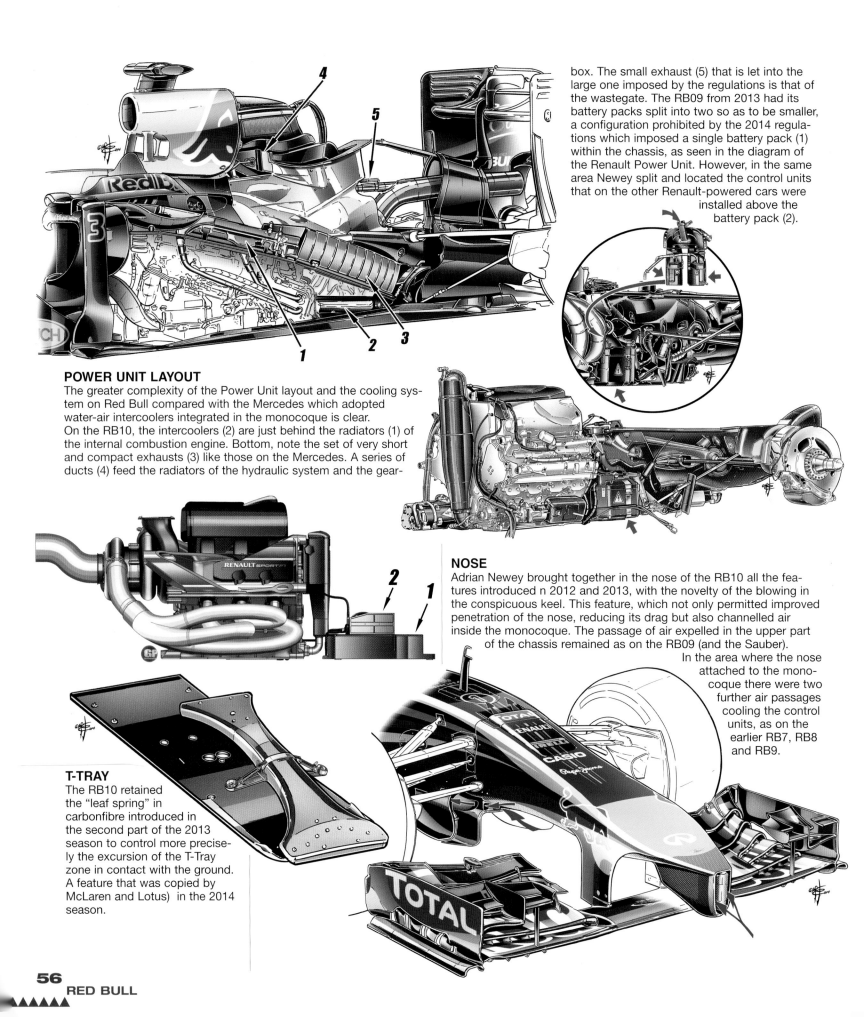

box. The small exhaust (5) that is let into the large one imposed by the regulations is that of the wastegate. The RB09 from 2013 had its battery packs split into two so as to be smaller, a configuration prohibited by the 2014 regulations which imposed a single battery pack (1) within the chassis, as seen in the diagram of the Renault Power Unit. However, in the same area Newey split and located the control units that on the other Renault-powered cars were installed above the battery pack (2).

POWER UNIT LAYOUT

The greater complexity of the Power Unit layout and the cooling system on Red Bull compared with the Mercedes which adopted water-air intercoolers integrated in the monocoque is clear.
On the RB10, the intercoolers (2) are just behind the radiators (1) of the internal combustion engine. Bottom, note the set of very short and compact exhausts (3) like those on the Mercedes. A series of ducts (4) feed the radiators of the hydraulic system and the gear-

NOSE

Adrian Newey brought together in the nose of the RB10 all the features introduced n 2012 and 2013, with the novelty of the blowing in the conspicuous keel. This feature, which not only permitted improved penetration of the nose, reducing its drag but also channelled air inside the monocoque. The passage of air expelled in the upper part of the chassis remained as on the RB09 (and the Sauber).
In the area where the nose attached to the monocoque there were two further air passages cooling the control units, as on the earlier RB7, RB8 and RB9.

T-TRAY

The RB10 retained the "leaf spring" in carbonfibre introduced in the second part of the 2013 season to control more precisely the excursion of the T-Tray zone in contact with the ground. A feature that was copied by McLaren and Lotus) in the 2014 season.

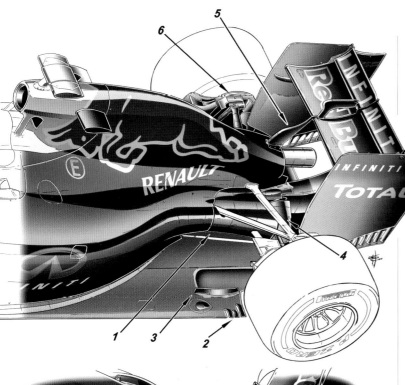

S-DUCT

Even with the low nose, Red Bull again featured an air passage between the lower and upper parts, present on the previous year's RB09. On the 2013 car, this passage was concealed within the nose and its presence was intuited by the fairing covering the brake fluid cylinders, flattened (and sacrificed so as to be able to create the ramp (the small circle shows the normal version form the 2012 RB08). The ingress for the air was created in the lower part of the chassis with small slots that in the detail drawing with the turning vanes removed can clearly be seen to be let into the lower part of the chassis to cool the electronic control units at the start of the sidepods.

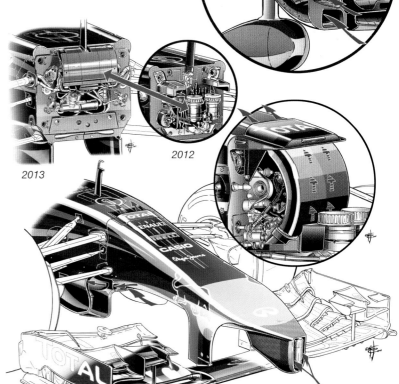

2013

2012

RB09 2013

RB9-RB10 COMPARISON

The revolution in the regulations led to the creation of a car that was very different, including the design of the sidepods, as seen in the comparison with those of the RB09 (2013). The RB10 lost the ramp-like descent and the air passage in the lower part, opting for rather angular side walls (1). The lower part, severely cut away, retained the slots (2) ahead of the rear wheels and a small vertical fin (3) shielding the tyres. The driveshaft is set within the fairing (4). The single rear wing support (5) had a boomerang shape. (6) The upper wishbone mount was shifted inboard and faired with an aerodynamic profile.

REAR VIEW

The enormous oval vent (1) in the end part of the sidepods was positioned very low, with the aerodynamic fairing (4) of the suspension placed practically halfway. New diffuser, cut away and rounded (2) in the area close to the wheels. In the 200 mm central zone there is a kind of vertical flap.

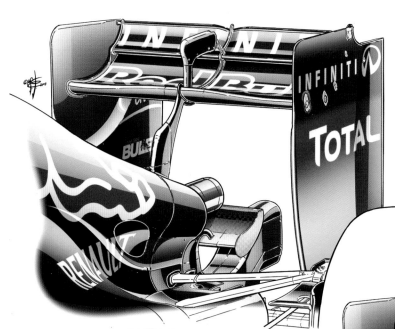

MONKEY SEAT
A n are where Red Bull went against the tide was that of the monkey seat which the team chose to place below the exhaust to improve the efficiency of the extractor profile. In order to introduce this feature, the protection structure had a clear S-shape.

SHANGHAI
Red Bull retained the new rear wing introduced in Melbourne and characterised by new slots in the endplates. They were no longer horizontal and placed above the main profile, but rather followed the line at the height of the dorsal part.

DIFFUSER
Another unique feature on the RB10 were these vortex generators, placed in the central part of the diffuser to increase the extraction of air and obviously difficult to spot when the car was in the pits.

SAKHIR: FRONT WING
In a desperate attempt to compensate for the reduced power of the Renault engine, Red Bull "simply" removed the cascades to reduce straight-line drag; similarly, at the rear, around a centimetre was trimmed off the flap in the rear wing so as to balance the car.

FOUR-POT CALIPER
Like Mercedes, Red Bull reprised the four-pot (rather than six-pot) rear brake caliper: a feature that both teams (Mercedes at the time being Brawn GP) had introduced and then abandoned in the 2009 season. Subsequently both Sauber and McLaren also adopted the feature.

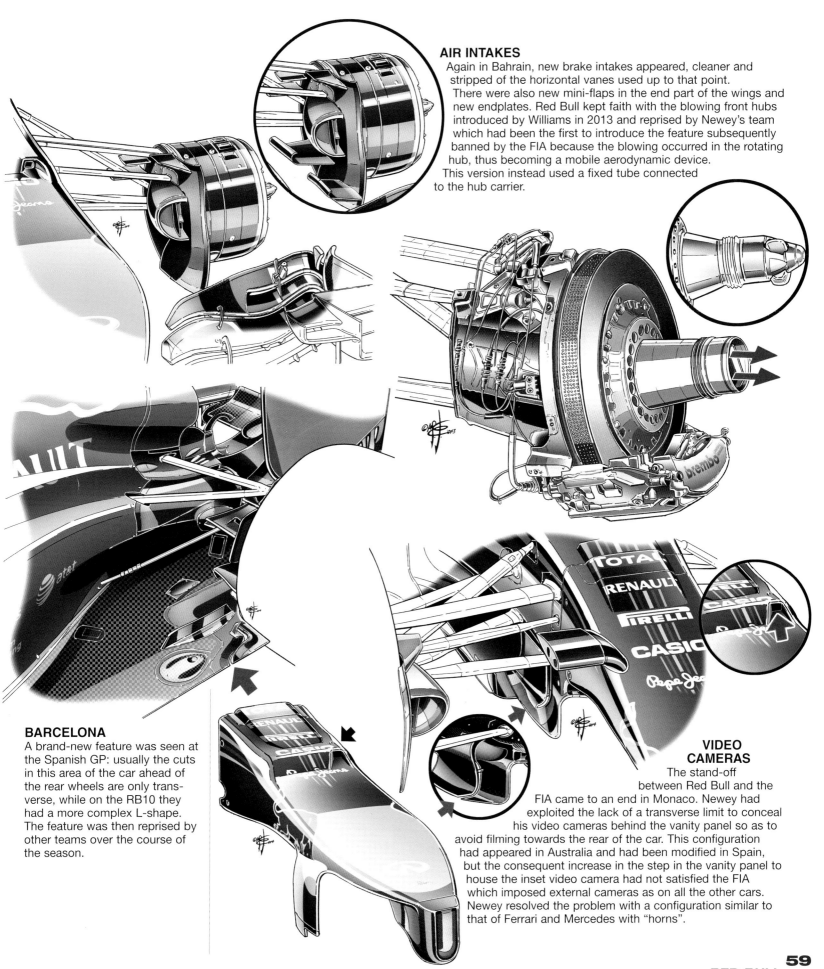

AIR INTAKES

Again in Bahrain, new brake intakes appeared, cleaner and stripped of the horizontal vanes used up to that point.

There were also new mini-flaps in the end part of the wings and new endplates. Red Bull kept faith with the blowing front hubs introduced by Williams in 2013 and reprised by Newey's team which had been the first to introduce the feature subsequently banned by the FIA because the blowing occurred in the rotating hub, thus becoming a mobile aerodynamic device.

This version instead used a fixed tube connected to the hub carrier.

BARCELONA

A brand-new feature was seen at the Spanish GP: usually the cuts in this area of the car ahead of the rear wheels are only transverse, while on the RB10 they had a more complex L-shape. The feature was then reprised by other teams over the course of the season.

VIDEO CAMERAS

The stand-off between Red Bull and the FIA came to an end in Monaco. Newey had exploited the lack of a transverse limit to conceal his video cameras behind the vanity panel so as to avoid filming towards the rear of the car. This configuration had appeared in Australia and had been modified in Spain, but the consequent increase in the step in the vanity panel to house the inset video camera had not satisfied the FIA which imposed external cameras as on all the other cars. Newey resolved the problem with a configuration similar to that of Ferrari and Mercedes with "horns".

MONACO
Doubling up of the monkey seat on the RB10, with two mini-profiles on the upper part of the central exhaust too.

SPA
The problem encountered by Ricciardo in Belgium with his right front brake was caused by a new, extremely light fixture (bell) designed to save unsprung weight. This feature was also associated with the fact that Spa, like Silverstone, is considered to be a "light" track for brakes and one on which Red Bull tried to go to the limit to privilege performance.

MONTREAL
In Montreal, this new rear wing endplate with a conspicuous vertical slot was rejected in favour of the version seen in Bahrain with only horizontal slots at the top and no vertical slot.

MONZA
Like Ferrari, Red Bull also reprised the front wing seen at Monza in 2013, accentuating the reduction in downforce not only through the elimination of the lateral upper flaps, but also the overturned L flaps that had been retained on the RB9 (highlighted by the arrow). The chord of the flaps was reduced.

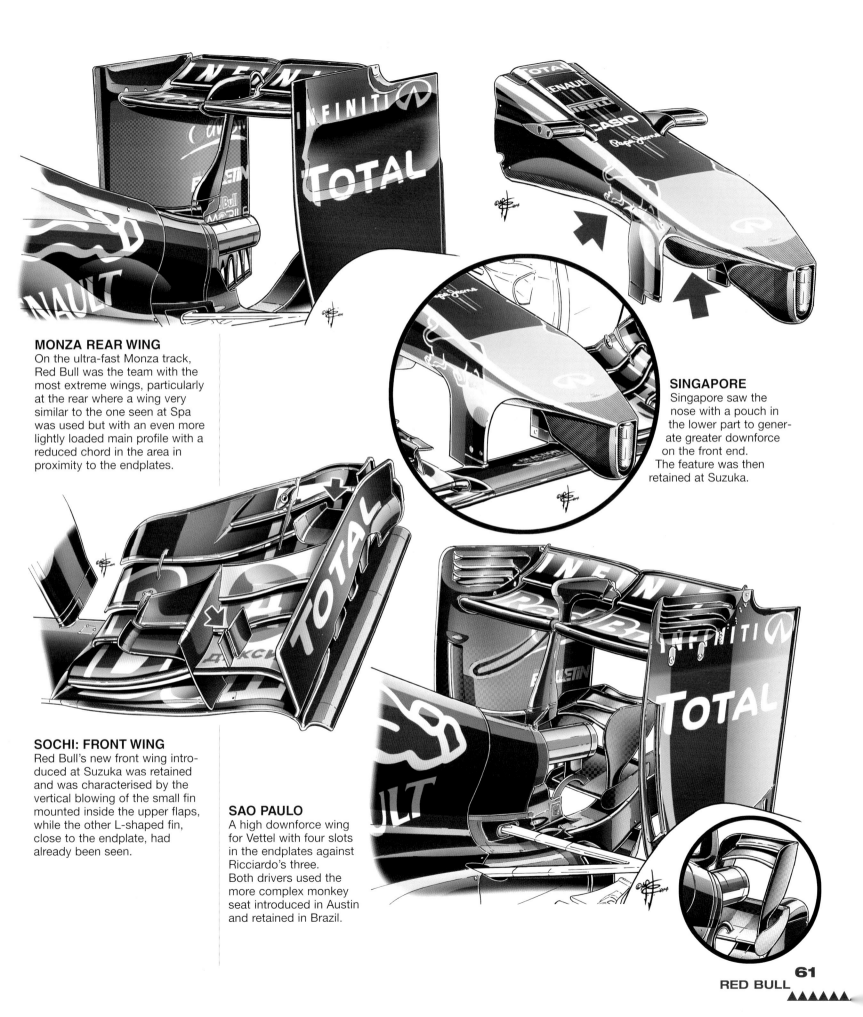

MONZA REAR WING

On the ultra-fast Monza track, Red Bull was the team with the most extreme wings, particularly at the rear where a wing very similar to the one seen at Spa was used but with an even more lightly loaded main profile with a reduced chord in the area in proximity to the endplates.

SINGAPORE

Singapore saw the nose with a pouch in the lower part to generate greater downforce on the front end. The feature was then retained at Suzuka.

SOCHI: FRONT WING

Red Bull's new front wing introduced at Suzuka was retained and was characterised by the vertical blowing of the small fin mounted inside the upper flaps, while the other L-shaped fin, close to the endplate, had already been seen.

SAO PAULO

A high downforce wing for Vettel with four slots in the endplates against Ricciardo's three. Both drivers used the more complex monkey seat introduced in Austin and retained in Brazil.

WILLIAMS

Williams was without doubt the team that made most progress with respect to 2013: the Grove-based team in fact was the protagonist in a remarkable turn around thanks to the new FIA regulations that revolutionised the cars with the adoption of the Power Units.

After a terrible year in which it finished in 9th place in the Constructors' Championship with just 5 points, Sir Frank's team, now directed by his daughter Claire, hoisted itself up to 3rd behind Mercedes and Red Bull Racing, but ahead of Ferrari on 320 points.

Felipe Massa and Valtteri Bottas actually closed out the front row of the grid for the Austrian GP, breaking the hegemony of the Silver Arrows, and over the course of the season achieved three 2nd places and six podium finishes.

The car was created under the technical direction of Pat Symonds, the former Benetton, Renault and Virgin engineer who from July 2013 had been seeking to optimise the work initiated by Mike Coughlan.

Having abandoned the naturally aspirated Renault V8 in favour of the Mercedes V6 Turbo, Williams could count on the best Power Unit available to client teams. This opportunity was facilitated by Toto Wolff, head of Mercedes Motorsport, as well as being a minor shareholder at Grove. Symonds revised the organization of the work, focusing the aerodynamic work for the FW36 on efficiency rather than downforce (which then proved to be wanting on slow tracks).

However, the objective was to create a car with little drag, capable of optimal speeds through the trap and therefore capable of attempting overtaking while also able to conserve fuel. This was a particularly important factor given that the Power Unit came with a restriction fuel tank capacity restriction of 100 kg. The FW36 was presented with a conspicuous proboscis nose and

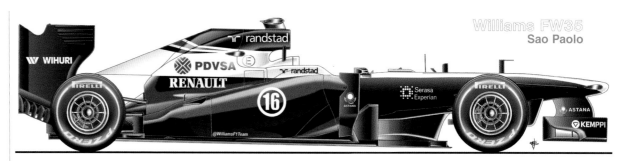

Williams FW35
Sao Paolo

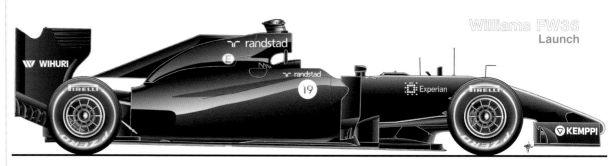

Williams FW36
Launch

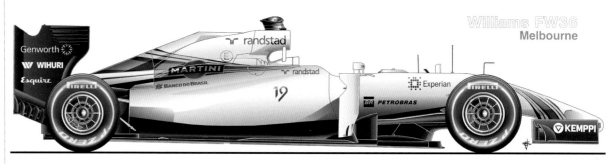

Williams FW36
Melbourne

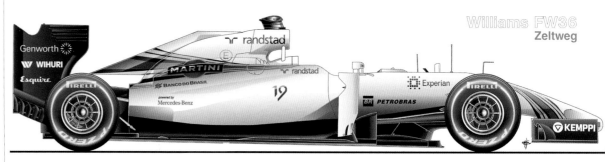

Williams FW36
Zeltweg

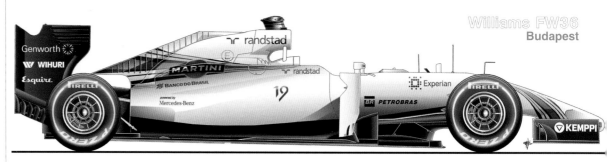

Williams FW36
Budapest

fairly large radiator mouths but sidepods that were very narrow towards the rear end so as to leave the necessary space in the Coke bottle area for the passage of the air flows towards the rear extractor. Williams adopted push-rod front and pull-rod rear suspension with a new geometry. The design dida away with a central rear wing pylon, with the two aerodynamic profiles mounted just above the diffuser, either side of the crash box.

As well as supporting the wing, this feature served to reproduce, at least in part, the effects of the beam wing the 2014 regulations had outlawed. The aerodynamic advantages were nonetheless greater than the inevitable increase in weight the feature entailed.

The Williams-made eight-speed gearbox was also new and boasted a titanium casing: this relatively conservative choice of material was made in view of the high temperatures predicted for the Power Units. In contrast with the Mercedes which located its water/air intercooler in the monocoque, on the FW36 a more traditional installation in the sidepods was preferred.

The Martini-striped white cars proved capable of exploiting the Pirelli tyres well and was not particularly affected by the mid-season banning of the FRIC systems as the one it had been using had not been as sophisticated as Brackley's. Pat Symonds went for substance over form, foregoing for example, the digital display with the McLaren Applied Technology LCD screen.

In Australia, interest had been aroused by the rear view mirror perfectly integrated in the three aerodynamic elements formed by the winglets either side of the cockpit. Shanghai saw the appearance of a new dorsal fin on the engine cover that had 18 vertical gill slots of varying lengths. This was an experiment that was to be reprised later in the season, in particular for the hottest Grands Prix. Barcelona saw the introduction of new bodywork capable of guaranteeing better cooling of the Mercedes engine without compromising the excellent efficiency of the car.

In Canada the front wing endplate featured a kind of "beak" in the final section, while the upper flaps with a vent between the two small profiles were retained. At the Red Bull Ring the FW36 presented a refinement; nothing to do with the McLaren-style "shutter" rear suspension, but the rear tie-rod near the brake intake became a true flap, as if it were an aerodynamic element of the brake duct.

At Hockenheim, the team revisited the engine cover tested in China that allowed better evacuation of the hot air from the radiators without overly penalising the efficiency of the FW36. Hunagry also saw the debut of a new rear wing equipped with a monkey seat to increase downforce. The brake intakes were also revised and equipped for the same reason with a greater number of fins, while a small flap appeared below the video camera, reprising a feature that had already been seen on the Ferrari F14T.

In Japan a comparison test was conducted with a new rear bodywork design tested on Bottas's car, while Massa remained faithful to the old configuration: the Finn had shorter and narrower sidepods.

The upper rear suspension mount was also different and protruded beyond the fairing.

Lastly, a front brake air intake different to the one used at Sochi was seen: the carbonfibre ear presented a vent that served to reduce the flow of air towards the brake intakes, improving the flow to be channelled towards the rear of the car.

POWER UNIT

Williams was the only Mercedes-powered team to threaten the works Silver Arrows, actually closing out the front row of the grid in Austria, thanks largely to the Stuttgart Power Unit.

Highlighted by the red arrow at the top, the oil reservoir partially concealed the large compressor placed in front of the engine. Located in the rear zone instead was the big turbine with the MGU-H in the V of the engine.

DEBUT

Making its debut in Jerez, the new FW35 sported a "neutral" blue livery.

Curiously, both Williams and Toro Rosso presented the same solution for fixing the rear wing and overcoming the abolition of the beam wing. The endplates were linked to the protection structures via a broad profile (2) located below the 150 mm limit, an an area in which the regulations prohibited the placing of bodywork elements. The external zone (1) of the extractor profile was very sophisticated with an arched section strongly inclined towards the outside. On the Williams the driveshaft (3) was not faired, while the tie-rod (4) was notably set further back and lower. (5) In the 2014 season the monkey seat increased from 150 mm to 200 mm in width.

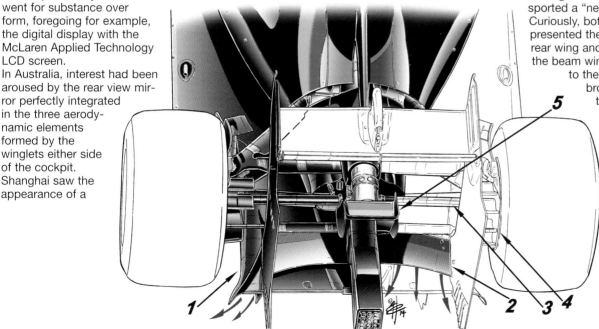

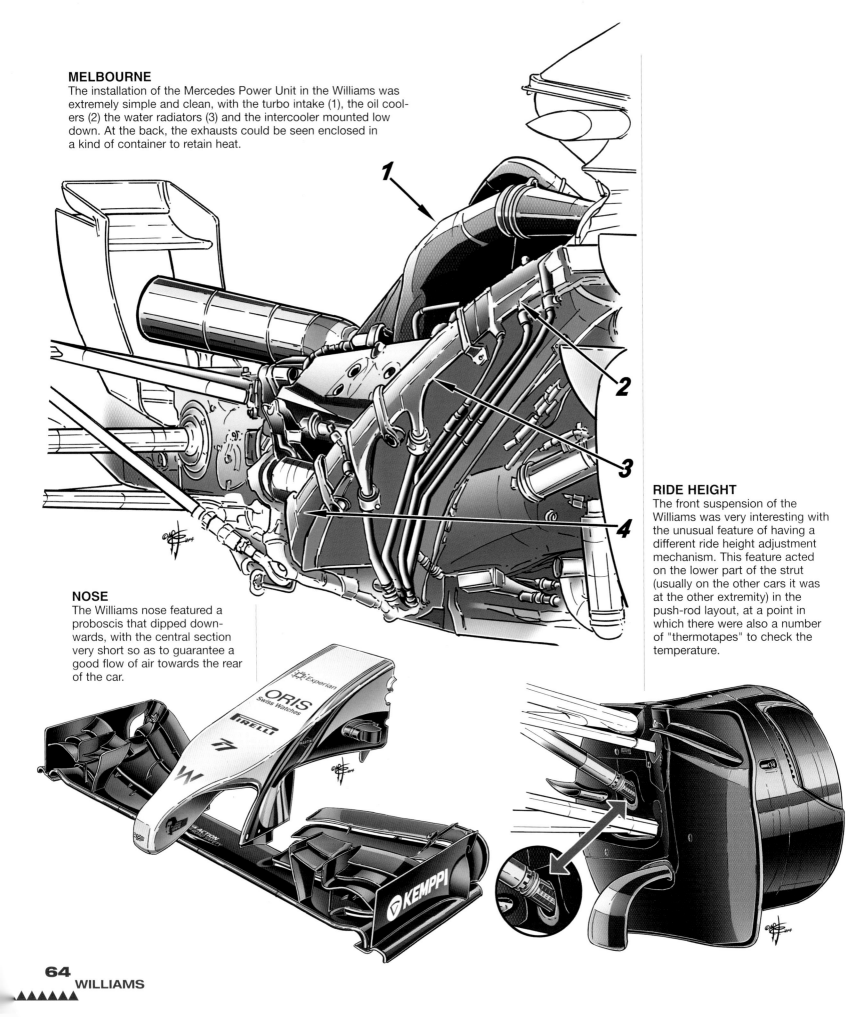

MELBOURNE

The installation of the Mercedes Power Unit in the Williams was extremely simple and clean, with the turbo intake (1), the oil coolers (2) the water radiators (3) and the intercooler mounted low down. At the back, the exhausts could be seen enclosed in a kind of container to retain heat.

NOSE

The Williams nose featured a proboscis that dipped downwards, with the central section very short so as to guarantee a good flow of air towards the rear of the car.

RIDE HEIGHT

The front suspension of the Williams was very interesting with the unusual feature of having a different ride height adjustment mechanism. This feature acted on the lower part of the strut (usually on the other cars it was at the other extremity) in the push-rod layout, at a point in which there were also a number of "thermotapes" to check the temperature.

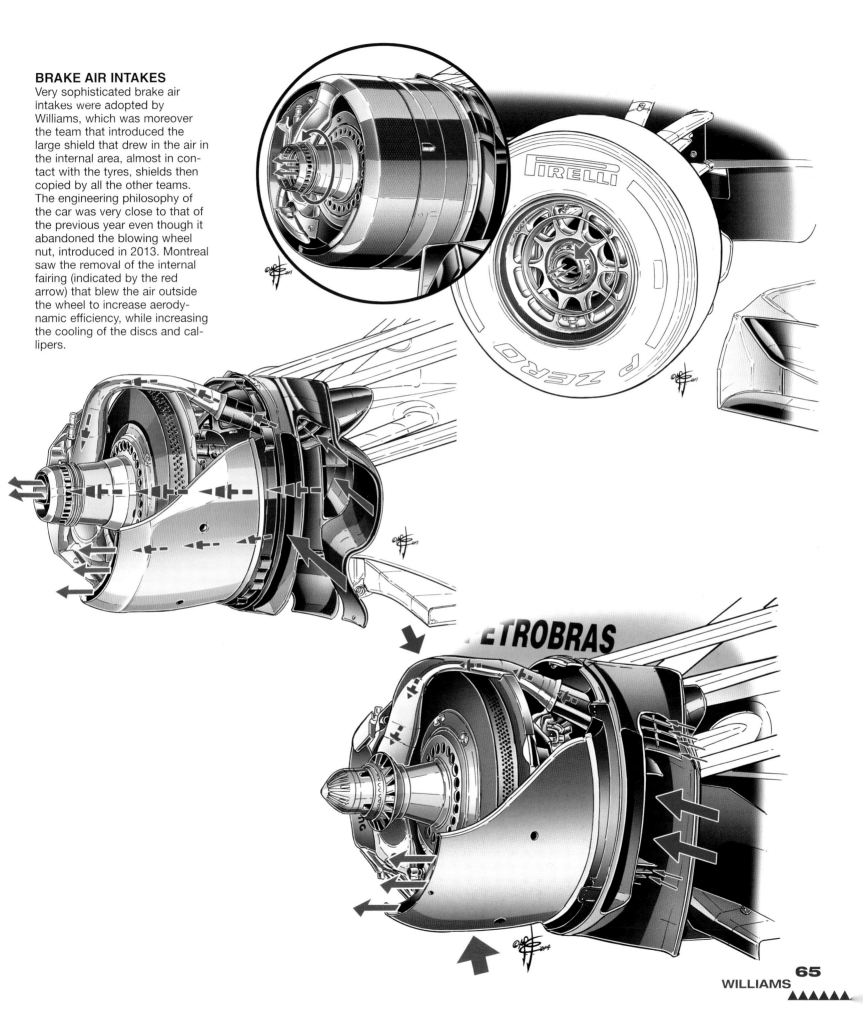

BRAKE AIR INTAKES

Very sophisticated brake air intakes were adopted by Williams, which was moreover the team that introduced the large shield that drew in the air in the internal area, almost in contact with the tyres, shields then copied by all the other teams. The engineering philosophy of the car was very close to that of the previous year even though it abandoned the blowing wheel nut, introduced in 2013. Montreal saw the removal of the internal fairing (indicated by the red arrow) that blew the air outside the wheel to increase aerodynamic efficiency, while increasing the cooling of the discs and callipers.

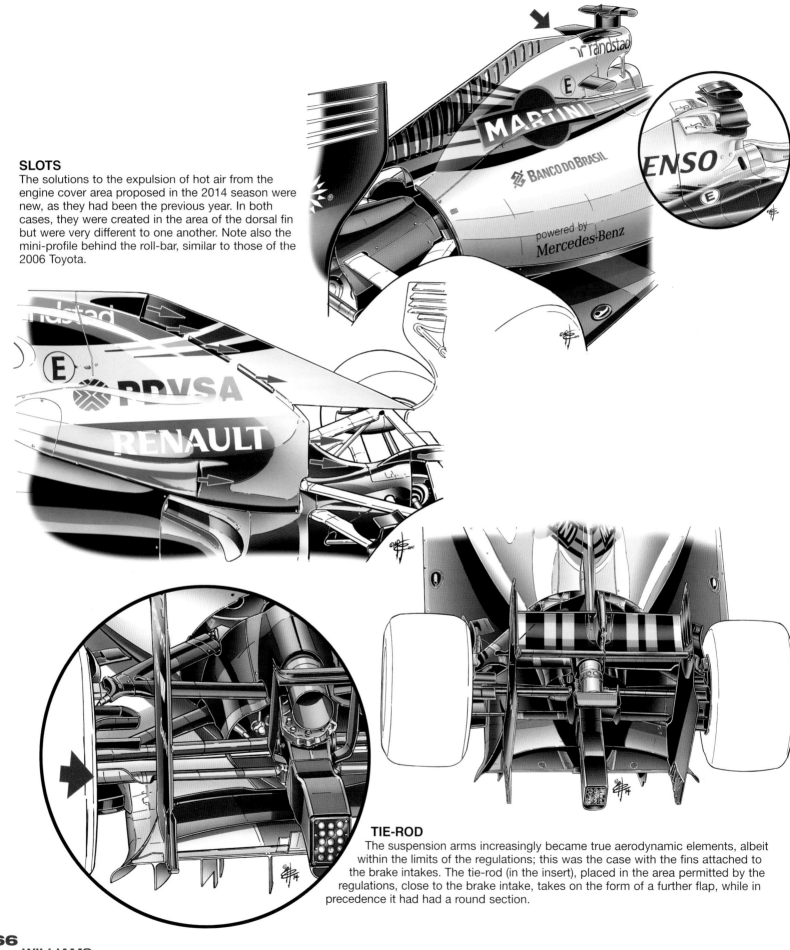

SLOTS

The solutions to the expulsion of hot air from the engine cover area proposed in the 2014 season were new, as they had been the previous year. In both cases, they were created in the area of the dorsal fin but were very different to one another. Note also the mini-profile behind the roll-bar, similar to those of the 2006 Toyota.

TIE-ROD

The suspension arms increasingly became true aerodynamic elements, albeit within the limits of the regulations; this was the case with the fins attached to the brake intakes. The tie-rod (in the insert), placed in the area permitted by the regulations, close to the brake intake, takes on the form of a further flap, while in precedence it had had a round section.

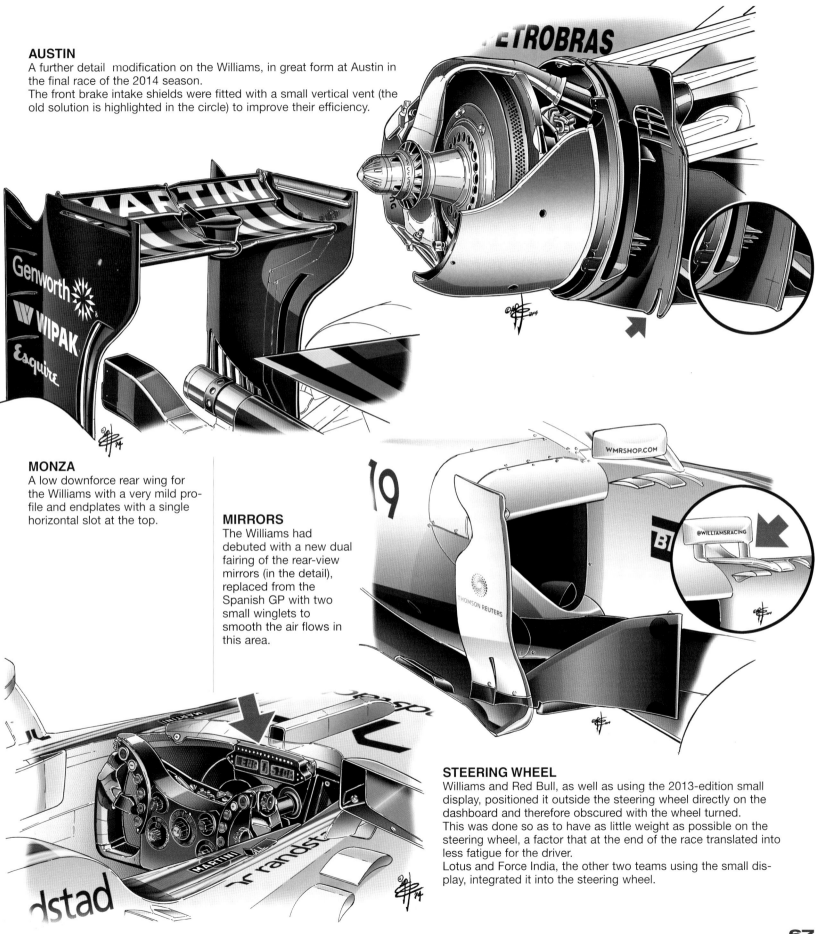

AUSTIN

A further detail modification on the Williams, in great form at Austin in the final race of the 2014 season.

The front brake intake shields were fitted with a small vertical vent (the old solution is highlighted in the circle) to improve their efficiency.

MONZA

A low downforce rear wing for the Williams with a very mild profile and endplates with a single horizontal slot at the top.

MIRRORS

The Williams had debuted with a new dual fairing of the rear-view mirrors (in the detail), replaced from the Spanish GP with two small winglets to smooth the air flows in this area.

STEERING WHEEL

Williams and Red Bull, as well as using the 2013-edition small display, positioned it outside the steering wheel directly on the dashboard and therefore obscured with the wheel turned.

This was done so as to have as little weight as possible on the steering wheel, a factor that at the end of the race translated into less fatigue for the driver.

Lotus and Force India, the other two teams using the small display, integrated it into the steering wheel.

FERRARI

CONSTRUCTORS' CLASSIFICATION			
	2013	2014	
Position	3°	4°	-1 ▼
Points	354	216	-138 ▼

It was back in 2009 when Ferrari last finished in 4th place in the Constructors' Championship, but at least that season the team did win a race. To find a year with a similar lack of success, we have to go way back to 1993; these two facts alone reveal the extent to which the 2014 season was an uphill climb for the Prancing Horse. In the year in which the engines (transformed into "Power Units") reclaimed a dominant role in the conferment of performance, Maranello was unable to honour the tradition whereby engines were always the strong suit of the Rosse. The project that brought together the two electric motors and the six-cylinder turbo engine got underway well behind schedule especially if we consider that Mercedes had instead been working on their Power Unit for around four years.

The most curious aspect, at least from an outside observer's point of view, is that in a year in which Adrian Newey demonstrated great concern for the increased importance acquired by engines and their reliability and management with respect to aerodynamics, at Maranello they went against the tide. Underlying the F14 T project was in fact an extreme aerodynamics package that even conditioned the choices made relating to the Power Unit and its components.

The very pronounced step in the lower part of the chassis should have been integrated with an elongated rear end that tapered as much as possible to create a so-called Coke bottle zone and a particularly efficient diffuser.

In order to achieve this three specific choices were made: the advancement of the internal combustion engine, the location of the intercooler inside the V of the engine and the placing of the oil reservoir in the gearbox spacer. This last was something of an innovation, even though effectively it represented a step back into the past of no less than 16 years. The oil tank in the gearbox spacer had in fact been abandoned on F1 cars in the late '90s after Stewart and Arrows had shifted it to the front of the engine in 1998, placing it in a niche created in the monocoque. A return to the past as had been the case in 2009, when Adrian Newey had reprised the pull-rod rear suspension layout.

This innovation had allowed the engine to be advanced and in theory allowed for better packaging of the various components. For the same reason, the exhausts now rose vertically so as to free up the lower area. This particular choice also led to a considerable lengthening of the wheelbase, clearly revealed by the dimensions of the gearbox casing. At the same time it significantly conditioned the efficiency of the Power Unit, penalised by the adoption of a smaller turbine than that of the Mercedes-powered cars; an "interesting" move but one that ended up conditioning the performance of the entire Power Unit. Above all the provision of additional power by the electric motor linked to the turbine (MGU-H) was inefficient compared with other cars equipped with Mercedes engine and was clearly at a disadvantage in terms of acceleration and maximum speed.

Ferrari also went against the tide in its choice of nose configuration, with no proboscis, flat, wide and obviously low in order to respect the limit of 185 mm from the reference plane imposed by the FIA for safety reasons. For

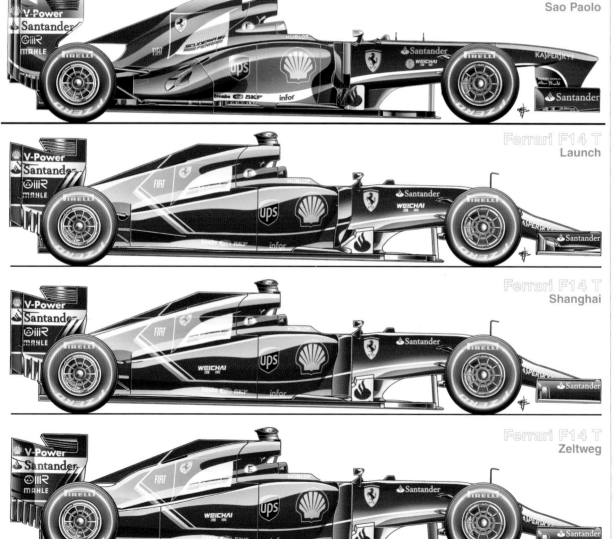

Ferrari F138
Sao Paolo

Ferrari F14 T
Launch

Ferrari F14 T
Shanghai

Ferrari F14 T
Zeltweg

the third consecutive season, Ferrari retained its controversial pull-rod front suspension layout and during the course of the championship in the search to improve the handling of the car attention focussed on the rear end, with sensors being applied to the suspension arms from the United States GP in Austin.

A great deal of work for almost every race went into the brake intakes and the blowing front hubs, introduced but not raced in Shanghai. Ferrari also experimented with the exhausts to improve the supply of heat to the MGU-H, also drawing of the work of Marussia on whose car the "bandaged" exhausts appeared before the F14 T (on which they debuted at Spa).

A new engine cover was presented in Canada but not raced, making its debut in the next GP in Austria where it was actually used in an even more closed version, lacking the dorsal mid-line vents tested on the Friday.

That occasion also saw the appearance of new turning vanes under the chassis and candelabra at the sides of the wider and redesigned sidepods.

At the third but last race of the season in Austin, Ferrari was already testing in view of the 2015 season, with a new rear wing concept, that was different in all its elements, but above all making a modification to the rear suspension geometry tested only by Raikkonen. Going back to the wing, it had a surprising dual vent in correspondence with the back of the main plane, new for the F14T but not for Red Bull which had already introduced the feature at the second race of the season in Malaysia.

The horizontal vents in the upper front part of the endplates were also new, as were the wing profiles. The single support pylon was also modified.

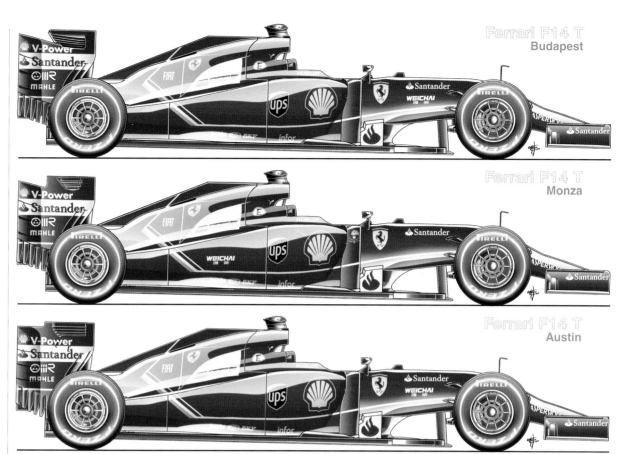

Ferrari F14 T
Budapest

Ferrari F14 T
Monza

Ferrari F14 T
Austin

OVERHEAD VIEW

(1) The nose of the F14T was low, flattened and shorter than that of the F138. (2) The front wing was located 7.5 cm from the external edge of the tyres and for this reason the endplates became even more curved and sophisticated. (3) As per the regulations, the video cameras are located in the upper part of the nose, close to the mounting point on the chassis, while previously they were placed strategically, as flaps with respect to the main profile. (4) Bridge turning vanes similar to those tested at the end of the 2013 season. (5) There was an incredible reduction in the width of the sidepods (highlighted in yellow) despite the more complex cooling requirements of the Power Unit. (6) The Coke bottle area was also more tapering. (7) All the heat from the sidepods was channelled to their end sections via two large circular vents. (8) Vertical rear wing support pylons returned with a new boomerang shape. (9) The new endplates represented an evolution of those seen in the 2013 season, with the confirmation of the presence of the fringes in the lower section.

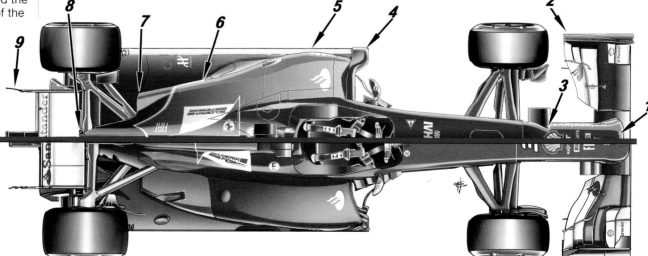

SIDE VIEWS

Ferrari presented an extreme interpretation of the new restriction on nose heights. In fact, the low "duck's bill" (1) was integrated with the decision to cut away the chassis (2-3) so as to get around the regulations and limit the toxic effects of the lowering of the monocoque while at the same time exploiting the lower aerodynamics to best effect. (4) The sidepods were of a similar size to those of the F138: despite the need for greater heat dispersal associated with the new Power Units, they had bridge turning vanes at the leading edge and fairly small intake mouths.
(5) The dynamic air intake was triangular in shape. (6) The tapering engine cover had a clear dorsal fin. (7) The boomerang-shaped vertical supports were also new, (8) as were the rear wing endplates.
(9) The hot air from the radiators was all channelled to the end zone of the sidepods.

FRONT VIEW

The F14T did not have a proboscis nose but rather (1) a flat, wide and obviously low form respecting the 185 mm limit imposed by the FIA for safety motives. (2) The front wing was 15 cm narrower, again because of the new regulations. (3) Both the endplates and the section of the wing from the main profile to the cascades were new. (4) For the third season running Ferrari retained pull-rod suspension at the front too. (5) The F14T uses bridge-type turning vanes at the leading edge of the sidepods. (6) The rear wing was also penalised by the regulations: it had to be contained within a "box" that was 2 cm lower; the beam wing lower profile was outlawed.
(7) The dynamic intake was smaller and triangular in shape.

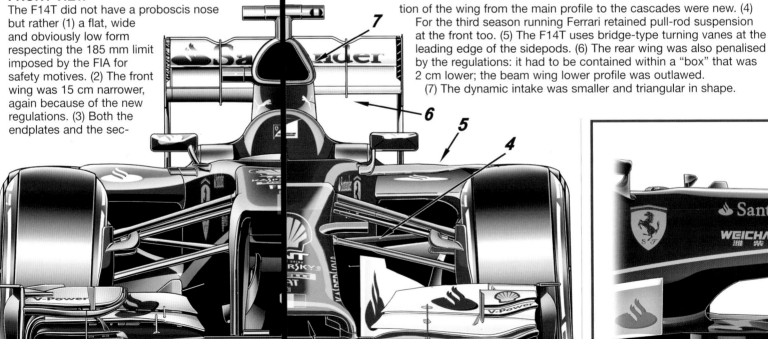
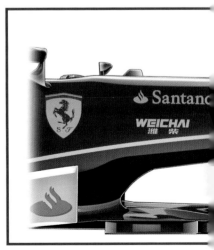

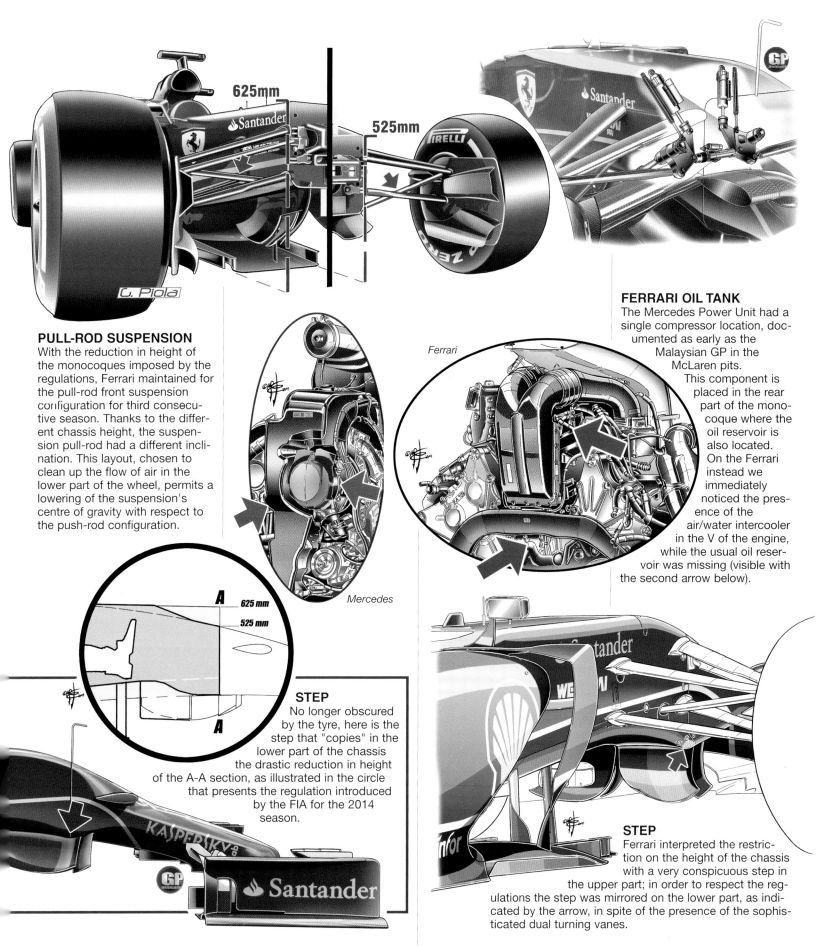

625mm

525mm

G. Piola

PULL-ROD SUSPENSION

With the reduction in height of the monocoques imposed by the regulations, Ferrari maintained for the pull-rod front suspension configuration for third consecutive season. Thanks to the different chassis height, the suspension pull-rod had a different inclination. This layout, chosen to clean up the flow of air in the lower part of the wheel, permits a lowering of the suspension's centre of gravity with respect to the push-rod configuration.

Mercedes

Ferrari

FERRARI OIL TANK

The Mercedes Power Unit had a single compressor location, documented as early as the Malaysian GP in the McLaren pits.
This component is placed in the rear part of the monocoque where the oil reservoir is also located. On the Ferrari instead we immediately noticed the presence of the air/water intercooler in the V of the engine, while the usual oil reservoir was missing (visible with the second arrow below).

A
625 mm
525 mm
A

STEP

No longer obscured by the tyre, here is the step that "copies" in the lower part of the chassis the drastic reduction in height of the A-A section, as illustrated in the circle that presents the regulation introduced by the FIA for the 2014 season.

STEP

Ferrari interpreted the restriction on the height of the chassis with a very conspicuous step in the upper part; in order to respect the regulations the step was mirrored on the lower part, as indicated by the arrow, in spite of the presence of the sophisticated dual turning vanes.

FERRARI REVOLUTION

The F14 T was a brand-new, courageous and in many ways nonconformist project but not equally positive in terms of results on the track.

Underlying the design was an extreme aerodynamics package that excessively conditioned the choices relating to the Power Unit. The very pronounced step in the lower part of the chassis should have been integrated with an elongated rear end that tapered as much as possible to create a so-called Coke bottle zone and a particularly efficient diffuser. As we have seen, there were three particularly innovative choices: the advancement of the internal combustion engine, the location of the intercooler inside the V of the engine and the placing of the oil reservoir in the gearbox spacer.

This last was a feature that had been abandoned on F1 cars after Stewart and Arrows had introduced the concept of placing the oil reservoir in a niche in the monocoque ahead of the engine in 1998. The new oil reservoir location created space in the area in front of the engine permitting an advanced position and a particularly compact and narrow rear mechanical installation. For the same reason, the exhausts now rose vertically so as to free up the lower area. This particular choice also led to a considerable lengthening of the wheelbase, clearly revealed by the dimensions of the gearbox casing. It did however compromise the efficiency of the Power Unit in that a particularly small turbine was adopted.

The MGU-K was also enclosed in the gearbox casing, as seen in the exposed engine drawing (see the blue arrow).

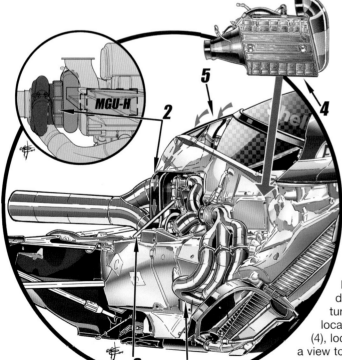

POWER UNIT LAYOUT

This drawing presents the Ferrari Power Unit layout (1), designed in view of the most compact installation possible, to the benefit of the aerodynamics, exploiting the slightly advanced position of the internal combustion engine.

For the same reason, the exhausts rose very close to the cylinder heads, with a drastic reduction of transverse bulk. (2) The electric motor group, compressor and turbine was located as on the Renault, despite speculation that the electric motor was located centrally. (3) Stiffening to eliminate turbine vibration. New intercooler position (4), located at the centre of the engine V (Mercedes placed it within the monocoque) with a view to saving space in the sidepods. (5) Air intakes for cooling the clutch.

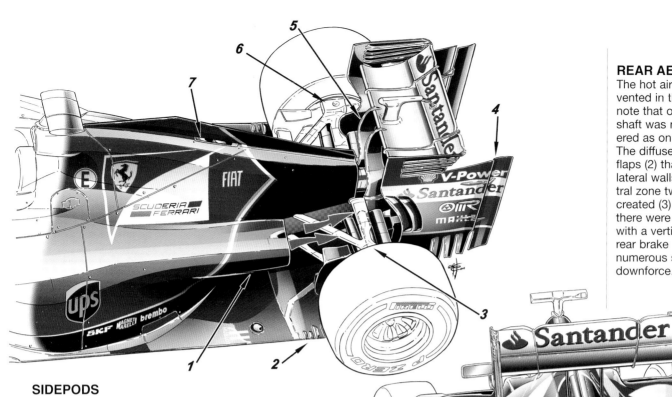

REAR AERODYNAMICS

The hot air from the sidepods all vented in the rear section (1); note that on the F14T the driveshaft was not completely covered as on the 2013 car. The diffuser featured two mini-flaps (2) that also ran along the lateral walls. In the 200 mm central zone two flared spoilers were created (3) while on the RB10 there were two very small ones with a vertical central part. The rear brake intakes (4) featured numerous small flaps to create downforce.

SIDEPODS

Despite the increase demand for hear dispersal associated with the Power Unit, the sidepods of the F14T were very compact with a wide, almost horizontal vent (1) in the end section. The slots (2) ahead of the rear wheels were retained. The driveshaft (3) is exposed, although partially faired by the suspension arms. New endplates for the rear wing presenting a vertical vent (4) close to the trailing edge. Dual boomerang (5) rear wing pylons (single on the Red Bull). (6) The upper wishbone mount was shifted inboard and faired with an aerodynamic profile. There was a supplementary vent (7) on the engine cover of the F14T to cool the clutch.

ENGINE COVER

The issue of heat is always at the centre of the modifications to the car for the Malaysian GP, a factor even more important last year given the greater need for heat dispersal of the Power Units. Ferrari adopted the spinal vents tested in Bahrain and paired with a larger central oval vent (in the circle the version seen in Melbourne).

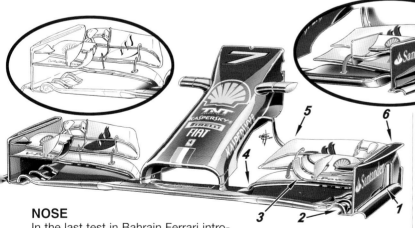

NOSE

In the last test in Bahrain Ferrari introduced the new wing for the first race in Australia. The endplates (1) were simpler, the main profile (2) was more curved and equipped with two vents, the new flap was raised (3) with the principal element (4) modified and vented. The other two flaps (5) were also new, with the second adjustable; the T-shaped element at the top of the endplate (6) was also new.

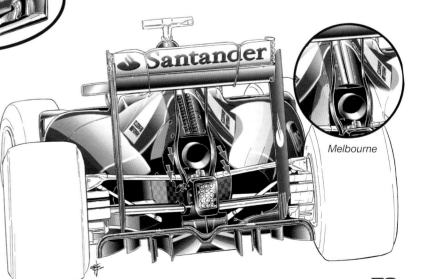

Melbourne

BLOWING HUBS

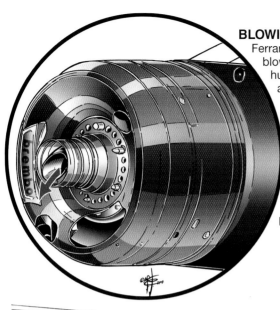

Ferrari presented an extreme version of the blowing in the central section of the front hubs, briefly used in 2013 by Red Bull and Williams. The feature was paired with enormous brake intakes that swerved to channel a great quantity of air from inside the wheel to the outside so as to improve the air flow towards the rear of the car. After a brief test ahead of Bahrain, the feature was incorporated on both cars.

MONTREAL

Ferrari abandoned the much lower and more tapering engine cover in order to privilege the greater heat dispersal guaranteed by the older version (in the circle). As can be seen, this cover presented large vents in the area ahead of the rear suspension, while the new version extended beyond the suspension arms in order to blow in the upper level of the extractor profile. Note also the hot air vent for the brakes inside the wheels, a feature also present in the old version.

ZELTWEG

On the Zeltweg track, Ferrari reinstated the aerodynamic package put to one side in Canada in order to improve cooling. The drawing of the new engine cover also shows the monkey seat, eliminated for qualifying and the race. Compared with Canada, this engine cover was used in a more extreme form, with the vents in the dorsal fin completely closed after the comparison tests conducted with the two versions on the Friday. Note the new brake intakes with the multiplication of the attached fins.

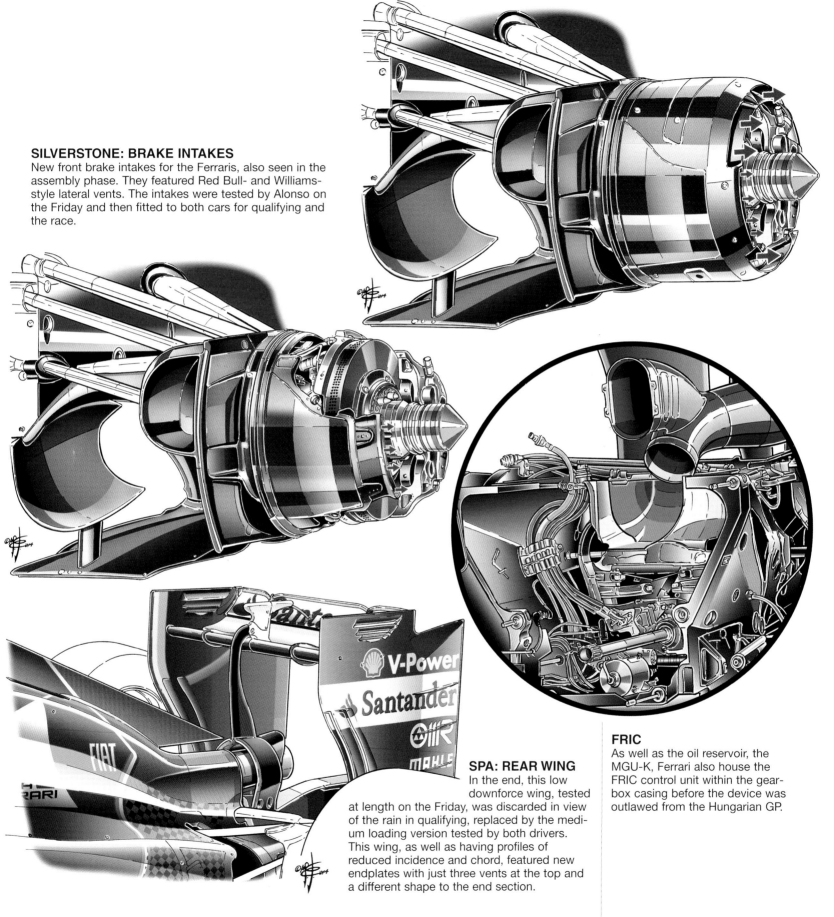

SILVERSTONE: BRAKE INTAKES

New front brake intakes for the Ferraris, also seen in the
assembly phase. They featured Red Bull- and Williams-
style lateral vents. The intakes were tested by Alonso on
the Friday and then fitted to both cars for qualifying and
the race.

FRIC

As well as the oil reservoir, the
MGU-K, Ferrari also house the
FRIC control unit within the gearbox casing before the device was
outlawed from the Hungarian GP.

SPA: REAR WING

In the end, this low
downforce wing, tested
at length on the Friday, was discarded in view
of the rain in qualifying, replaced by the medium loading version tested by both drivers.
This wing, as well as having profiles of
reduced incidence and chord, featured new
endplates with just three vents at the top and
a different shape to the end section.

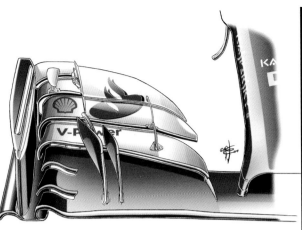

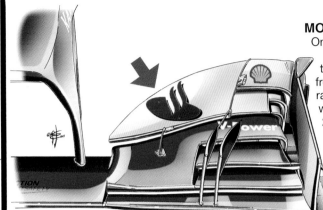

MONZA FRONT WING

On the F14T the upper flaps were eliminated in favour of two vertical turning vanes from the front wing already raced in 2013. The assembly was naturally applied to the 2014 main profile and flap which were not modified. In 2013, a new main profile and a single flap had been raced.

SINGAPORE

On the Singapore track which is particularly hard on braking systems, Ferrari fitted 1000-hole Brembo discs, with five holes being aligned horizontally.

AUSTIN

A new rear wing configuration introduced by Ferrari at Austin and used by both drivers. It differed in all details and above all in the shape of the endplates which also presented a new (for Ferrari) dual vent capable of energising the flow of air in the lower part of the profiles. This feature had already been introduced by Red Bull at the second race of the season in Malaysia.

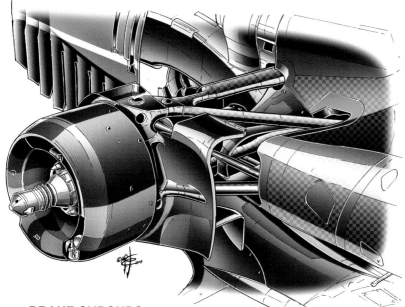

BRAKE SHROUDS

Under close observation in the final races of the season, the F14T's rear suspension became a rolling laboratory for the harvesting of data to be used for the 2015 project. Note the brake shrouds completely closed externally with the hot air venting internally in a kind of "mine" created among the numerous fins applied to create downforce.

REAR SUSPENSION

A comparison between the left-hand wishbone of the two F14Ts used in practice on the Friday. The traditional wishbones with the integrated fairing in carbonfibre compared with the one fitted (on the left only) to Raikkonen's car, which presented two removable cuffs created through rapid prototyping to house sensors.

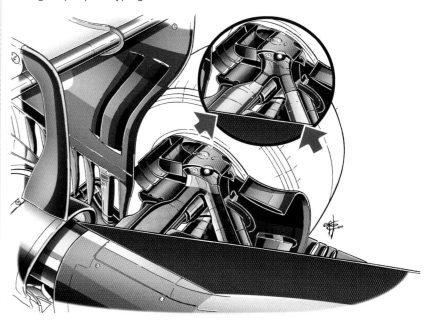

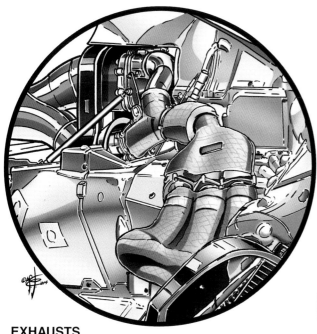

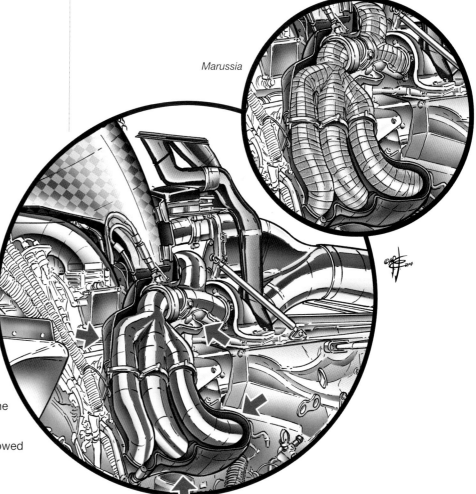

Marussia

EXHAUSTS

At the Belgian GP, Ferrari modified its exhausts, which were different to those seen on the Marussia in previous races. On the F14T, in fact, the pipes were not "bandaged" with a special tape to retain heat that was then transferred to the turbine, but were encased in an insulating material similar to that used by Mercedes on the W05 Hybrid from the start of the season.
This modification was worth around 12 kW in extra energy (around 15 hp), extremely useful on a track like Spa that allowed the engine to run flat out for 70% of each lap.

F138 - F14 T COMPARISON

A comparison between the last Ferrari of the generation powered by 2400 cc, naturally aspirated V8 engines, the F138, and the first of the new F1 era, the F14 T.

This last saw the return of turbocharging, with the adoption of a 1600 cc V6 combined with two electric motors using energy recovered from the brakes (the old KERS transformed into MGU-K) and the heat of the turbo (MGU-H). The F14 was thus a conceptually new F1 car, with slightly narrower wings (15 cm less) and a lower nose to improve safety in the case of a T-bone collision between two cars, to mentioned just the two most important changes to the regulations.

The reduction in width of the front wing, particularly evident in the front view comparison, gave plenty of food for thought to the aerodynamicists of the various teams who had to reduce the toxic effects of the front wheel with wings terminating close to the middle of the tyres.

The external appearance of the cars thus changed significantly, starting with the nose, with Ferrari eschewing the pointed or proboscis design in favour of a flat, square-cut configuration nicknamed the duckbill (originally assigned to a Barnard-designed car from 1989). The chassis was also subjected to significant changes, with Ferrari opting for the most drastic solution to the reduction of the height of the front bulkhead by 10 cm. The sidepods were very similar despite the significant increase in the demand for heat dispersal required by the new Power Unit. Another fairly conspicuous feature was the abolition of exhaust blowing and the imposition of a single tail pipe. The lower profile or beam wing that served to improve the efficiency of the extractor profile while also acting as a rear wing support was also abolished. With the exception of Williams and Toro Rosso, the teams all adopted vertical single or dual element vertical pylons.

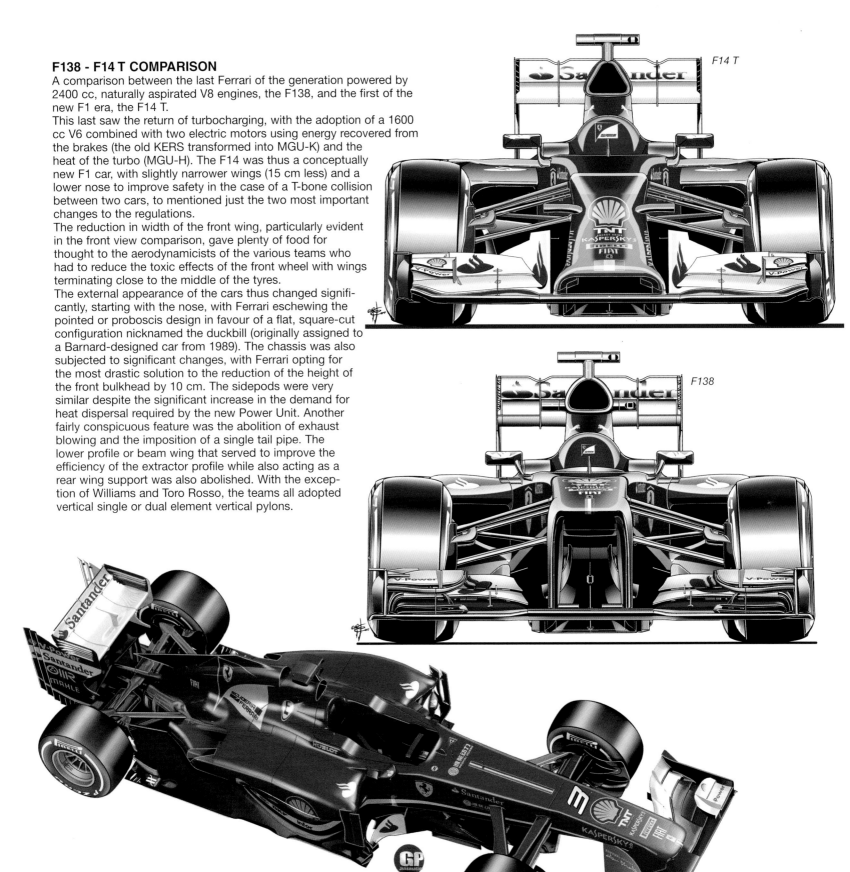

F14 T

F138

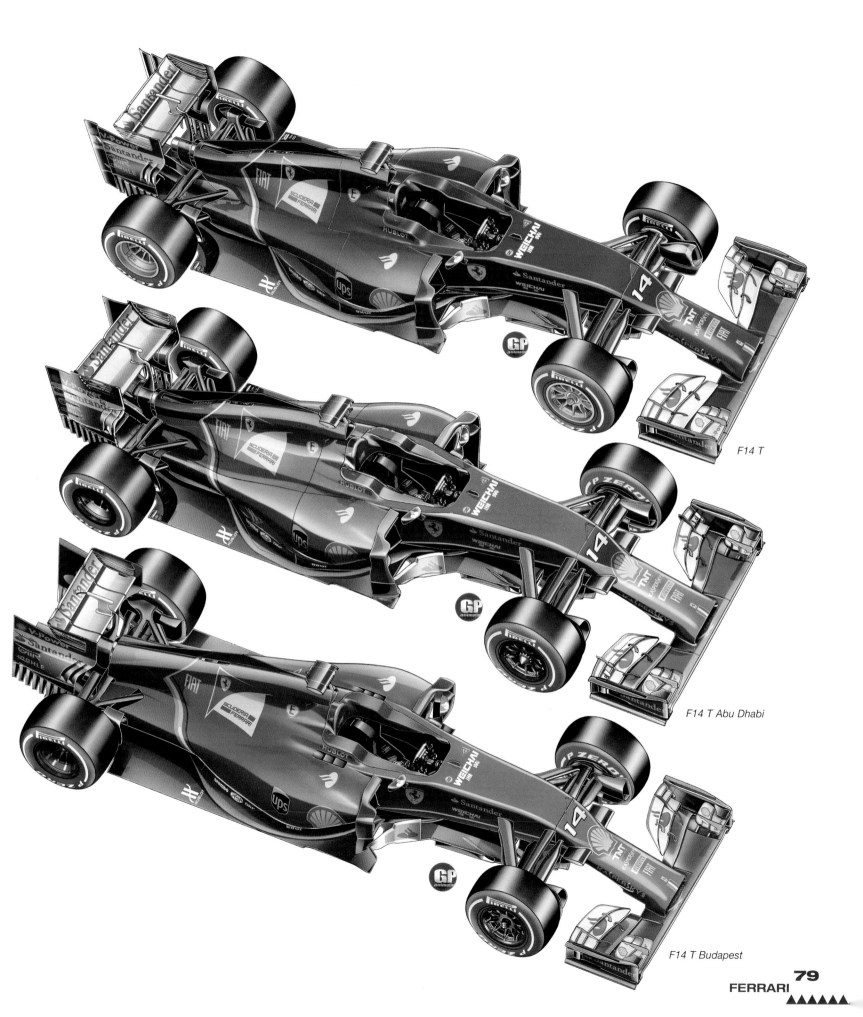

F14 T

F14 T Abu Dhabi

F14 T Budapest

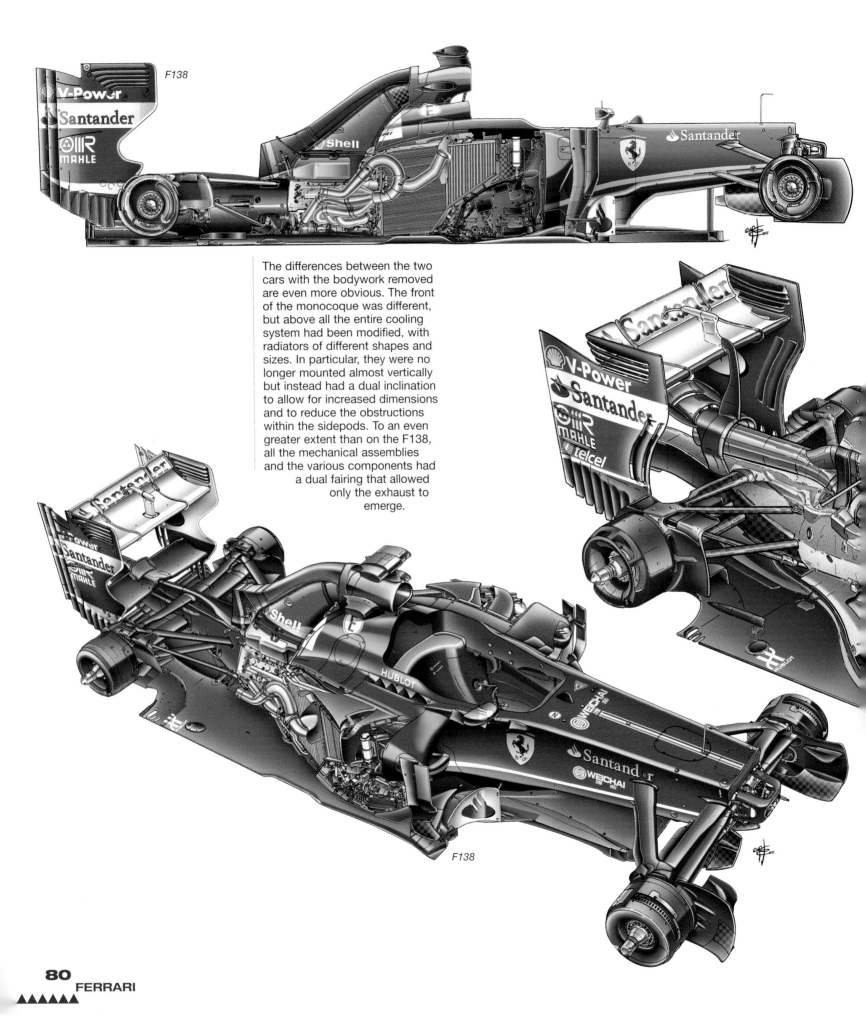

F138

The differences between the two cars with the bodywork removed are even more obvious. The front of the monocoque was different, but above all the entire cooling system had been modified, with radiators of different shapes and sizes. In particular, they were no longer mounted almost vertically but instead had a dual inclination to allow for increased dimensions and to reduce the obstructions within the sidepods. To an even greater extent than on the F138, all the mechanical assemblies and the various components had a dual fairing that allowed only the exhaust to emerge.

F138

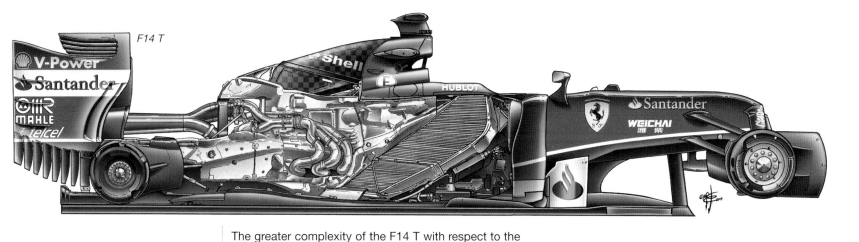

F14 T

The greater complexity of the F14 T with respect to the F138 emerges in this comparison, even though the true revolution enacted at Maranello remains concealed in these drawings. We are referring to the location of the oil reservoir within the gearbox casing, a decision that broke with the tradition of placing the reservoir between engine and chassis, in niche in the rear bulkhead.
The F14 T was intended to be a car with extreme aerodynamics, but this design choice significantly penalised the mechanical side of the car, imposing compressor and turbine dimensions that were too small compared with those of its rivals.

F14 T

McLAREN

CONSTRUCTORS' CLASSIFICATION			
	2013	2014	
Position	5°	5°	=
Points	122	181	+59▲

A poor season for McLaren despite the support of the best power unit available on the market: not a single win for the Woking-based team and above all a significant gap in the final Constructors' Championship with respect to the Mercedes-powered Williams: 181 points against 320…

And yet the season had begun so well with Magnussen and Button respectively second and third behind Rosberg's Mercedes in the first Grand Prix in Australia. While this episode remained iso-lated it did demonstrate that McLaren had succeeded in achieving a good level of overall reliability. In terms of perfor-mance, the signals were not so positive: the severe aerodynamic restrictions imposed by the regu-lations in fact created consider-able difficulties, especially the different alignment of the front wing endplates with respect to the wheels.

The 15 cm reduction in the maxi-mum width of the wing placed the endplates in the worst possi-ble position with respect to the wheels, making the task of directing the flow of air towards the centre and rear of the car without suffering from the inter-ference of the turbulence created by the rotating tyres much more difficult.

The low nose, which had appeared on the MP4/29's debut guaranteed good loading of the front axle but penalised the quali-ty of the flow to the rear axle. By the first race in Australia a new high nose had been pre-pared and crash tested in order to improve the overall aerody-namic balance. As for the restric-tions on the rear wing and in par-ticular the ban of the lower pro-file, McLaren introduced on the MP4/29 one of the most con-spicuous and unusual novelties of the season, that is the so-called "shutters" or fairings applied to the rear suspension, designed and positioned so as to work in synergy with the diffuser, increasing its efficiency.

With the reduction in the height of the chassis the pull-rod front suspension was also abandoned and therefore only used by McLaren in the 2013 season. Among other things, the new lay-out allowed improved structural stiffness and a slight weight sav-ing. One of the objectives of the MP4/29 project was that of cre-ating a light car capable of exploiting the 7 kg of ballast per-mitted by the regulations to allow the car to be adapted to the dif-ferent characteristics of the Pirelli tyres. Another new feature (in reality one drawn from the past) was that of relating to the saw-tooth leading and trailing edges

McLaren MP4/28
Sao Paolo

McLaren MP4/29
Launch

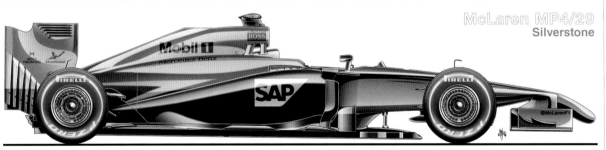

McLaren MP4/29
Silverstone

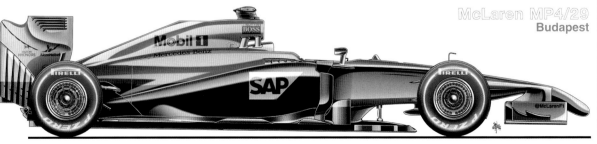

McLaren MP4/29
Budapest

P4/28-MP4/29 COMPARISON

McLaren came up with its own interpretation of the low nose, adopting a fairly high square-cut design, followed by a kind of long, narrow "point" (1) so as to respect the regulations while ensuring a good air flow towards the rear axle. (2) The front wing was com-pletely new, while the suspension (3), following the pull-rod experi-ment, returned to a push-rod lay-out. (4) The cockpit was advanced to allow the engine to be set fur-ther forwards too and have a very narrow rear end. (5) The shape of the sidepods was completely new with a notable narrowing in the so-called Coke bottle area (6). (7) A Red Bull-style L-shaped cut for the stepped bottom ahead of the rear wheels. (8) All the hot air vents from two conspicuous ducts flush with the rear suspension. (9) The suspension elements were of the rear wing. This feature had already been seen in 2004 and 2005 on the Williams and Renault.

The MP4/29 could have been fitted with the blowing hubs but the feature was never used during the course of the season.

The issue of the front wing and the aerodynamic balance represented the fil rouge of the team's technical development throughout the championship.

Following the minor revolution in the first race in Melbourne, a new front wing arrived for Sepang. Another arrived in Spain where improvements to the front suspension and a new diffuser were also introduced. The same was the case in Austria, while Germany saw the so-called "toothed" rear wing. Lastly, in Singapore the car was fitted with a new front wing and diffuser.

A vast development programme that did not, however, bring significant increments in performance, above all with respect to rivals equipped with identical Mercedes Power Units, as in the case of Williams.

It should be noted that at McLaren, in parallel with the development of the 2014 car, a programme was also launched for a hybrid car designed for the Honda Power Unit.

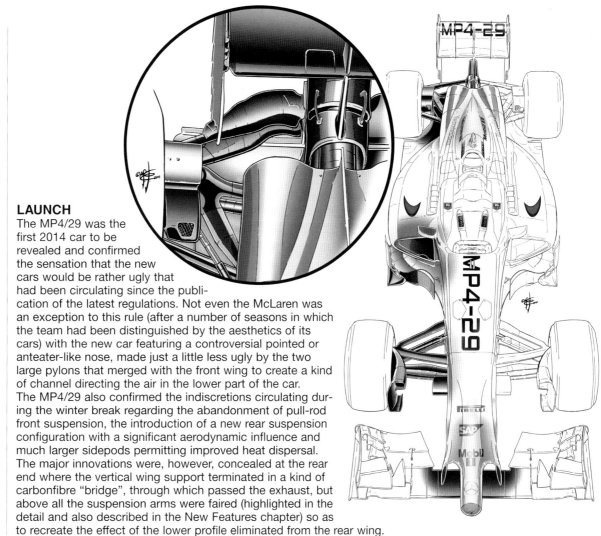

LAUNCH

The MP4/29 was the first 2014 car to be revealed and confirmed the sensation that the new cars would be rather ugly that had been circulating since the publication of the latest regulations. Not even the McLaren was an exception to this rule (after a number of seasons in which the team had been distinguished by the aesthetics of its cars) with the new car featuring a controversial pointed or anteater-like nose, made just a little less ugly by the two large pylons that merged with the front wing to create a kind of channel directing the air in the lower part of the car.

The MP4/29 also confirmed the indiscretions circulating during the winter break regarding the abandonment of pull-rod front suspension, the introduction of a new rear suspension configuration with a significant aerodynamic influence and much larger sidepods permitting improved heat dispersal.

The major innovations were, however, concealed at the rear end where the vertical wing support terminated in a kind of carbonfibre "bridge", through which passed the exhaust, but above all the suspension arms were faired (highlighted in the detail and also described in the New Features chapter) so as to recreate the effect of the lower profile eliminated from the rear wing.

designed to have a significant influence over the rear aerodynamics. In practice, two large fairings work in synergy with the trailing edge of the diffuser. (10) Another new feature was the dual toothed leading edge to the flap and the trailing edge of the main profile; this last reprised a similar feature seen on the Williams at Monza in the 2004 season. On that occasion, however, the teeth were seen only on the trailing edge of the flap.

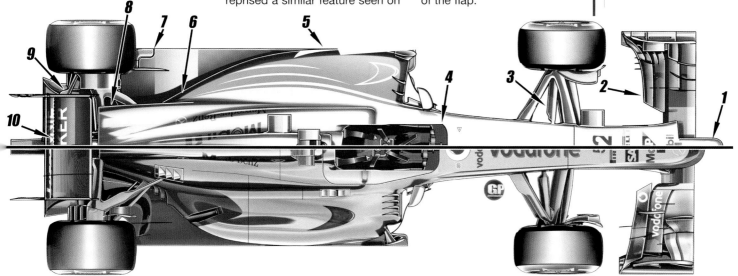

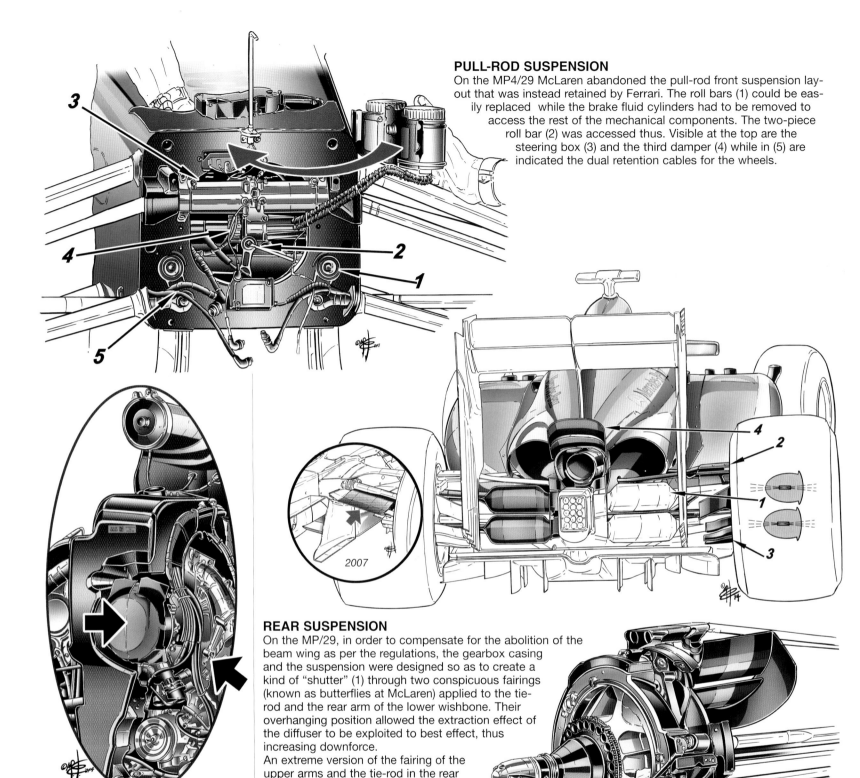

PULL-ROD SUSPENSION

On the MP4/29 McLaren abandoned the pull-rod front suspension layout that was instead retained by Ferrari. The roll bars (1) could be easily replaced while the brake fluid cylinders had to be removed to access the rest of the mechanical components. The two-piece roll bar (2) was accessed thus. Visible at the top are the steering box (3) and the third damper (4) while in (5) are indicated the dual retention cables for the wheels.

REAR SUSPENSION

On the MP/29, in order to compensate for the abolition of the beam wing as per the regulations, the gearbox casing and the suspension were designed so as to create a kind of "shutter" (1) through two conspicuous fairings (known as butterflies at McLaren) applied to the tie-rod and the rear arm of the lower wishbone. Their overhanging position allowed the extraction effect of the diffuser to be exploited to best effect, thus increasing downforce.
An extreme version of the fairing of the upper arms and the tie-rod in the rear suspension in order to create true aero-dynamic profiles: this was a feature that Newey had introduced when he was at McLaren in 2007. The only restriction imposed by the regulations was that of respecting the 3.5:1 ratio between the width and thickness of the arms.
The upper wishbone mount (2) also had aerodynamic functions as did the numerous fins placed on the brake intakes (3). (4) The monkey seat was instead a two-piece element and enclosed the exhaust.

COMPRESSOR

The first confirmation of the new compressor location on the Mercedes engines, separated from the turbine and mounted at the front of the engine together with the oil reservoir, came in the McLaren pits. Even though it was covered with adhesive tapes, it generous dimensions were evident.

FOUR-POT CALIPER

With the reduction in braking power on the rear axle (around 30% less), some teams adopted four-pot calipers like this McLaren version, made exclusively for the team by the Japanese firm Akebono.

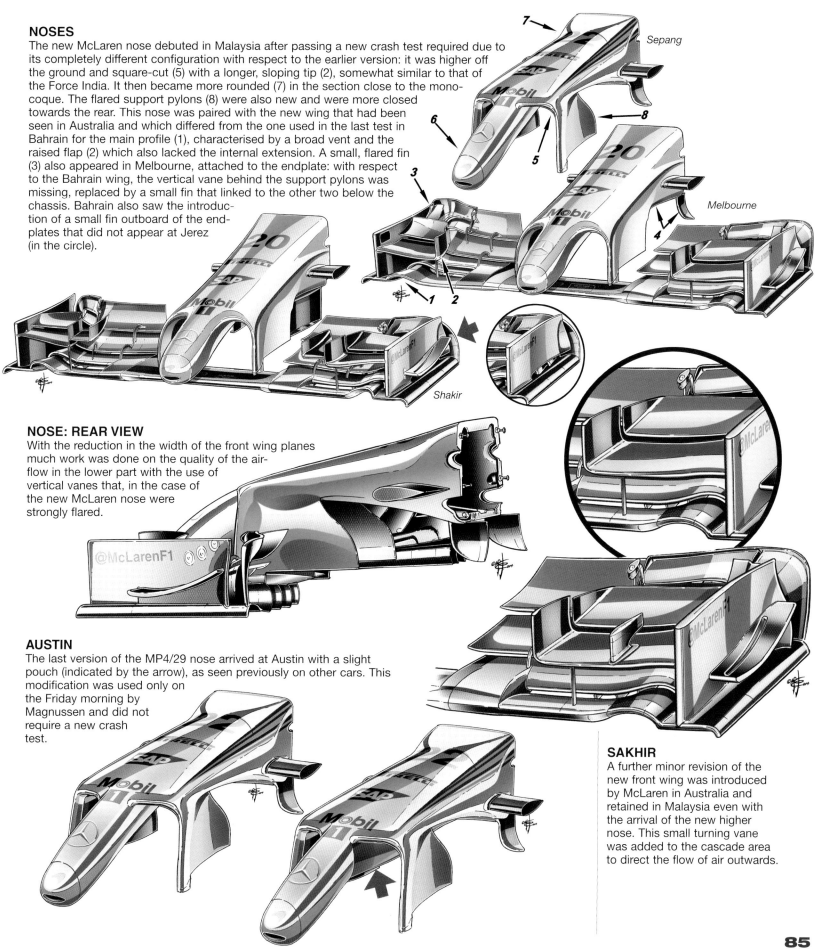

NOSES

The new McLaren nose debuted in Malaysia after passing a new crash test required due to its completely different configuration with respect to the earlier version: it was higher off the ground and square-cut (5) with a longer, sloping tip (2), somewhat similar to that of the Force India. It then became more rounded (7) in the section close to the monocoque. The flared support pylons (8) were also new and were more closed towards the rear. This nose was paired with the new wing that had been seen in Australia and which differed from the one used in the last test in Bahrain for the main profile (1), characterised by a broad vent and the raised flap (2) which also lacked the internal extension. A small, flared fin (3) also appeared in Melbourne, attached to the endplate: with respect to the Bahrain wing, the vertical vane behind the support pylons was missing, replaced by a small fin that linked to the other two below the chassis. Bahrain also saw the introduction of a small fin outboard of the endplates that did not appear at Jerez (in the circle).

Sepang

Melbourne

Shakir

NOSE: REAR VIEW

With the reduction in the width of the front wing planes much work was done on the quality of the airflow in the lower part with the use of vertical vanes that, in the case of the new McLaren nose were strongly flared.

AUSTIN

The last version of the MP4/29 nose arrived at Austin with a slight pouch (indicated by the arrow), as seen previously on other cars. This modification was used only on the Friday morning by Magnussen and did not require a new crash test.

SAKHIR

A further minor revision of the new front wing was introduced by McLaren in Australia and retained in Malaysia even with the arrival of the new higher nose. This small turning vane was added to the cascade area to direct the flow of air outwards.

ZELTWEG

Refinement of the brake intakes with features that also reprised those of the previous season continued at Zeltweg too where this rear brake intake made its debut with a new rounded section (1), also equipped with cooling mouths separated by a kind of vertical bulkhead (2). Their task was to divide the flows in this area, while at the same time enhancing the aerodynamics and cooling functions. The discs (3) had diameters reduced by 7% while two mini-fins providing downforce can be seen (4). The cut in front of the wheels equipped with a kind of flap (5) was also new.

MONTREAL

On the medium-fast Montreal track, Button tried the single fairing of the lower rear suspension wishbone on the Friday before returning to the standard version (in the circle) used by his teammate.

HOCKENHEIM

This was a new McLaren feature because although it vaguely resembled the teeth in the trailing edge of the Williams flap from 2014 (subsequently copied by Renault and Honda), it had a very different function. The dual row of teeth appeared both in the trailing edge of the main profile and the leading edge of the flap. The feature simulated a wider DRS opening (fixed at 7 cm), improving the maximum speed once the flap was open.

Williams Monza 2004

SILVERSTONE

McLaren practically copied the flared slot (previously it had a straight cut) in the area ahead of the front wheels, introduced by Red Bull in Spain (in the detail), firstly on Button's car only and then on both.

SPA

The low downforce version of the wing also had the sawtooth feature, but only on the leading edge of the flap, while the version introduced in Germany had also had teeth on the trailing edge of the main profile. Note also the absence of the monkey seat and endplates without the small turning vanes that had characterised the wing used in Germany.

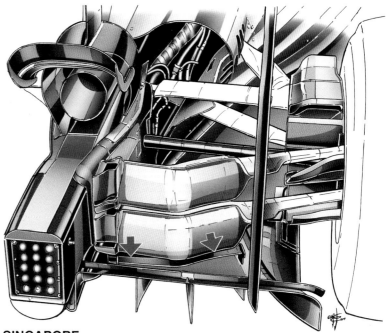

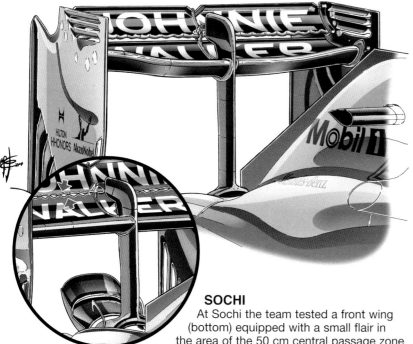

SINGAPORE

At Singapore, the modification seen on the McLaren aroused no little surprise, with the addition of a new mini-flap below the first of the two shutters fairing the two levels of the suspension arms. This feature had never previously been seen and was designed to improve the downforce on the rear axle of the MP4/29.

SOCHI

At Sochi the team tested a front wing (bottom) equipped with a small flair in the area of the 50 cm central passage zone (neutral as per the regulations) and the lateral profiles. The feature was used to study the air flows in correlation with the new regulations on the shape of the noses to be brought in by the FIA for the 2015 season.

Abu Dhabi

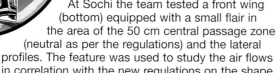

Sochi

ABU DHABI

The endplates also lost the most sophisticated and complicated feature of the MP4/29, adopting a single element curving outwards slightly as on the Red Bull. Note also the new turning vanes below the monocoque which were also closer to those of the RB10 than the earlier version, which was then preferred for qualifying and the race.

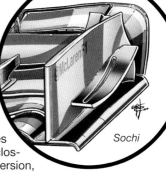

Sochi

Abu Dhabi

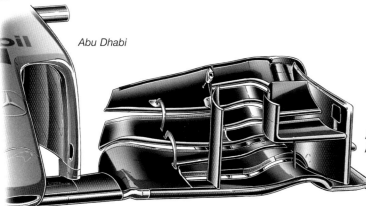

ABU DHABI

Abu Dhabi saw the debut of the new front wing designed by Peter Prodomou, which in practice replicated the features hitherto realised for Red Bull. In the comparison with the McLaren-style Sochi front wing (bottom), it can be seen that there was not a single element in common, from the main profile through to the flaps and in particular the cascades. As was predictable, this new wing unbalanced the car despite the modifications made to the turning vanes below the monocoque and the brake intakes.

FORCE INDIA

CONSTRUCTORS' CLASSIFICATION			
	2013	2014	
Position	6°	6°	=
Points	77	155	+98▲

2014 saw Force India continue to establish itself in Formula 1, once again finishing in 6th place in the Constructor's Championship, as in 2013 and 2011, while more than doubling its points from 77 to 155.
The Silverstone-based team capitalized on its excellent working relationship with Mercedes, using not only the PU106A Power Unit, but also the new eight-speed transmission. The technical director Andy Green opted for the best six-cylinder 1.6 Turbo on the market and was able to take advantage, especially at the start of the 2014 season, of an important technical advantage that allowed the small Anglo-Indian team to achieve a series of important results.
The strengths of the VJM07 were once again its speed and great aerodynamic efficiency, factors that frequently allowed it to compete alongside the Williams in the search for outright speed through the trap.
The designing of the VJM07 around the Mercedes Power Unit had begun very early, back in 2013, when the team successfully interpreted the greatest upheaval in the regulations of the modern era with simple, rational features. Despite the lowering of the nose imposed by the FIA, the Force India designers managed to cut away the chassis below the nose so as to increase the air flow towards the rear diffuser.
The VJM07 thus earned a place in the history books as the car with the most "unusual" trunk-like nose. An anti-aesthetic feature that aroused considerable debate (even though Force India was by no means the only team to adopt this type of proboscis), but which proved to very functional.
Force India got off to an excellent start to the season, at one point sitting in 2nd place in the Constructors' Championship before slipping back to its customary position. A car that was good straight out of the box thanks to good design work then

Force India VJM06
Sao Paolo

Force India VJM07
Launch

Force India VJM07
Hockenheim

lacked the economic resources and organizational structure to compete with the top teams: it is no mystery that Force India does not have its own wind tunnel and has to try to accumulate hours in the tunnels available.
The VJM07 also proved to be a very parsimonious car in terms of wear on its Pirelli tyres; this meant that while it possessed great race pace, it was instead limited when it came to the flying qualifying lap. Almost all of the 2014 cars were born overweight due to the adoption of the Power Units, but this was not the case with the Force India.
To compensate for Nico Hulkenberg's greater weight, a programme was immediately set in place to shave kilos off the chassis. The German driver was already able to use the lighter chassis in Australia and the team benefited greatly from that expe-

rience as they could use part of the ballast at the front to better balance the car, helping restrict tyre wear. The VJM07 also respected all the cooling parameters required by the Mercedes engineers whilst others opted for extreme configurations in the interests of aerodynamic advantages, a reason why Force India never suffered serious reliability problems. With its relatively limited budget, the Silverstone-based team had to carefully calibrate the evolutions that appeared during the course of the season.
In China, for example, FRIC made its debut while in Barcelona modifications were made to the mechanisms of this new feature and aerodynamic changes deriving from the Bahrain tests were introduced in Shanghai. Specifically, vertical turning vanes were fitted to the side of the sidepods and various

rear wing elements were fitted with small turning vanes inclined upwards and used to increase downforce.
The horizontal vents were also modified with a downward flare at the end.
The most extensive aerodynamic package was introduced in Austria: a new nose, recognisable thanks to the more curving wing support pylons with the nose attachment points being set further back. With this design it proved possible to increase the flow of air in the lower part of the nose so as to channel it towards the rear diffuser and again increase the aerodynamic loading. The lower bulb was also more tapered, which inevitably meant a new FIA homologation crash test had to be passed. Silverstone saw the appearance of a single central support pylon for the rear wing, while the main

profile retained an upwards flare in the central part of the leading edge, with a larger flap.

No less than eight horizontal turning vanes were placed on the endplates in the final section, while there were two vertical vents with just three horizontal slots in the upper part, slanting down at the rear.

At Hockenheim there was an engine cover without the two ears behind the roll-bar but equipped with a visible dorsal fin. The ERS radiators were moved to the rear: this modification failed to produced the results hoped for.

The VJM07 suffered greatly from FIA's ban on FRIC, a feature in which the team had invested heavily. On the Ardennes switchback it was therefore necessary to install an arched monkey seat to channel the hot exhaust gases and generate downforce without creating excessive drag.

Two rear wings instead appeared at Monza: the Belgian version with three horizontal vents in the upper part and one with the endplates lacking gills in the upper area but which retained the two vertical vents on the leading edge and the small radial turning vanes at the rear.

For Singapore there was instead a revision of the front wing endplate: a small curved winglet was fitted to the external part to increase aerodynamic loading.

A high downforce rear wing appeared in Austin: the main plane had a gullwing dished leading edge, while a Gurney flap was fitted to the mobile flap. The endplates featured five horizontal flaps with the package being completed with a different monkey seat.

NOSE

One of the most extreme noses among the 2014 cars was that of the Force Indias: high and square-cut in the central section and terminating in a fairly long proboscis. There was a major evolution at the Austrian GP, with the lateral pylons strongly inclined forwards. This also led to the adoption of a different anchorage point on the main profile.

REAR WING

From the beginning of the season the rear wing endplates were very sophisticated, characterised by these small appendices on the trailing edge. The high slots at the front were also new and introduced from the Chinese Grand Prix.

SINGAPORE

In Singapore, Force India made significant modifications above all to the front wing; after two years the endplates were simplified with a single vent rather than the three present since 2013. A small semi-horizontal fin was added in the front section. The circle shows the earlier configuration.

HOCKENHEIM

What was virtually a B version of the Force India was introduced at Hockenheim, with a new engine cover and new sidepods.

The revision was prompted by the shifting of the gearbox radiator (highlighted by the second red arrow) from the end of the engine cover, which required a second intake, to immediately behind the main radiator.

There were notable advantages in terms of clean aerodynamics, to the benefit of the new rear wing also introduced in Germany.

Nonetheless, for the following races Force India went back to the old configuration.

TORO ROSSO

CONSTRUCTORS' CLASSIFICATION			
	2013	*2014*	
Position	8°	7°	+1▲
Points	33	30	-3▼

For Scuderia Toro Rosso 2014 was a season of alternate fortunes; the statistics say that it was an improvement on the previous year as the team finished a notch higher in the constructors' championship in 7th place, but it did so with just 30 points rather than the 33 of 2013 and above all well back from Force India in 6th with an advantage of no less than 125 points. The ambition of the Faenza-based team was to improve in relation to the investment made given that it now had the sixth highest budget in Formula 1, but the team led by Franz Tost had to come to terms with a Renault Power Unit that had serious reliability problems early on in the season. Its best result was Vergne's fine 6th place in the Singapore GP. Following the technical revolution of 2013, the STR9 was born out of the work conducted by the technical director James Key and the chief designer Luca Furbatto.

The fact that the Piemontese engineer no longer figured in Key's plans aroused a sensation and he actually left Toro Rosso before the new car had made its debut in Melbourne.

The STR9 represented a clean break with the past due to the revolution in the regulations that imposed the adoption of 6-cylinder turbocharged engines equipped with ERS and strict aerodynamic restrictions.

Toro Rosso opted for the Renault power unit, abandoning the Ferrari engines it had used since 2007. The decision had been taken by the powers that be at Red Bull in the interests of rationalisation - sharing the same Power Unit with Red Bull Racing creating the possibility of synergy in the development of the rear end of the car. In reality, the two teams owned by Dietrich Mateschitz interpreted the packaging of the Power Unit very differently, with there being little in common if not the gearbox ratios, while the Toro Rosso's eight-speed unit retained an aluminium casting with a carbonfibre spacer.

The STR9 was the first 2014 car to take to the track on 24 January during the filming day at Misano that preceded the official launch in the pit lane at Jerez three days later. Extreme features were avoided on the STR9, with the Renault Power Unit being housed in spaces that were not as tight as those of the Red Bull RB10. At first sight, what caught the eye was the long proboscis extending a kind of keel under the nose that remained fairly high, interpreting like the other teams the regulation designed to prevented an effective flow airflow beneath the chassis, with its ugly beak-like appendix.

The chassis was of a traditional design and the front suspension retained the push-rod layout even though the arms were no longer inclined, to the benefit of more efficacious geometries. The front wing was immediately fitted with endplates designed to shield the front wheels as much as possible. The STR9 was characterised by sidepods with rather small triangular radiator inlets that flared at the bottom, revealing a fairly deep underbody step. The Renault V6 was fitted with an air/air intercooler, a feature that required larger radiator packs, hence the swelling in the coachwork behind the driver should come as no surprise.

The air cooling the intercooler and the ERS radiator came from the second intake on the airbox. The triangular upper intake fed

Toro Rosso STR8
Sao Paolo

Toro Rosso STR9
Melbourne

Toro Rosso STR9
Zeltweg

Toro Rosso STR9
Sao Paolo

the engine while the second, lower aperture was created for the radiators. An interesting idea that privileged aerodynamics over the ideal location of the packs. The sidepods were relatively narrow at the end, displaying a very accentuated Coke bottle shape, with the hot air vents either side of the transmission. The engine cover was distinguished by a small dorsal fin. With the abolition as per the regulations of the lower profile known as the beam wing, it was interesting to note that the rear wing support had no central pylons, but relied on a profile mounted on the underbody on which sat the endplates characterised by a long vertical vent. In the central section was a complex monkey seat enclosing the single exhaust. The rear suspension retained the pull-rod layout. The Romagna-built car, in contrast with the RB10s that had suffered serious cooling problems among others during winter testing, lapped fairly consistently with the Renault Power Unit, albeit in detuned form to restrict reliability problems and with the battery recharging frequently playing up. The STR9 was born overweight hence prior to Melbourne James Key launched a weight saving programme and in Australia we saw a straight rear wing with a single pylon; however, this feature was not raced and failed to appear at Sepang too. The nose introduced

in the final test session in Bahrain instead made its debut. A third rear wing also appeared in Bahrain, but it had a fixed main profile saving over three kilograms in weight. The European debut in Barcelona saw the nose introduced in Melbourne even more cut away in the lower section to ensure a greater flow of air towards the rear end. At Monaco, Toro Rosso changed the gears (a possibility permitted by FIA just once over the course of the season) for higher ratios. The lightweight exhausts endured an unsuccessful debut, causing the retirement of the two drivers after sparkling performance in testing. In Canada there was a preview of the new rear suspension designed to reduced tyre degradation and increase traction, but a breakage in Austria was apparently due to a design fault that was immediately corrected. The Red Bull Ring saw an evolved version of the STR9 with new smaller and lighter radiators and completely redesigned sidepods. The front wing was also new and characterised by a doubling up of the profiles in the outside section, creating a cascade of no less than five vents. The mounts for the vanes and the upper flaps above the main profile were also modified. The gradual improvements made to the Renault Power Unit allowed performance to be increased on fast circuits such as

Spa and Monza too. On the road circuit the Faenza-built car qualified in the top 10. The nose with the perforated bulb made its debut in Japan. It should have appeared in Singapore, but had yet to pass the crash test allowing it to be homologated and hence debuted at Suzuka where it could also count on the S.Duct that drew air from below the tip and channelled it to the upper part of the nose, improving the air flows.

DOUBLE AIR INTAKE

A brand new feature with the double airbox intakes. The upper triangular aperture was the classic intake for the engine while the lower one was dedicated to the radiator packs with the intercooler and the ERS radiator which was raised with respect to the traditional radiators.

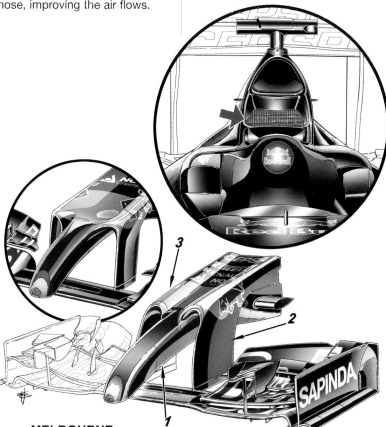

MELBOURNE

At the first race of the season in Australia Toro Rosso conducted a comparison test with the two noses available before opting for the new one introduced during the final test in Bahrain which had required a new crash test. The novelty concerned the central section (1) with the longer proboscis. The vertical pylons (2) were inclined backwards to merge with the shorter, narrower and arching central section (3). This nose was retained through to the Spanish GP where a version that was more cut away in the lower section was introduced.

JEREZ

The Toro Rosso presented a series of new features with the rear wing attached with a broad aerodynamic profile (1) like that of the Williams. The monkey seat (2) was very conspicuous with two levels, the upper part featuring curved profiles and large endplates. The diffuser (3) was cut away on the outside at 45°. The driveshafts (4) were set inside the fairings of the tie-rod and the rear arm of the lower wishbone. There was a very large hot air vent (5). The shape of the Coke bottle zone (6) was very different with respect to that of its Red Bull cousin. The taper began much earlier and was straighter.

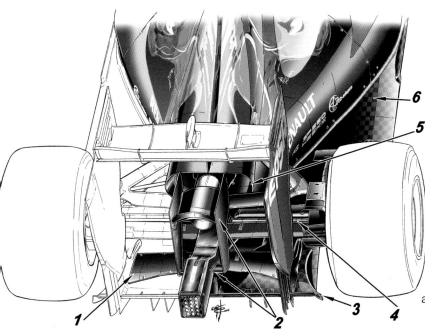

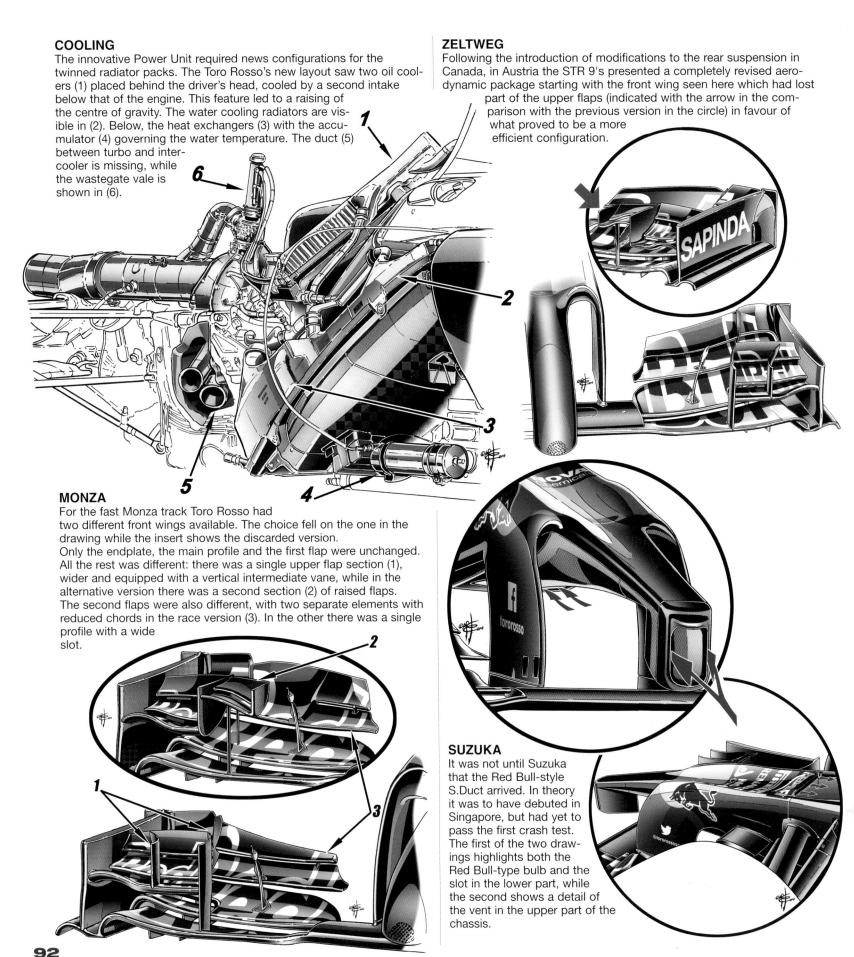

COOLING

The innovative Power Unit required news configurations for the twinned radiator packs. The Toro Rosso's new layout saw two oil coolers (1) placed behind the driver's head, cooled by a second intake below that of the engine. This feature led to a raising of the centre of gravity. The water cooling radiators are visible in (2). Below, the heat exchangers (3) with the accumulator (4) governing the water temperature. The duct (5) between turbo and intercooler is missing, while the wastegate vale is shown in (6).

ZELTWEG

Following the introduction of modifications to the rear suspension in Canada, in Austria the STR 9's presented a completely revised aerodynamic package starting with the front wing seen here which had lost part of the upper flaps (indicated with the arrow in the comparison with the previous version in the circle) in favour of what proved to be a more efficient configuration.

MONZA

For the fast Monza track Toro Rosso had two different front wings available. The choice fell on the one in the drawing while the insert shows the discarded version.
Only the endplate, the main profile and the first flap were unchanged. All the rest was different: there was a single upper flap section (1), wider and equipped with a vertical intermediate vane, while in the alternative version there was a second section (2) of raised flaps. The second flaps were also different, with two separate elements with reduced chords in the race version (3). In the other there was a single profile with a wide slot.

SUZUKA

It was not until Suzuka that the Red Bull-style S.Duct arrived. In theory it was to have debuted in Singapore, but had yet to pass the first crash test. The first of the two drawings highlights both the Red Bull-type bulb and the slot in the lower part, while the second shows a detail of the vent in the upper part of the chassis.

LOTUS

The 2014 season was particularly difficult for Lotus with the team tumbling from 4th place in the Constructors' Championship in 2013 to 8th, with a terrible collapse in the number of points conquered: from 325 to just 10. This was a quite remarkably negative result for the Enstone team, which in 2013 had been accustomed to competing for podium positions. The E22 instead struggled to qualify from Q2 and at times even Q1. Things were no better in the actual races, with Lotus having to settle for two 8th places obtained by Romain Grosjean as their best finishes of the year. Financial problems joined forces with technical and organizational difficulties to banish this prestigious team to the tail end of the grid. The eagerly awaited car conceived around the Renault Energy Power Unit missed the first winter test at Jerez as certain components were not yet ready. Economic problems then delayed its appearance until the dual Bahrain session ahead of the World Championship.

In what was the greatest upheaval in the regulations in the recent history of F1, Lotus was therefore prevented from lapping with any regularity, Major (negative) upheavals among the staff saw James Allison leave the technical direction of Lotus for Ferrari in early September 2013, with the chief aerodynamic engineer Dirk de Beer following him to Maranello. Moreover, the most experienced wind tunnel staff went to Williams and McLaren, while Jarrod Murphy, the head of CFD, accepted an offer from Mercedes. Nick Chester therefore found himself having to take on the role of technical director in the midst of a rebuilding operation that involved significant shrinkage in staff numbers.

The Lotus E22, with its unusual asymmetric double tusk nose, was developed by de Beer through to the end of 2013 before being inherited by Nicola Hennel, a former Ferrari man. An unfortunate car that aroused considerable debate over its extreme features, but which brought precious little satisfaction. The initial problems with the Renault Power Unit delayed development; the French six-cylinder's lack of power and reliability also partially hid the failings of the unusual black and gold car. The walrus nose with the tusks of different lengths was designed to allow a greater flow of air below the tub, air that would be then channelled towards the rear diffuser, but this feature proved to be one of the most critical on the car.

The E22 had other asymmetrical features as well as the nose: this was the case with the sidepods, characterised by large radiator packs and hot air vents at the rear that were visibly differentiated, but also the mono-pylon supporting the rear wing which as well as being steeply inclined towards the rear was also slightly shifted with respect to the single central exhaust.

Every team supplied with Renault engines could choose how its Power Units were installed: the Lotus engineers underestimated the issue of cooling, with the radiator pack mounted in a chevron formation open towards the front, and opted for a water-air intercooler that was too small and penalised the efficacy of the MGU-H, obtaining less hybrid power than the other teams equipped with the same French Power Unit. Only from the

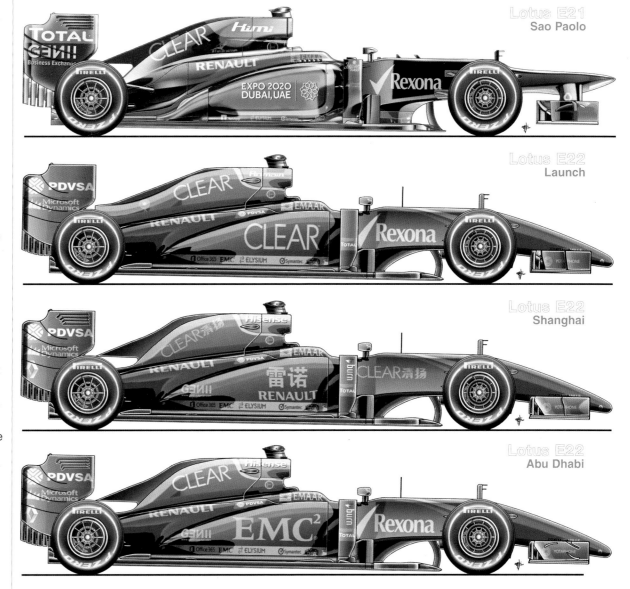

Lotus E21
Sao Paolo

Lotus E22
Launch

Lotus E22
Shanghai

Lotus E22
Abu Dhabi

Spanish GP onwards did things improve: the progress made by the French engineers was enhanced by a larger intercooler that in turn was added to the aerodynamics package composed of a new underbody and a new front wing that allowed Maldonado to qualify in 5th place. The E22 proved to be a poorly balanced car lacking in downforce, especially at low speeds. As early as Australia, Nick Chester had introduced a splitter under the two-pronged nose in an attempt to improve front-end grip, while he had opened a conspicuous on either side to vent hot air and cool the electronic control units. Five inclined "skittles" appeared in Malaysia acting as flow vanes but proved unsatisfactory. Sakhir saw the introduction of a brake air intake with three small triangular flaps in the upper part of the duct, used to direct the flows behind the front wheel, avoiding toxic turbulence at the entrance to the radiator mouths.

In China the Enstone engineers focussed on the rear end with a new Red Bull-style diffuser equipped with flow vortex generators mounted in the central part of the tunnel. Modifications were also made to the engine cover with a large fin following the work on the shrinking of the airbox.

At Monaco attention instead turned to the brakes: the brake duct split the cooling and aerodynamic functions.

Canada saw the debut of the low downforce aerodynamic package, with very lightly loaded front and rear wings. The rear wing in particular presented a particularly mild main profile including the leading edge, while there were only two horizontal vents and five turning vanes

mounted in a fan configuration towards the top. Also of note was the debut of a new exhaust system designed to improve the efficacy of the Renault Power Unit.

In terms of aerodynamics, compared with Silverstone modifications were made to the front wing endplate ahead of the German GP with the addition of an arching triangular flap.

At Spa instead, the engine cover created a sensation, with its widened rear section particularly evident on the left-hand sidepod (which contained the turbo inter-

cooler), which penalised the aerodynamic efficiency of the E22.

At Sochi the monkey seat mounted on a rear wing support was no longer asymmetric like the Singapore version.

This was the beginning of a process of "normalization" that led at Austin to the appearance of a new nose in place of the double tusk version. A nose that respected FIA's 2015 regulations that was also seen at Abu Dhabi in slightly modified form.

The E22's season in any case proved to be disastrous: the

Enstone team paid a heavy price for the ban on blowing exhausts, a technical feature that had rewarded the research conducted by Nick Chester, and was similarly penalised by the ban on the use of FRIC from the German GP. The hydraulically-interconnected suspension had been continually developed over the previous five years, allowing Lotus to control ride heights and obtain the maximum aerodynamic loading.

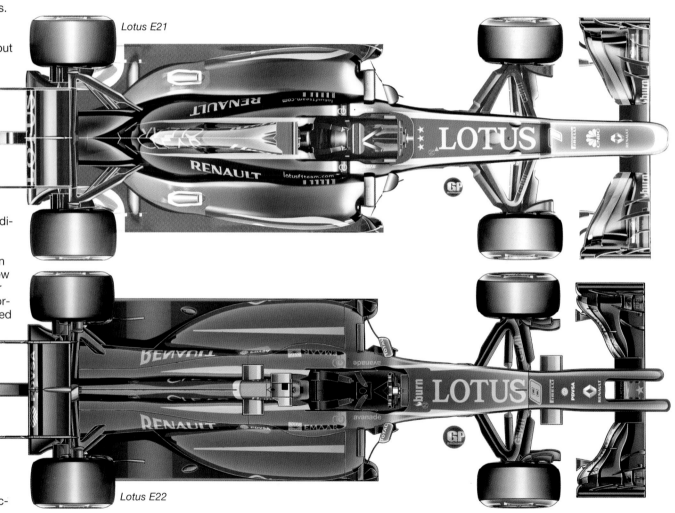

Lotus E21

Lotus E22

OVERHEAD COMPARISON

The prize for the most original car went to the E22, the first to be fitted with a nose with two points that were moreover asymmetric, with the right-hand tusk with a structural role being longer and the one destined to respect the regulations regarding the height of the nose and to pass the frontal crash test. This was not the only asymmetry on the E22 as the vent in the end part of the sidepod was also wider on the left (containing the intercooler) than the right. The exhaust, central on all cars, was shifted to the right with respect to the rear wing support pylon.

NOSE

Without doubt, Lotus was the team that presented the most unusual car, with its asymmetric nose (1) longer on the right than the left. The two extensions also served as mounts (1) for the front wing (2) and as turning vanes, slightly curving inwards. The three-piece endplates (3) were very sophisticated and aligned sharply towards the inside (as highlighted by the yellow band) to shield the front wheels as much as possible. The difference in the length between the two extensions is also clearly evident in the view from below.

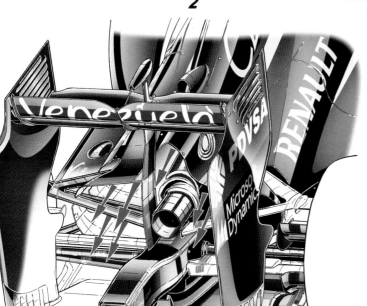

ASYMMETRIC EXHAUST

The E22 was also asymmetric at the rear. This was due to the fact that the left-hand sidepod contained both the radiators and the intercooler and the vent for the hot air in the end section was consequently wider than the one on the right. The exhaust was also placed to the right of the central pylon.

ENGINE COVER

The greater demand for heat dispersal associated with the complex Power Units required right from the presentation of the car this small intake in the area of the dorsal fin, along with a supplementary vent.

SEPANG

The issue of the great heat is always at the centre of the modifications made to the cars in view of the Malaysian GP, an aspect accentuated this year by the greater demands for heat dispersal of the Power Units. There was a new vent let into the left-hand sidepod that served to evacuate the hot air from the intercooler located in that area.

BRAKE INTAKES

The wing recued to 1650 rather than 1800 mm meant that the endplates were necessarily set closer to the chassis, making it more difficult to direct the flow towards the outside of the front tyres. One area almost brushed the inside of the tyre where new features were introduced including these small triangular fins destined to "clean" the airflow towards the central part of the car.

AUSTIN

On Grosjean's car at Austin Lotus experimented on the Friday morning with a nose without the double tusk in view of the 2015 season regulations that were to ban the extreme designs used up to then by most teams. This nose was tested again at the final two rounds of the championship was never raced.

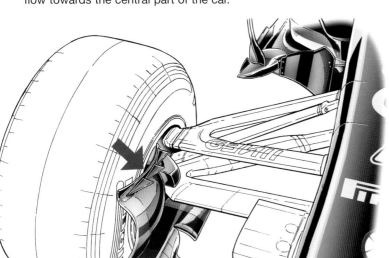

HOCKENHEIM

New two- rather than three-piece endplates (right-hand insert) for Lotus, with the initial section with a compound flare as in the previous season (left-hand insert), both in the initial section at the top and in the end section. The previous version is seen in the insert.

2013

HIGH DOWNFORCE NOSE

This nose was tested on the high downforce tracks. It was introduced in Malaysia and featured a low-mounted horizontal splitter topped by vertical "skittles": this was another feature that aroused considerable interest and perplexity with regard to its efficiency.

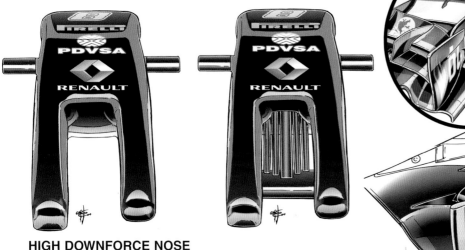

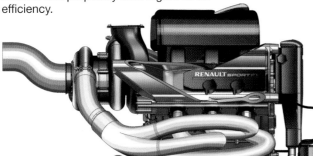

RENAULT ENERGY F1 2014

This is the diagram supplied by Renault of its 1600 cc V6 turbo engine. The compressor/turbine assembly is located at the end of the cylinder heads. The large battery pack and the control units were located at the front of the engine, within the fuel tank area.

MARUSSIA

In the most difficult season in the history of modern F1, Marussia succeeded in conquering its first points in the Constructors' Championship, points that allowed it to finish in 9th place ahead of the more prestigious Sauber and on more than one occasion to reach Q2 in qualifying. Such an achievement was largely down to the driving talent of Jules Bianchi who at Monaco had achieved that 9th place as well as technical motives. Both Marussia and Sauber had bought into the daring technical configuration adopted at Maranello, with the oil reservoir located in the gearbox casing. According to the terms of their contract, as well as the engines (in this case the Power Units) they also had to use the same transmission. Pat Symonds, who subsequently joined Williams, laid the foundation for a decent albeit simple car, capable of acting as the starting point for development that progressed with a certain consistency in spite of the team's very restricted budget. It was by no means a coincidence that the splendid result in Monaco closely followed the introduction in the preceding Go in Spain, improvements to the front suspension that allowed the MR03 to gain half a second a lap.

The team went through a tricky patch when the abolition of FRIC (the hydraulic interconnection of the suspension between the two axles) from the Hungarian GP meant that it had to find a way of adapting its car. The final major evolution came at the Belgian GP, with the MR03 significantly improved in terms of stability under braking. Then came the absurd tragedy at Suzuka where the team risked dropping out of the World Championship; it was the points gained by the tragically unfortunate Jules Bianchi that actually allowed the team to confirm its participation in Formula 1 in the 2015 season.

EXHAUSTS

Marussia frequently conducted tests on behalf of Ferrari, especially in the area of the exhausts. In order to avoid the dispersal of heat, initially (in Bahrain) the Marussia was fitted with small carbonfibre shields (highlighted with the red arrow), while in Germany the exhausts were "bandaged" with a kind of tape to retain heat and guarantee more energy for the MGU-H.

Marussia MVR02
Sao Paolo

Marussia MVR03

SAUBER

CONSTRUCTORS' CLASSIFICATION			
	2013	2014	
Position	7°	10°	-3▼
Points	57	0	-57▲

The 2014 season was the worst in the history of Sauber, with the team failing to earn a single championship point and falling to 10th place in the Constructors' standings, losing no less than three positions with respect to 2013 and paying a drastic price for the adoption of the Power Unit.

The C33 proved to be an ill conceived car for a number of reasons: the Swiss car adopted the Ferrari Power Unit which proved to be uncompetitive but above all a number of technical features that severely conditioned the choices of a team hitherto always capable of getting the best out of the limited economic resources at their disposition.

The location of the oil tank and the MGU-K in the gearbox casing, for example, imposed a layout that was different to the usual configuration, with the engine further forwards so as to have a weight distribution that respected the regulations.

The car was born heavy due to the excessive weight of both engine and chassis.

At the start of winter testing, Sauber suffered considerable problems with the fine-tuning of the integrated brake by wire system made by Sauber themselves and Ferrari. At the rear in fact, discs of a smaller diameter and four- rather than six-pot callipers as fitted to the F14 T had been adopted. This choice derived from the fact that the ERS made a contribution to braking with the MGU-H recharging.

The first important development of the C33 was seen at the Spanish GP, the first race of the European season: Gutierrez's car was lightened by 15 kg thanks to painstaking work that concerned almost every area of the car: new sidepods, with slightly smaller and lighter radiators but still fabricated with micro-tubes and the cooling of the control units was improved with new intakes to safeguard the electronics.

The nose was also lightened and equipped with a modified front wing with the endplates featuring a McLaren-type small fin.

The engine cover and the turning vanes were also modified.

Large brake intakes then appeared at Monaco: there were radial grilles with no less than six apertures at the front between the rubber and the carbonfibre brow.

In Canada, on the low/medium downforce circuit, Sauber introduced a rear wing with a curving section in proximity to the endplates and a dipped configuration towards the outside.

A Gurney flap was mounted on the flap that in turn caught the eye with two V's in proximity to the ribs. The venting of the hot air from the radiators was also revised with a more closed engine cover.

Silverstone saw modifications to the turning vanes with three vertical elements and the vanes outboard of the sidepods: in this phase two vortex generators were introduced, attached to the endplates and working in harmony with the foot of the candelabra having a raised border.

In Hungary, given the low average speeds of the circuit, an engine cover with an ample aperture at the rear was fitted, similar to the one seen at Hockenheim, with the aim of dispersing the heat of the Power Unit and avoid compromising the reliability of the 058/3 engine.

Two front wings appeared at Spa: one milder and one with a greater aerodynamic loading. The slipperiest version was fitted with a final flap with a reduced incidence and surface area with respect to the one that had to produce more vertical thrust.

At Monza Sauber too obtained from Ferrari the exhaust insulation that Marussia had adopted in experimental form.

The tail pipes of the 059/3 were "bandaged" so as to avoid the dispersal of heat from the gases that drove the turbine.

This feature allowed the engine to produce around 10 extra horsepower. The rear wing was very mild, with the main profile almost flat and a low incidence flap fitted with a Gurney flap.

On the Singapore street circuit the team looked for more downforce with a different front wing equipped with a longer fin outside the endplate and a larger footplate within the main profile in proximity to the endplate with a sharper flare.

There were novelties at the rear too with the bodywork being widened and lengthened at the end of the sidepods so as to

Sauber C32
Sao Paolo

Sauber C33
Launch

Sauber C33
Abu Dhabi

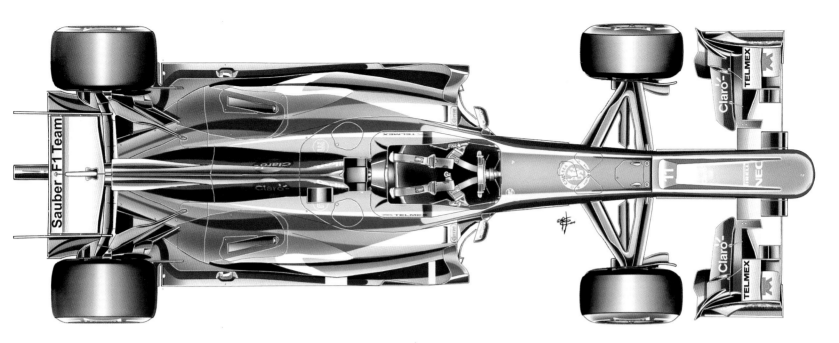

improve cooling of the Ferrari Power Unit.

This last modification was also made so as to exploit to better effect the flows of hot air and increase aerodynamic loading while making the rear diffuser

more effective. The fin on the engine cover was then revised. Numerous updatess during the course of the World Championship therefore, none of which served to gain a single point for Sauber.

C32 TOP VIEW
In the 2014 season, Sauber was unable to present a brand-new car as had been the case in 2013 with the C32 which had attracted attention as the narrowest car in the field: no less than 10 cm each side, as highlighted by the yellow dashes.

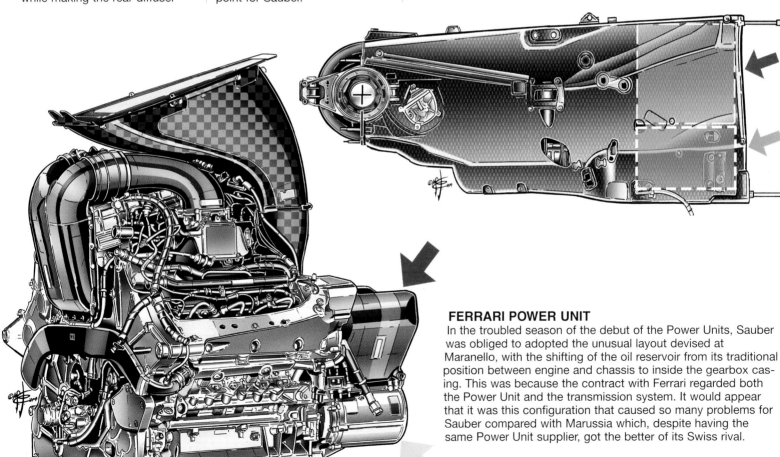

FERRARI POWER UNIT
In the troubled season of the debut of the Power Units, Sauber was obliged to adopted the unusual layout devised at Maranello, with the shifting of the oil reservoir from its traditional position between engine and chassis to inside the gearbox casing. This was because the contract with Ferrari regarded both the Power Unit and the transmission system. It would appear that it was this configuration that caused so many problems for Sauber compared with Marussia which, despite having the same Power Unit supplier, got the better of its Swiss rival.

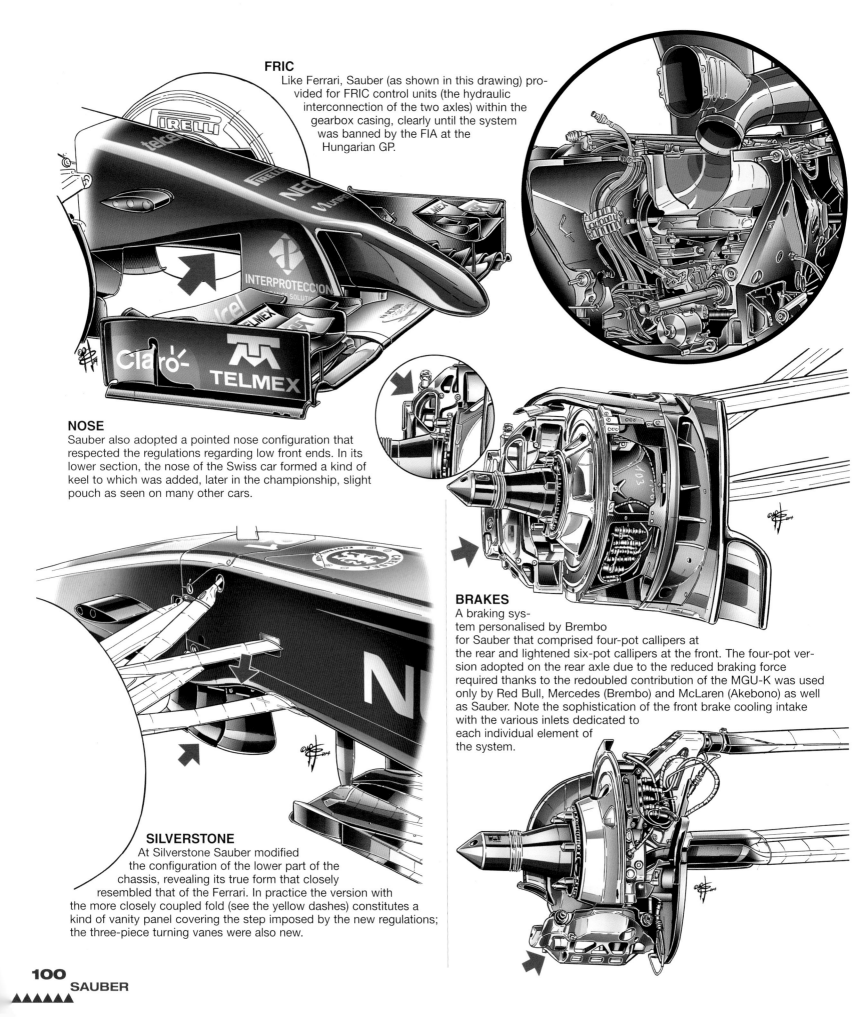

FRIC

Like Ferrari, Sauber (as shown in this drawing) provided for FRIC control units (the hydraulic interconnection of the two axles) within the gearbox casing, clearly until the system was banned by the FIA at the Hungarian GP.

NOSE

Sauber also adopted a pointed nose configuration that respected the regulations regarding low front ends. In its lower section, the nose of the Swiss car formed a kind of keel to which was added, later in the championship, slight pouch as seen on many other cars.

BRAKES

A braking system personalised by Brembo for Sauber that comprised four-pot callipers at the rear and lightened six-pot callipers at the front. The four-pot version adopted on the rear axle due to the reduced braking force required thanks to the redoubled contribution of the MGU-K was used only by Red Bull, Mercedes (Brembo) and McLaren (Akebono) as well as Sauber. Note the sophistication of the front brake cooling intake with the various inlets dedicated to each individual element of the system.

SILVERSTONE

At Silverstone Sauber modified the configuration of the lower part of the chassis, revealing its true form that closely resembled that of the Ferrari. In practice the version with the more closely coupled fold (see the yellow dashes) constitutes a kind of vanity panel covering the step imposed by the new regulations; the three-piece turning vanes were also new.

CATHERAM

CONSTRUCTORS' CLASSIFICATION			
	2013	2014	
Position	11°	11°	=
Points	0	0	=

The complexity of the new formula with the Power Units imposed by the FIA delivered a knock-out blow to a team which had already shown its limitations with the traditional naturally aspirated V8s. Caterham had come close to folding after the British GP due to a lack of liquidity, despite boasting a technical staff that should have guaranteed it a greater level of competitiveness. The team had planned to start the season with a solid car that would allow it to achieve reliability and then work on performance gradually with features more appropriate to an F1 car. Unfortunately, the chronic, devastating budget problems prevented this project from taking shape. The resulting CT05 was perhaps the ugliest and least competitive car in the history of modern F1. It was disconcerting above all for the configuration of its nose, with heavy square-cut shapes that initially appeared to suggest a temporary solution. Minor improvements appeared in Spain, but the turning point, if you can call it that, came at Spa with a more attractive and less bulky nose introduced at the behest of the technical director John Illey. However, even this move was not sufficient to render the CT05 competitive and the team, afflicted by the usual economic problems, was obliged to desert both the United States and Brazilian GPs and then merely make up the numbers in the last race in Abu Dhabi.

Caterham CT05
Melbourne

Caterham CT05
Abu Dhabi

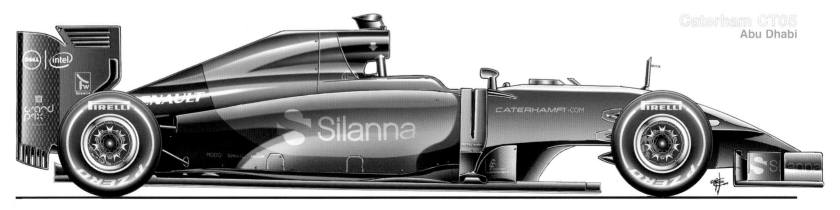

New REGULATIONS

Following the revolution in the F.1 regulations in 2014, the FIA decided on significant modifications for the following season. The most conspicuous aspect was the elimination of the noses, in reality long proboscises, that featured on last year's cars, the motivations that led to this particular decision being substantially associated with safety and aesthetics. Those bee stingers really were hard on the eyes and could also be dangerous in that in the case of a front to rear shunt, the nose could slip under the rear chute of the forward car, act as a lever and lift the rear end which could then strike the helmet of the driver behind. As it had done in 2013, with the introduction of the stepped nose and the following year with the regulation regarding low noses, the Federation moved to ban the horrible features devised by many teams. In theory the outlawed designs were the two-pronged Lotus nose and the finger, or proboscis, noses of the Williams, McLaren, Force India, Sauber, Toro Rosso, Marussia and Caterham

cars. This was achieved by modifying the dimensions of the nose with the length increased from the 750 mm of 2014 to the current 850, with the areas of three different cross sections being defined. The first is of 60,000 mm2, but above all a second section of 20,000 mm2 was imposed 750 mm from the front axle and another of 9,000 mm2 at the tip, with widths defined for the deformable structure of 330 mm in the central zone and 140 mm at the extremities.
It was thought that very long noses would be seen, but instead both Williams and Force India initially presented a kind of stub that effectively allowed the section to be drastically reduced and consequently the air flow in the lower section to be improved.
The stub guarantees a kind of Venturi effect in the neutral central zone, with the front wing that has to have a neutral profile for the central 50 cm, allowing minimal downforce to be obtained at this point too. This is a very delicate zone, which determines the behaviour of the flows to the central part of the car through to the diffuser, hence the need to come up with new configurations guaranteeing greater aerodynamic efficiency. The stub was then adopted by Sauber, Toro Rosso, Manor and Red Bull itself, while Mercedes and Lotus opted for a short nose without the stub. Only Ferrari and McLaren went with a

long, low nose design. There is still the possibility of exploiting the passage of air between the lower and upper parts of the nose reintroduced by Sauber in the 2012 season.
The text of the regulations still permits an opening in the lower part with the unvaried restriction of 150 mm from the front axle, as prescribed in art. 37.8 of the technical regulations. Lastly, in order to avoid the ruse devised by Adrian Newey in 2014, with the video camera placed inside the vanity panel in order to prevent unwanted shots of the central part of the car, a restriction was introduced with respect to the longitudinal axis which translated into a minimum distance between the two cameras of 150 mm.

However, the most important novelties concerned the Power Unit sector. Above all, their reduction from five to four per driver over the course of the season. With a calendar of 19 races, each unit has to cope with at least five Grands Prix in order to avoid penalties such as 10 grid positions when a team fits the fifth power unit or five positions for each component of the power unit: CPU, battery, MGU-H, MGU-K and turbocharger. The engineers were allowed to update the engine using the 32 development tokens with Mercedes spending 25 for the homologation of the PU106B at the end of February, while Ferrari used three less and Renault just 20.
The others are available to be spent over the

NOSE REGULATIONS 2015 ART. 15.4.3

The finger of the 2014 car has become a knuckle, as seen in the version depicted above, following a more linear interpretation of the regulations. The possibility of passing from 330 mm at the B section to just 135 mm at the C section was exploited. In fact, along with the extreme section of 9,000 mm2 with a minimum width of 135 mm at 850 mm from the front axle, Art. 15.4.3 introduced a further section of 20,000 mm2 at 750 mm from the same axle with a maximum width of 330 mm.

A

B C

750mm

850mm

60000 mm²
330mm
135mm
750mm
850mm
20000 mm²
9000 mm²

MERCEDES AND FERRARI

The 2014 Mercedes nose was to prove to be 50 mm too short as shown in the overhead view; the Stuttgart firm in fact fielded a design fairly similar to that of the 2014 season but with a regulation length while, in theory, the

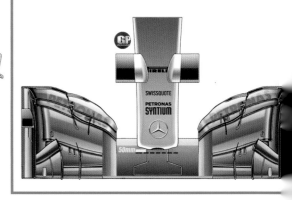

50mm

course of the season, so Mercedes have seven, Ferrari 10 and Renault 12. The newcomer Honda instead, debuting with the six-cylinder RA615 H supplied exclusively to McLaren, has been given nine tokens, representing the average of those remaining to the other constructors. Only Mercedes has proved capable of respecting the scheduled rotations, with the German team's first unit being used for six race weekends, equivalent to over 4,100 km, a true record for F1! Renault and Honda have instead suffered severe reliability problems and Ferrari decided to anticipate the first replacement in view of making recourse to a fifth unit.

Among the restrictions introduced for 2015 is the requirement for the gearbox to last six Grands Prix, one more than in the past, while the entire season must be disputed with a single gear train chosen at the beginning of the year; in 2014, instead, the teams could change at least once during the championship. In the early races of the season the Federation scrutineers noted that certain teams had found a way of bypassing the fuel flow meter. In order to close off the loophole, from the race in Shanghai the FIA decided to measure the fuel flow both upstream and downstream of the control system. Evidently, this provision was insufficient given that in Barcelona a further modification imposed a constant fuel flow of between 90 and 100 kg/s with the engine under power. The federation's technicians also decided on even more severe aerodynamic regulations and from the Canadian GP, the flaps on the front wings were allowed to flex no more than 3 mm when subjected to a static load of 60N; that is to say, 6.1 kg.

PROHIBITED FEATURES ART. 15.4.3

The anti-aesthetic features such as the Lotus double tusk, which proved to be very uncompetitive, and the finger-proboscis-anteater noses adopted in the 2014 season by

McLaren, Williams, Force India, Sauber, Toro Rosso, Marussia and Caterham were to all intents and purposes banned.

Ferrari nose could have been retained with modifications that would not have completely changed its form but Maranello instead opted for a very long, low design.

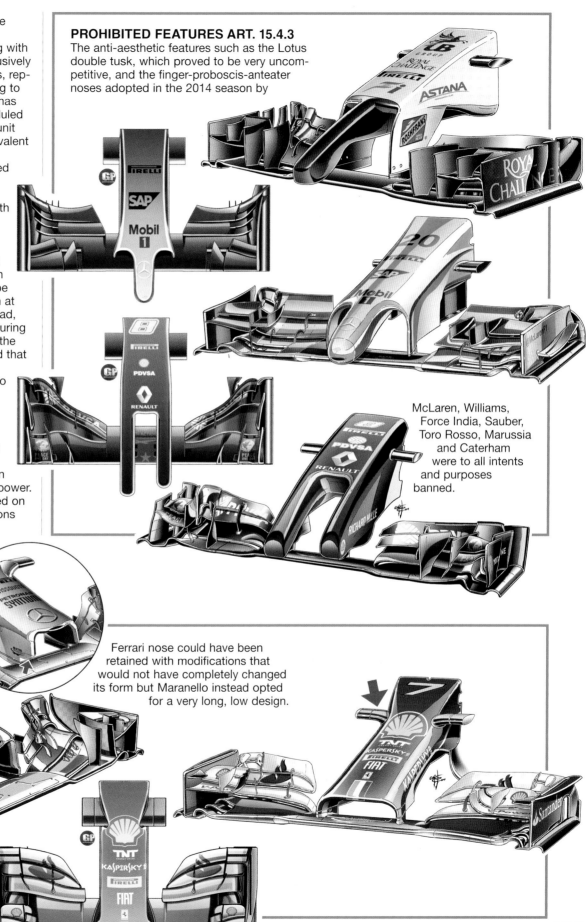

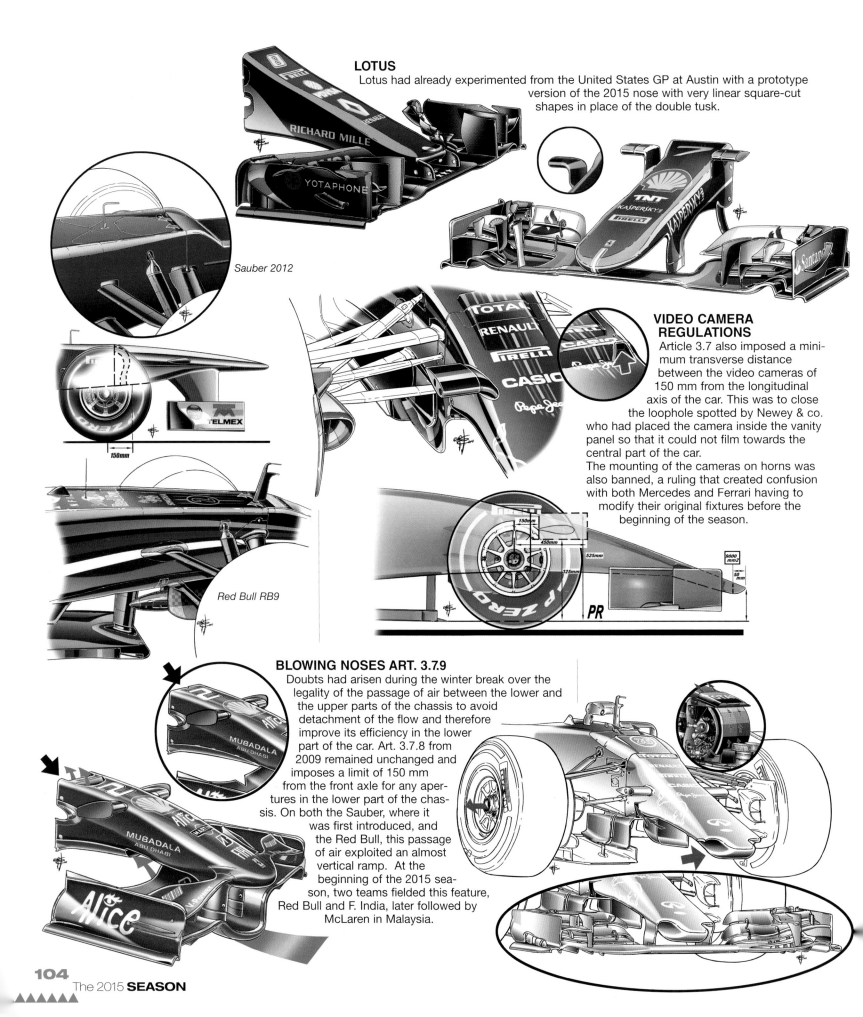

LOTUS

Lotus had already experimented from the United States GP at Austin with a prototype version of the 2015 nose with very linear square-cut shapes in place of the double tusk.

Sauber 2012

150mm

Red Bull RB9

VIDEO CAMERA REGULATIONS

Article 3.7 also imposed a minimum transverse distance between the video cameras of 150 mm from the longitudinal axis of the car. This was to close the loophole spotted by Newey & co. who had placed the camera inside the vanity panel so that it could not film towards the central part of the car.

The mounting of the cameras on horns was also banned, a ruling that created confusion with both Mercedes and Ferrari having to modify their original fixtures before the beginning of the season.

150mm
450mm
525mm
325mm
9000 mm2
50 mm

PR

BLOWING NOSES ART. 3.7.9

Doubts had arisen during the winter break over the legality of the passage of air between the lower and the upper parts of the chassis to avoid detachment of the flow and therefore improve its efficiency in the lower part of the car. Art. 3.7.8 from 2009 remained unchanged and imposes a limit of 150 mm from the front axle for any apertures in the lower part of the chassis. On both the Sauber, where it was first introduced, and the Red Bull, this passage of air exploited an almost vertical ramp. At the beginning of the 2015 season, two teams fielded this feature, Red Bull and F. India, later followed by McLaren in Malaysia.

The possible evolutions of the Power Units through to 2020

Power unit element	engineering details	token	2015	2016	2017	2018	2019 + 2020
crankcase	space between cylinders, engine cover, crankcase ribs	2	■				
crankcase	all bore dimensions relating to the water cooling passages	3					■
cylinder head	everything associated with the above mentioned modifications	2					■
combustion	all elements defining combustion. Includes manifolds, pins, combustion chambers, valve geometry, valve opening and closing times, injector jets, coils, plugs. excludes: valve positions	3					■
valve axis position	includes the angle of inclination, excludes movement along the axis	2					■
valve guides	from the valve to the cam: position and geometry, exhaust inlet. includes the valve return to the cylinder head	2					■
valve guide-camshaft	From the cam to the valve gear. Geometry with the exception of the cam profile. Includes the damping system linked to the camshaft. Inlet exhaust.	1					■
valve guide	includes position and geometry of the valvegear and the vibration dampers	2					■
covers	rocker covers	1					■
crankshaft	main bearing diameter	2					■
crankshaft	main bearings	2					■
gudgeon pins	includes bearings associated with the pins	2					■
pistons	includes bearings and rollers	2					■
pneumatic valves	includes air pressure regulating device	1	■				
auxiliary controls	from the controls to the power source. Includes the position of the controls as permitted	3					■
oil pressure pump	includes filter. Excludes internal parts not in contact with the pump body	1					■
oil scavenging pump	any oil scavenging system	1					■
oil scavenging	oil degasser, oil reservoir, scavenging oil reservoir	1					■
water pump	includes Power Unit water passages	1					■
injection system	fuel system components (high pressure fuel tubes, injection rails, fuel injectors, accumulators). Excludes injection jets	2					■
air intake	air box. Excludes turbocharging pressure, intake manifolds throttle valves and associated parts	1					■
air intake	intake manifolds and throttle valves and associated parts	1					■
air intake	intake manifolds and throttle valves and associated parts	1					■
turbocharging pressure	between compressor entrance and exit	2					■
turbocharging pressure	turbocharging pressure	2					■
turbocharging pressure	between exhaust flange and turbine entrance	1					
turbocharging pressure	actuators connected to the wastegate	1					■
electrical system	fixing of electrical components to the engine (cabling, sensors, alternator). Excludes actuators, plugs and coils	1					■
injection	coils, control unit	1					■
lubrication	all parts where oil circulates at high pressure (gear pump, passages, accessories)	1					■
MGU-H	complete. Internal parts including bearings and external casing	2					■
MGU-H	position, connection to the turbine	2					■
MGU-H	power electronic controls	1					■
MGU-K	complete. Internal parts including bearings and external casing	2					■
MGU-K	position, connection to turbine	2					■
MGU-K	power electronic controls	1					■
ERS	cabling	1					
ES	battery cells	2					■
ES	BMS	2					■
ERS cooling/lubrication	cooling and lubrication systems	1					■
heat treatment of friction surfaces		1					■
rotary or movement seals		1					■

■ *procedure that cannot be undertaken*

POWER UNITS AND TABLE

The FIA allowed the teams to update their Power Units by freely using their 32 development tokens, the value of which is highlighted in the drawing and the table.

New features **2015**

Following the great upheaval in the regulations introduced in 2014, Mercedes has continued to dominate the scene in the 2015 Formula 1 World Championship in both sporting and technical terms. Ferrari, however, has returned to the centre of attention thanks to greater competitiveness with respect to the revolutionary but rather ineffective F14 T from 2014 and above all thanks to certain new features that characterise the SF15T. Some of these actually came to light only after a number of races, as had been the case the previous season with the Mercedes that had monopolised the technical notes regarding the early races in 2014.
After the confirmation of the return of the oil tank to the classic position between engine and chassis rather than between engine and gearbox, it was in the area of the transmission that an all-new feature was introduced. Rather

than the oil reservoir, the gearbox casing of the SF15T, which last year had been much longer, conceals the passage of the exhausts with two lateral loops in the carbonfibre structure along with a central hole in the upper part.
A solution never previously seen in Formula 1. An aperture that we documented with a drawing of the Sauber whose contract with Maranello involves the use of the Power Unit

and the same transmission as the SF15T. Among other things, the gearbox is taller with the differential raised, a trend that has also been observed on other cars such as the Mercedes and Red Bull and, in a more extreme version, on the McLaren.
All this in order to privilege aerodynamics with a very efficient diffuser and a central end zone that is very narrow like the keel of a sailing boat. This feature also privileges power delivery with the optimised exhaust length.
While the 2014 season was experienced above all in terms of the search for the best way of exploiting and managing the complex Power Units, with cars created in certain cases almost more a rolling test benches, the new season immediately opened with a return to aerodynamic refinements starting with the choice of nose lengths, the only aspect of the cars that was subject to a variation in the regulations as documented in the 2015 Regulations chapter.

Sauber

Ferrari

Sauber

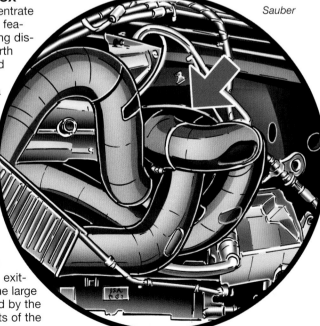

EXHAUST IN THE GEARBOX

The Ferrari SF15T is a concentrate of extreme and interesting features. The most interesting discovery came at the fourth race of the season and concerned the gearbox area. This was a discovery we first made observing the transmission of the Sauber which under the terms of their contract is the same as the Ferrari's. In the interests of improved aerodynamics, the exhaust manifolds were compacted low down and entered the gearbox spacer, exiting from the upper part with the large tail pipe with dimensions imposed by the regulations. In practice, the exhausts of the

The second most important innovation came from a second division team, Force India, which in the tests following the Austrian GP fielded a nose with previously unseen holes, a feature that in effect combines the advantages of the two short and long noses while astutely respecting the regulations to the letter.

However, it has to be noted that from the debut of the 2015 cars, novelties have been seen above all in the area of aerodynamics, with new features such as the engine air intakes on the Lotus or the curious brake intake shields on the McLaren, a team that has continued its research into rear suspen-

sion with an aerodynamic function. Again in this area, at the Austrian GP Toro Rosso faired the rear suspension wishbones with an extreme design that recalls the configuration of the Mercedes front end from the 2014 season onwards.

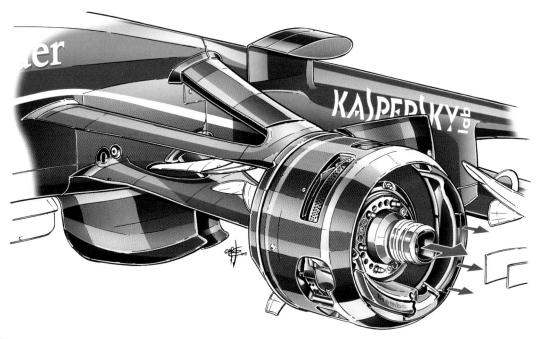

FERRARI

The SF15 T was the first car from Maranello with underslung brake calipers, albeit not in as extreme a configuration as on the Red Bull where they are completely horizontal. On the Ferrari the calipers are instead angled at about 30°. This feature combines well with the pull-rod suspension to concentrate more weight as low as possible. Note the blowing hub and the hot air vent directed towards the outside. In the 2015 season the central vent is also present on the Red Bull and the McLaren which also has it as an option on the rear hubs.

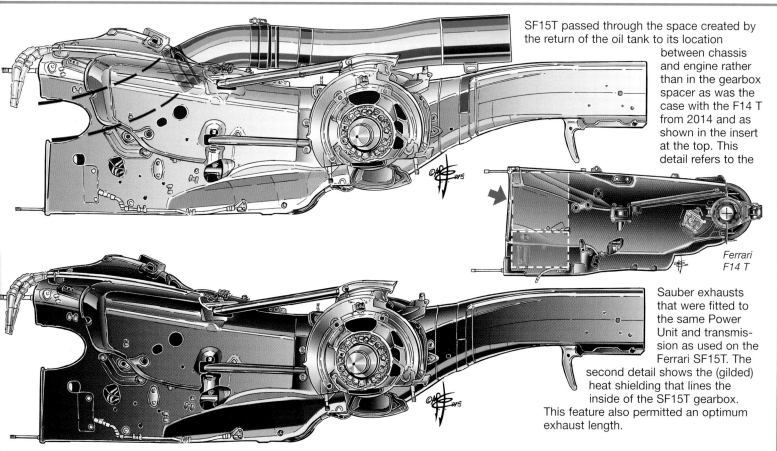

SF15T passed through the space created by the return of the oil tank to its location between chassis and engine rather than in the gearbox spacer as was the case with the F14 T from 2014 and as shown in the insert at the top. This detail refers to the

Ferrari F14 T

Sauber exhausts that were fitted to the same Power Unit and transmission as used on the Ferrari SF15T. The second detail shows the (gilded) heat shielding that lines the inside of the SF15T gearbox. This feature also permitted an optimum exhaust length.

FORCE INDIA

Surprisingly, in testing after the Austrian Grand Prix it was Force India that introduced a new feature that was destined to attract followers: that of the nostrils in the nose of the VJM 08. The design was based on the nose with the long finger from the previous season with two tubes being formed to feed the lower area of the car. The feature is perfectly legal because it respects the minimum and progressive section dimensions and above all because, in accordance with art. 3.7.8 the ground cannot be seen from a vertical observation point.

The two ducts have an inclination of 45°. The view from above reveals a kind of spoon that not only prevents a view of the ground but also directs the flow towards the bottom of the car and increases the efficiency of the S-Duct visible in the drawing top left. In practice, this feature permits great downforce on the front end, as with the long noses, without diminishing the efficiency of the flow towards the rear end as with the short noses.

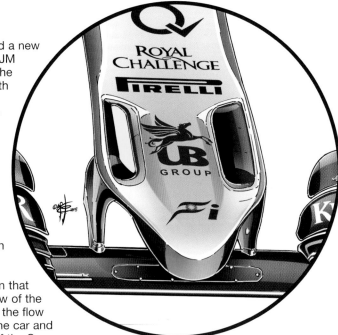

LOTUS AIRSCOOP

There was a previously unseen position for the two ear intakes on the Lotus, set lower down where there was less risk of upsetting the air flow to the rear wing. Usually the additional intakes were placed either on the upper part (Ferrari 2014 and Mercedes 2013) or either side (Mercedes 2014). In theory this new position should permit more efficient aerodynamics.

McLAREN: REAR SUSPENSION

Another new feature for the rear suspension of the 2015 McLaren that had already seen the introduction of an innovative feature last year. In both cases, the extent to which aerodynamics were privileged and dictated the adoption of the new configuration is clear. The lower wishbone has in fact been set as far back as possible, beyond the rear axle to allow the rear arm to work in synergy with the diffuser. For the first time its anchorage (red arrows) is on the impact protection structure rather than the gearbox. Last year in this area McLaren had adopted the previously unseen feature of shutters applied to the suspension arms (see insert) to compensate for the abolition of the beam wing.

McLAREN

The new MP4-30 is particularly sophisticated with a long, low nose combined with the win already seen in part at Abu Dhabi in 2014 and that references the wings designed by Prodomu for Red Bull. The shape of the brake air intakes is very unusual and they draw air from between the tyre and the shrouding that has an indent in the central part where there is a greater flow of air towards the inside of the wheel. It should be noted that the MP4-30 also has blowing hubs.

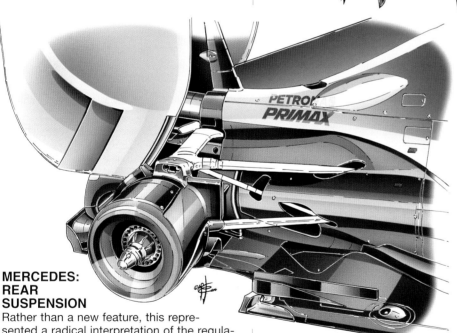

MERCEDES: REAR SUSPENSION

Rather than a new feature, this represented a radical interpretation of the regulations in order to improve the rear aerodynamics. Mercedes took an extreme approach to the possibility of fixing the rear suspension wishbones not directly onto the hub carriers but onto a plate, in this case significantly raised, both to obtain a different suspension geometry and to free up for aerodynamic purposes the lower area of the brake intake which has increasingly become an element designed to create downforce, in this case on the rear axle.

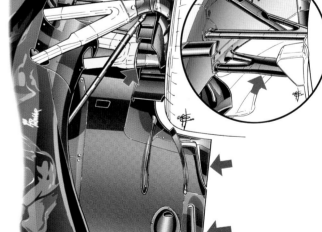

TORO ROSSO

The extreme feature introduced to the rear suspension at the Austrian Grand Prix by Toro Rosso was instead new. Not just the upper arm raised Mercedes style, but above all the lower wishbone that exploits the concept of the wide base wishbone in the front suspension, introduced as a major innovation by the Stuttgart firm the previous season. This configuration has been copied at the front for the 2015 by Ferrari and Force India and introduced for the first time at the rear on the STR 1 (highlighted in yellow in the drawing).

2015 **EVOLUTION**

The great innovation of the 2015 World Championship was the return to F1 of Honda in the role of exclusive supplier of Power Units to McLaren, reprising a pairing that had enjoyed major success in the late Eighties with four world titles won by Ayrton Senna and Alain Prost.

A new research centre has been constructed at Sakura entirely devoted to development of the Formula 1 project, while the European base is located at Milton Keynes in Great Britain. Plans for the completion of the structure severely delayed development of the RA615 H six-cylinder turbo, in part because the staff led by Yasuhisa Arai had no Formula 1 experience as the project had been started from scratch with no technical ties to the past. Honda put its faith in Gilles Simon, the Frenchman who for 10 years had been head of the Ferrari engine department in the Schumacher era; he launched an extreme design that initially presented severe reliability problems. The turbocharging system is unique among the modern Formula 1 Power Units. The Japanese manufacturer decided to locate the compressor in the V of the six-cylinder, in correspondence with the second pair of cylinders, separating it from the IHI turbine and placing the MGU-H between the two linked by a shaft. The idea was to create

an innovative packaging layout for the Power Unit that would allow the MP4-30 to have a very compact rear end, benefitting aerodynamics. The ERS radiator was therefore mounted above the internal combustion engine to guarantee very short pipework and ducts and to save weight. However, in contrast with the Mercedes, which is equipped with a large compressor cantilevered from the engine on the chassis side, Honda preferred a less bulky configuration designed to spin at the high speeds permitted by the regulations, 125,000 rpm, a limit never reached by the other constructors who only just exceeded the 100,000 threshold. While at Brixworth the engineers have focussed on the charging of the cylinders with a greater air flow, at Sakura they have concentrated on augmenting the speed of the fluids. However, problems have emerged concerning overheating and the longevity of the materials with repeated breakages of the turbocharging system and the MGU-H, problems that have severely delayed the development of the RA615 H. The Japanese have in fact concentrated on the search for reliability and in the first part of the season have avoided spending tokens on the development of the V6. The FIA has given all constructors 32 tokens they can spend on development of their 2014 Power

Units, allowing the modifications to be introduced during the course of the season. In order to homologate the 2015 unit, Mercedes has spent 25 units, Ferrari 22 and Renault just 20. It was difficult to establish how many tokens should be given to the Honda, which made its debut in Melbourne. In the end a compromise solution was representing the average number of tokens remaining for the other engine constructors: Mercedes 7, Ferrari 10 and Renault 12. Honda was therefore granted 9 tokens. The FIA World Council met in Mexico City in July and decided that in order to facilitate access to new constructors the possibility of using a fifth Power Unit would be granted in the first year. It should be remembered that each driver has just four units at his disposition over the course of the season, with grid position penalties imposed for exceeding this number. The measure was retroactive for Honda. It was a pity that when the two drivers, Fernando Alonso and Jenson Button arrived, they had already used the fifth engine. The sixth unit will not therefore be penalised when it is fitted to the MP4-30s. The number of teams did not increase given that Caterham dropped out after having produced in 2014 perhaps the ugliest and least competitive car in the history of modern Formula 1. Elsewhere, the 2015 season was one of adjustment with the only modification to the technical regulations concerning the shape of the noses, as detailed in the section devoted to the 2015 regulations.

McLAREN HONDA MP4-30

Honda came up with a Power Unit layout that was different to both that of Mercedes and that of Ferrari and Renault. The Japanese put the compressor in the V of the six-cylinder engine, separating it from the IHI turbine with the MGU-H in the middle linked via a shaft. Ferrari and Renault instead kept the compressor and turbine together while Mercedes separated the two at either end of the engine. The idea was that of creating an extreme packaging layout for the Power Unit that would allow the MP4-30 to have a very compact rear end so as to favour aerodynamics, as can be seen in the comparison view from above.
1) The MP4-30 began the season with a low, very wide and rounded nose.
2) The Red Bull-inspired front wing was all-new.
3) The steering arm was aligned with the upper wishbone and the brake cooling intakes were also very new.
4) The sidepods were cut away at the front and above all in the central-rear section (5) to improve the flow of air to the rear.
6 The rear suspension was innovative with the lower wishbone set notably further back and faired.
7 The MP4-30 had a longer wheelbase, as highlighted in yellow.
8) New diffuser.

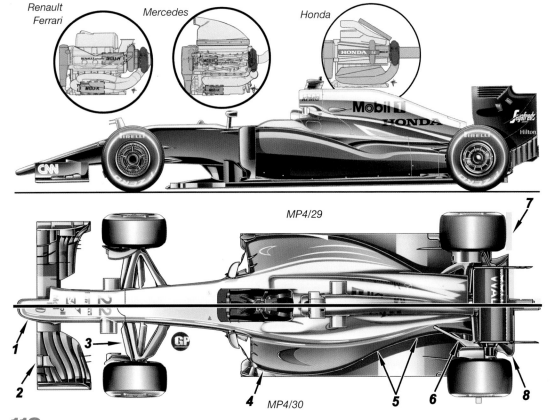

Renault
Ferrari

Mercedes

Honda

MP4/29

MP4/30

SF15 T - F14 T:
SIDE VIEW COMPARISON

The SF15T represents an almost complete break with the preceding F14T and was distinguished by the Alfa Romeo badge in place of the Fiat logo, referencing the origins of the Scuderia.

The droplet-shaped nose (1) was very long and the endplates were also new. For the first time the front brake callipers are underslung to exploit to the full the lowering of the centre of gravity guaranteed by the pull-rod suspension layout.

(3-4) The chassis has a gentler slope like that of the 2014 Mercedes with the tub dipping before that of the F14T as can be seen in the side view comparison.

New turning vanes (5) ahead of the sidepods like the vertical versions.

(6) The sidepods started higher and more rounded, with the lower part sharply cut away.

In the lower part of the air intake (7) there is a second mouth, as on the 2014 Toro Rosso.

A great deal of work has been done on the Power Unit (8), adopting a larger turbine-compressor assembly and improving the efficacy of the MGU-H thanks in part to a new exhaust configuration.

The whole rear end (9) is very closed and tapered.

The new rear wing introduced in Austin (10) boasted a new feature in the lower section. Immediately behind the rear wheels horizontal fringes (12) have been installed to improved the downforce generated by the new Red Bull-style diffuser (11).

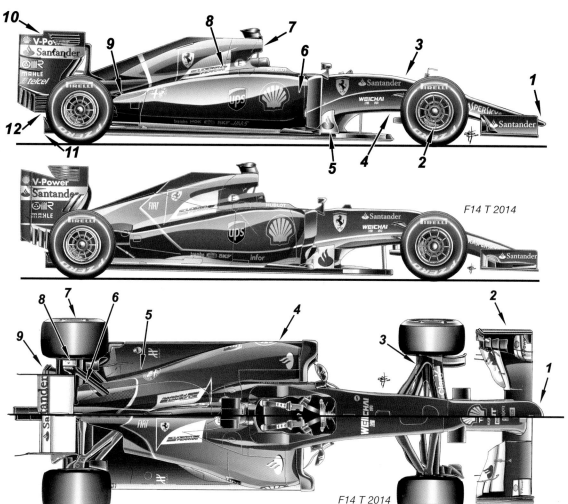

F14 T 2014

F14 T 2014

PULL-ROD SUSPENSION

For the fourth season Ferrari went with a pull-rod layout, naturally revised an corrected with respect to the one illustrated in the animation frame. This configuration permits better front aerodynamics. All the other cars instead use the push-rod layout.

TOP VIEW COMPARISON

The SF15T has distinguished itself at the car with the longest nose (1) in the field, of a fairly sophisticated shape in its lower section, a kind of V-shaped droplet dealing with initial management of the air flows in the lower part of the car.

The front wing is all new from the simpler endplates (2) inwards.

Interesting new features appeared in the area of the front suspension where a very narrow lower wishbone (3) was adopted in the wake of Mercedes' 2014 innovation.

A lot of work was done on cooling with the sidepods larger at the front (4) and tapering sharply in the Coke bottle area (5) and directing all the hot air to the rear end (6).

The wheelbase (7) was lengthened by around 5 cm.

The aerodynamic influence of the front and rear suspension (8) was also studied.

UNDERSLUNG BRAKES

On the SF15T for the first time the front brake callipers are underslung to exploit to the full the lowering of the centre of gravity guaranteed by the pull-rod suspension layout. For many seasons this was a feature adopted only by Red Bull. Note also the blowing wheel nut in a more extreme version than that of the F14T. The circle instead illustrated the less stepped configuration of the lower part of the chassis providing aerodynamics less sensitive to ride height variations.

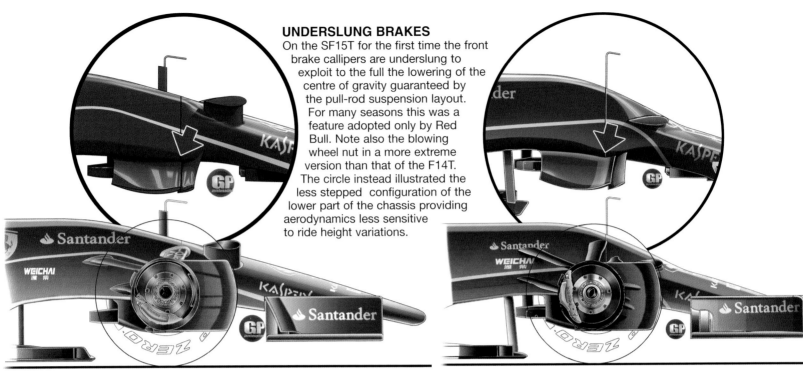

TUNING FORK LOWER WISHBONE

Ferrari adopted the innovative narrow lower wishbone introduced by Mercedes in 2014. This design allows a large aerodynamic profile to be created that acts in synergy with the front aerodynamic package. Mercedes itself has retained the feature, albeit with the steering arm set low and faired to increase the aerodynamic effect of the configuration.

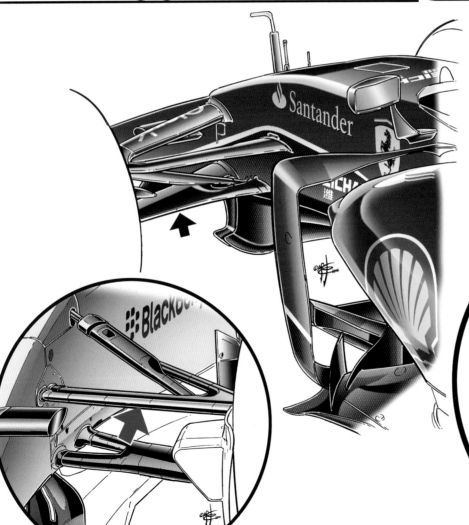

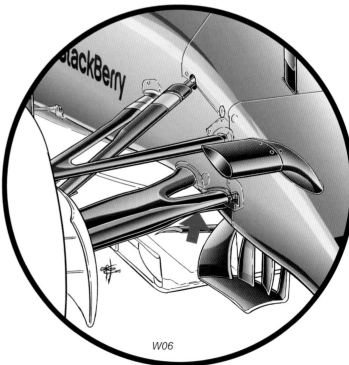

W05

W06

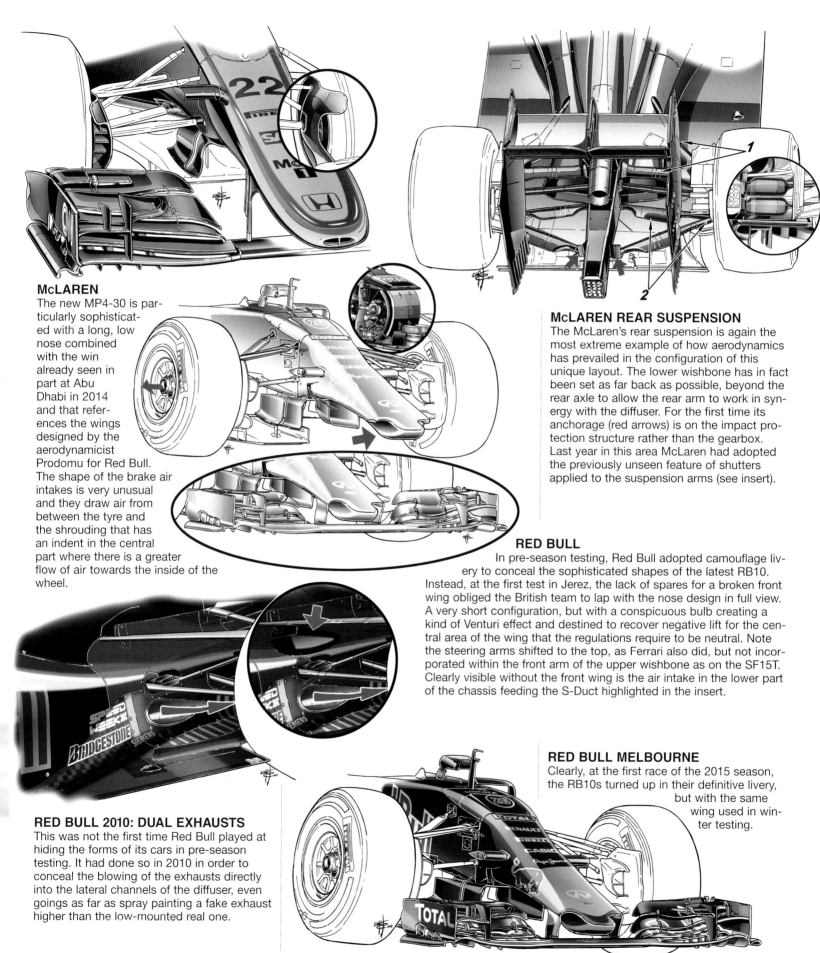

McLAREN

The new MP4-30 is particularly sophisticated with a long, low nose combined with the win already seen in part at Abu Dhabi in 2014 and that references the wings designed by the aerodynamicist Prodomu for Red Bull. The shape of the brake air intakes is very unusual and they draw air from between the tyre and the shrouding that has an indent in the central part where there is a greater flow of air towards the inside of the wheel.

McLAREN REAR SUSPENSION

The McLaren's rear suspension is again the most extreme example of how aerodynamics has prevailed in the configuration of this unique layout. The lower wishbone has in fact been set as far back as possible, beyond the rear axle to allow the rear arm to work in synergy with the diffuser. For the first time its anchorage (red arrows) is on the impact protection structure rather than the gearbox. Last year in this area McLaren had adopted the previously unseen feature of shutters applied to the suspension arms (see insert).

RED BULL

In pre-season testing, Red Bull adopted camouflage livery to conceal the sophisticated shapes of the latest RB10. Instead, at the first test in Jerez, the lack of spares for a broken front wing obliged the British team to lap with the nose design in full view. A very short configuration, but with a conspicuous bulb creating a kind of Venturi effect and destined to recover negative lift for the central area of the wing that the regulations require to be neutral. Note the steering arms shifted to the top, as Ferrari also did, but not incorporated within the front arm of the upper wishbone as on the SF15T. Clearly visible without the front wing is the air intake in the lower part of the chassis feeding the S-Duct highlighted in the insert.

RED BULL 2010: DUAL EXHAUSTS

This was not the first time Red Bull played at hiding the forms of its cars in pre-season testing. It had done so in 2010 in order to conceal the blowing of the exhausts directly into the lateral channels of the diffuser, even goings as far as spray painting a fake exhaust higher than the low-mounted real one.

RED BULL MELBOURNE

Clearly, at the first race of the 2015 season, the RB10s turned up in their definitive livery, but with the same wing used in winter testing.

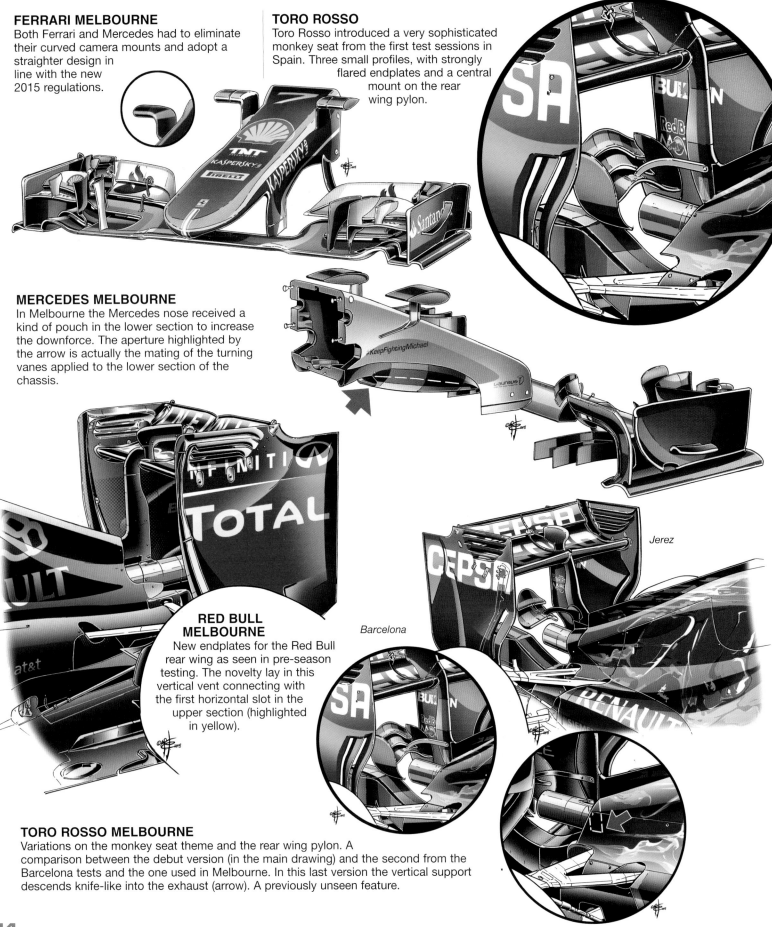

FERRARI MELBOURNE

Both Ferrari and Mercedes had to eliminate their curved camera mounts and adopt a straighter design in line with the new 2015 regulations.

TORO ROSSO

Toro Rosso introduced a very sophisticated monkey seat from the first test sessions in Spain. Three small profiles, with strongly flared endplates and a central mount on the rear wing pylon.

MERCEDES MELBOURNE

In Melbourne the Mercedes nose received a kind of pouch in the lower section to increase the downforce. The aperture highlighted by the arrow is actually the mating of the turning vanes applied to the lower section of the chassis.

RED BULL MELBOURNE

New endplates for the Red Bull rear wing as seen in pre-season testing. The novelty lay in this vertical vent connecting with the first horizontal slot in the upper section (highlighted in yellow).

Jerez

Barcelona

TORO ROSSO MELBOURNE

Variations on the monkey seat theme and the rear wing pylon. A comparison between the debut version (in the main drawing) and the second from the Barcelona tests and the one used in Melbourne. In this last version the vertical support descends knife-like into the exhaust (arrow). A previously unseen feature.

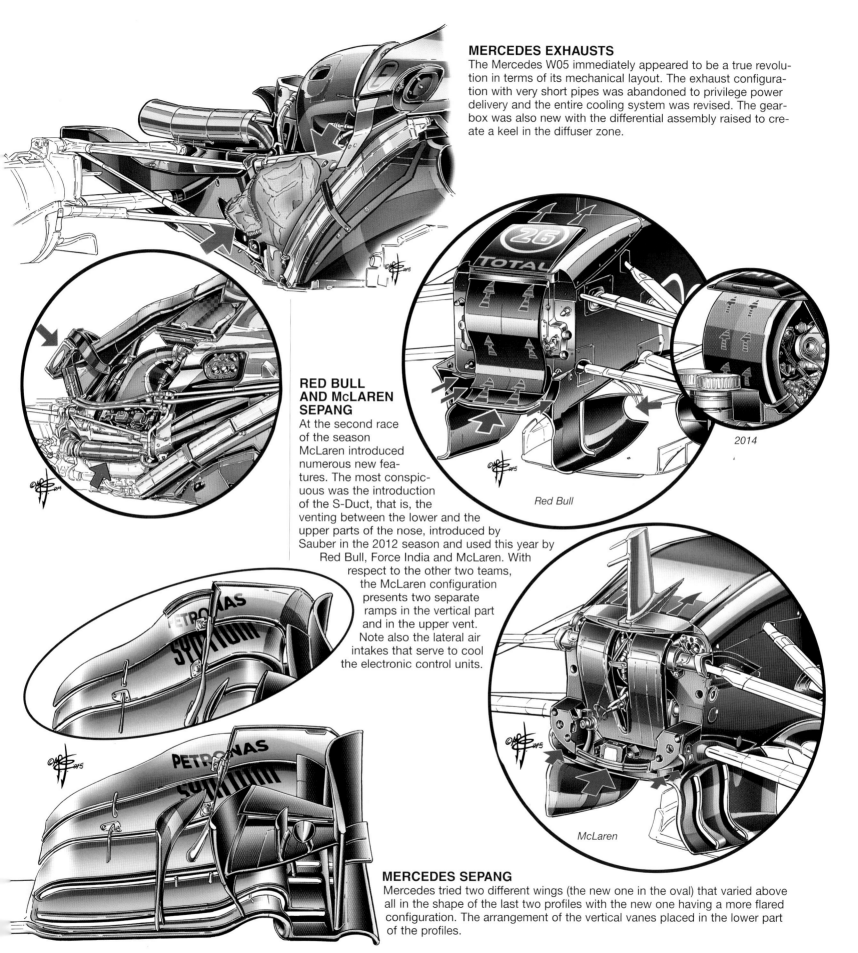

MERCEDES EXHAUSTS

The Mercedes W05 immediately appeared to be a true revolution in terms of its mechanical layout. The exhaust configuration with very short pipes was abandoned to privilege power delivery and the entire cooling system was revised. The gearbox was also new with the differential assembly raised to create a keel in the diffuser zone.

RED BULL AND McLAREN SEPANG

At the second race of the season McLaren introduced numerous new features. The most conspicuous was the introduction of the S-Duct, that is, the venting between the lower and the upper parts of the nose, introduced by Sauber in the 2012 season and used this year by Red Bull, Force India and McLaren. With respect to the other two teams, the McLaren configuration presents two separate ramps in the vertical part and in the upper vent. Note also the lateral air intakes that serve to cool the electronic control units.

2014

Red Bull

McLaren

MERCEDES SEPANG

Mercedes tried two different wings (the new one in the oval) that varied above all in the shape of the last two profiles with the new one having a more flared configuration. The arrangement of the vertical vanes placed in the lower part of the profiles.

FERRARI OIL TANK

At the third race of the season we finally grasped one of the key points of the revolution undertaken with respect to the old F14T. We are referring to the return to the past, that is, to the location of the oil tank (1) between engine and gearbox, as on all the other cars. The team therefore abandoned the unique and in the end unsuccessful location at the rear of the engine, inside the gearbox, that underlay the F14T layout. This return to the traditional location allowed the installation of the Power Unit and its accessories to be as compact as possible while conserving unchanged other elements such as the intercooler (2) location within the V of the engine and visible, as on the F14T, in the front view of the 6-cylinder engine removed from the chassis. Also unaltered was the position of the electric motor combined with the turbine, the MGU-H, and the disposition of the compressor and the turbine although both were updated in terms of the their physical dimensions. Lastly, the exhausts (3) were also different and avoided last year's fashion introduced by Mercedes for short pipes in order to privilege a layout that guaranteed good power delivery from the internal combustion engine without penalising the supply of heat for the MGU-H.

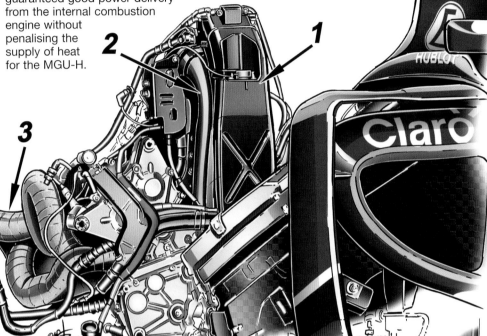

FERRARI SHANGHAI

Ferrari tried two different engine covers, with the dashed line showing the version with the larger central vent as used in Malaysia. Note that the driveshaft, which on the F14T had been fully faired, is instead partially exposed (red arrow).

MERCEDES SHANGHAI

The wing introduced in China by Mercedes was extremely sophisticated, above all with respect to its policy of the previous season reprised this year by other teams. There was an increase in the number of slots in the peripheral area close to the endplates and the section and arc of the various profiles has become more angular and pronounced.

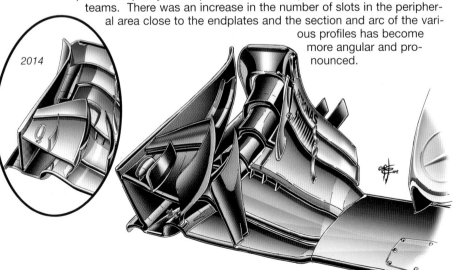

2014

SAUBER SHANGHAI

A new front wing but only for Nasr's Sauber, clearly of the Mercedes school but new in all its details. Inboard of the cascade is a single vertical fin like that on the Ferrari. The fin outside the endplate is different in shape and shorter.

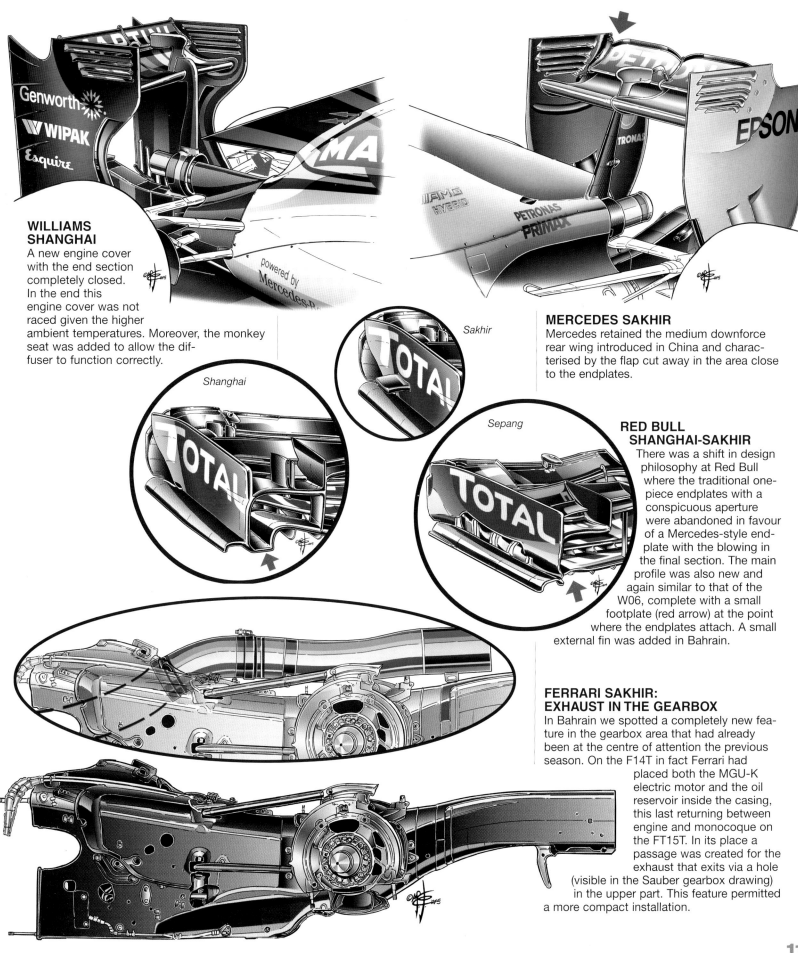

WILLIAMS SHANGHAI

A new engine cover with the end section completely closed. In the end this engine cover was not raced given the higher ambient temperatures. Moreover, the monkey seat was added to allow the diffuser to function correctly.

Sakhir

Shanghai

Sepang

MERCEDES SAKHIR

Mercedes retained the medium downforce rear wing introduced in China and characterised by the flap cut away in the area close to the endplates.

RED BULL SHANGHAI-SAKHIR

There was a shift in design philosophy at Red Bull where the traditional one-piece endplates with a conspicuous aperture were abandoned in favour of a Mercedes-style endplate with the blowing in the final section. The main profile was also new and again similar to that of the W06, complete with a small footplate (red arrow) at the point where the endplates attach. A small external fin was added in Bahrain.

FERRARI SAKHIR: EXHAUST IN THE GEARBOX

In Bahrain we spotted a completely new feature in the gearbox area that had already been at the centre of attention the previous season. On the F14T in fact Ferrari had placed both the MGU-K electric motor and the oil reservoir inside the casing, this last returning between engine and monocoque on the FT15T. In its place a passage was created for the exhaust that exits via a hole (visible in the Sauber gearbox drawing) in the upper part. This feature permitted a more compact installation.

McLAREN DIFFUSOR

Both McLaren drivers used the new diffuser, which in China had at the last minute and in a single example (Button). The area of the lateral channel near the wheel was very different with a forward-facing L-shaped Gurney flap.

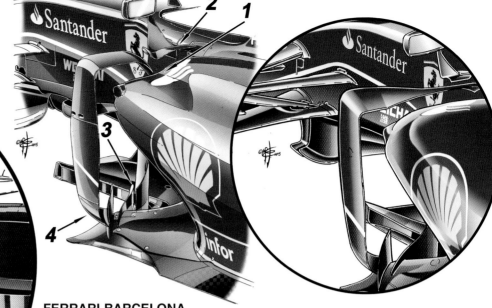

FERRARI BARCELONA

The most eye-catching novelties of the aerodynamic package introduced by Ferrari in Barcelona were concentrated in the area around the start of the sidepods of the SF15T which were strongly flared (1) and fitted with a new horizontal fin (2), while the vertical boomerang was no longer a one-piece element. The turning vanes ahead of the sidepods were equipped with two vents (3) while the vertical vanes had a new shape.

RED BULL

After four crash tests, Red Bull could finally use its short nose that was very similar to that of its Toro Rosso cousin which had been running it since the first race of the season. It is around 10 cm shorter, as revealed by the inclination of the vertical supports. This configuration permitted a good air flow in the lower section that feeds the diffuser.

FERRARI DIFFUSER

There L-shaped mini-flaps in the lateral ramp of the diffuser in the area attached to the wheel were new. This area was at the centre of attention as seen in the novelties introduced in Bahrain on the McLaren with the trailing edge of the diffuser flipped up in a forward-facing L. The mount for the vertical flange on the extractor profile was also new.

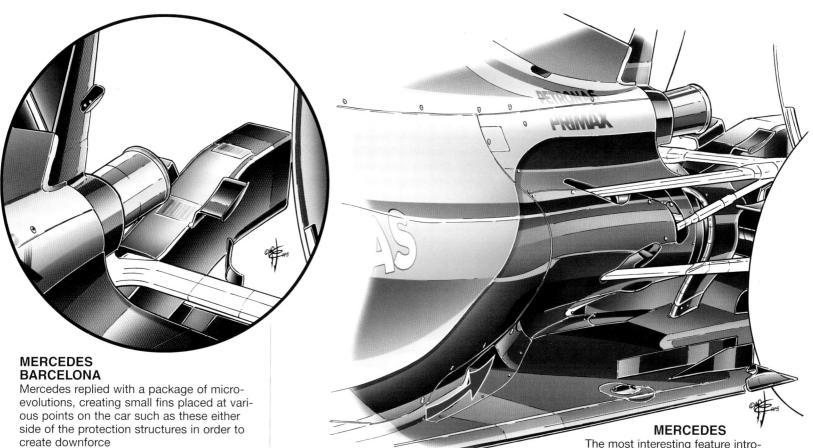

MERCEDES
BARCELONA

Mercedes replied with a package of micro-evolutions, creating small fins placed at various points on the car such as these either side of the protection structures in order to create downforce everywhere.

McLAREN

By Spain, McLaren had already introduced its new livery and modified the front suspension by removing the fairings from the lower wishbone, as we have shown in the comparison with the original version (left). The part of the diffuser close to the wheels had already been modified in Bahrain.

MERCEDES

The most interesting feature introduced by Mercedes concerns this air intake which might not be dedicated solely to the cooling of the rear end which, in its turn, is more tapered, especially in the lower part. In many ways it recalls the vent in the central area of the Red Bull diffuser from two years ago.

FERRARI

The detail highlights the mini-flaps positioned in the zone almost in contact with the rear wheel to create mini-vortices that enhance the efficiency of the diffuser.

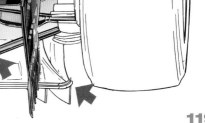

McLAREN AND FERRARI BRAKES MONACO

Vettel's SF15T featured these oval holes in the front brake shrouds (in the Ferrari drawing partially disassembled) which McLaren had introduced at the beginning of the season on its MP4-30. Note the new shape of the McLaren brake intakes.

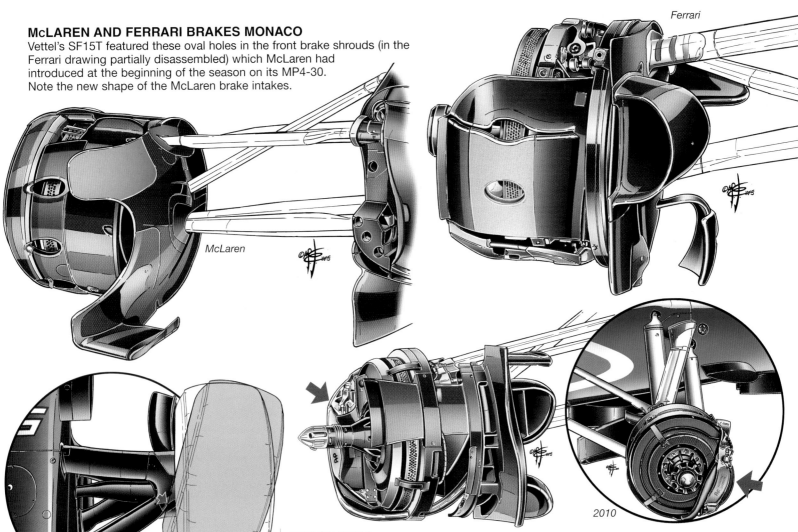

Ferrari

McLaren

2010

FORCE INDIA

Finally, after six seasons, Force India has eliminated the absurd location of the brake calipers beyond the front axle introduced in 2010. This feature had a negative effect on the cooling of the calliper. The new configuration was first seen a Monaco, a circuit particularly critical for brake cooling.

FERRARI MONACO

In order to lap on the streets of the principality, all the teams increased the steering radius from 14° to 22°. At this pointed a small portion of the front suspension wishbone had to be cut away to prevent the wheel from fouling the arm and blocking the steering.

RED BULL

The prize for the most important modification goes to Red Bull which raised the mounting point of the upper wishbone on the hub carrier in order to obtain a different camber recovery and improved traction. The insert shows a detail of the hub carrier with the modified upper wishbone mounting plate.

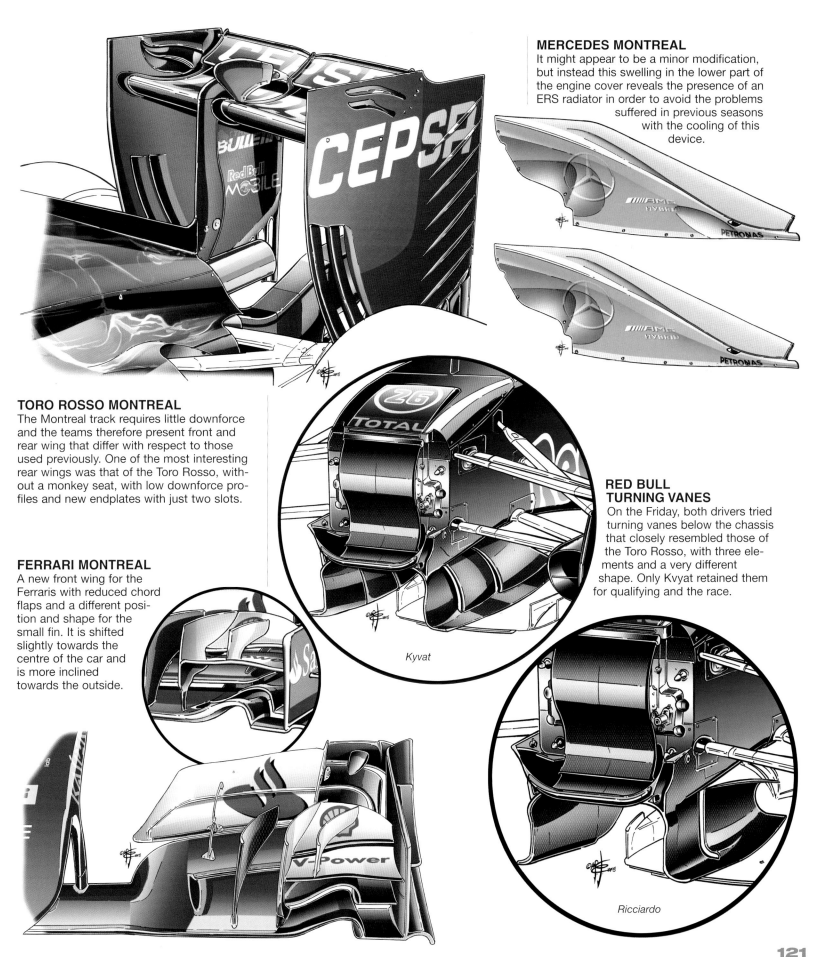

MERCEDES MONTREAL

It might appear to be a minor modification, but instead this swelling in the lower part of the engine cover reveals the presence of an ERS radiator in order to avoid the problems suffered in previous seasons with the cooling of this device.

TORO ROSSO MONTREAL

The Montreal track requires little downforce and the teams therefore present front and rear wing that differ with respect to those used previously. One of the most interesting rear wings was that of the Toro Rosso, without a monkey seat, with low downforce profiles and new endplates with just two slots.

FERRARI MONTREAL

A new front wing for the Ferraris with reduced chord flaps and a different position and shape for the small fin. It is shifted slightly towards the centre of the car and is more inclined towards the outside.

RED BULL TURNING VANES

On the Friday, both drivers tried turning vanes below the chassis that closely resembled those of the Toro Rosso, with three elements and a very different shape. Only Kvyat retained them for qualifying and the race.

Kvyat

Ricciardo

RED BULL BRAK INTAKES

Red Bull retained the small intake introduced at Monaco and dedicated to the cooling of the underslung calliper with the addition of a Mercedes-style small, tightly curved shield in the lower part with the aim of increasing the flow of air towards the braking system.

MERCEDES EXPOSED DISCS

For the first time this season Mercedes used front brake shrouds that were completely open at the front to improved dispersal of heat from the Carbon discs with four aligned holes.

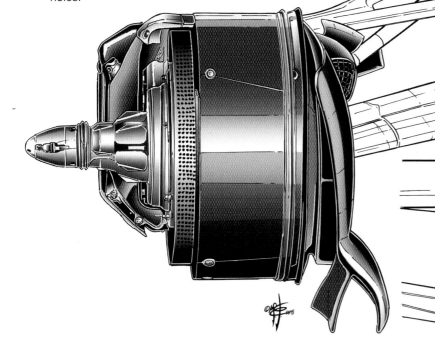

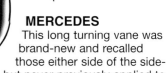

MERCEDES

This long turning vane was brand-new and recalled those either side of the side-pod mouths, but never previously applied to the brake intakes.

MERCEDES

Mercedes took an extreme approach to the possibility of fixing the rear suspension wishbones not directly onto the hub carriers but onto a plate, in this case significantly raised, both to obtain a different suspension geometry and to free up for aerodynamic purposes the lower area of the brake intake which has increasingly become an element designed to create downforce, in this case on the rear axle.

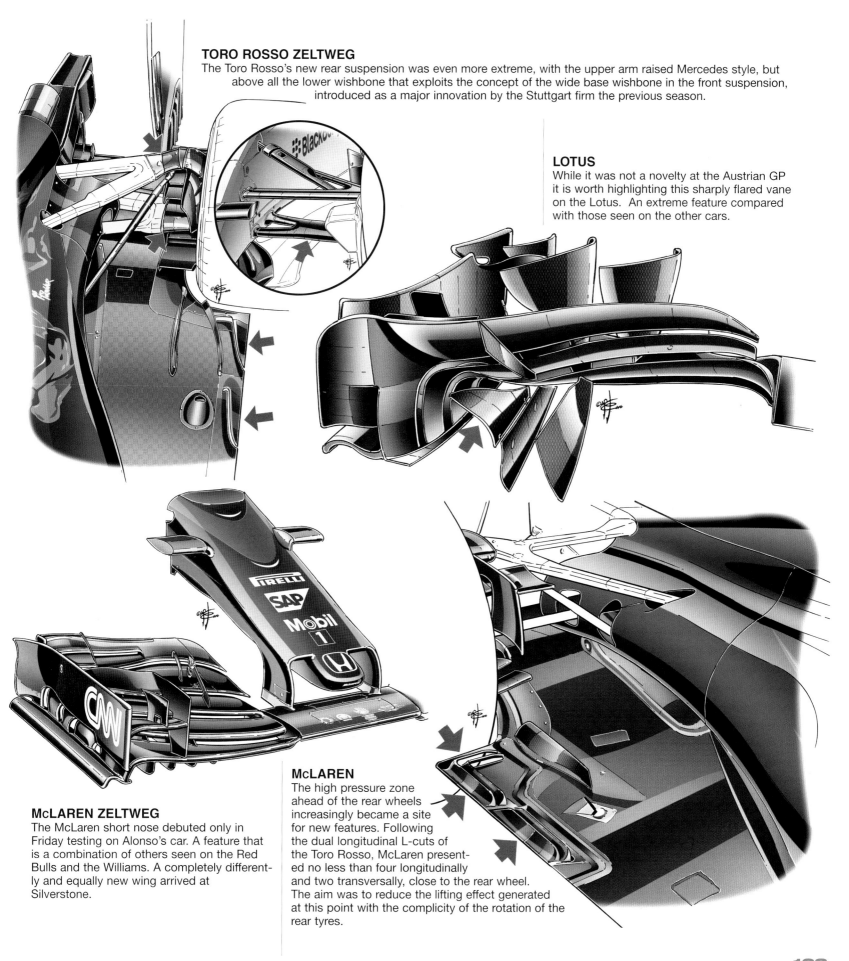

TORO ROSSO ZELTWEG

The Toro Rosso's new rear suspension was even more extreme, with the upper arm raised Mercedes style, but above all the lower wishbone that exploits the concept of the wide base wishbone in the front suspension, introduced as a major innovation by the Stuttgart firm the previous season.

LOTUS

While it was not a novelty at the Austrian GP it is worth highlighting this sharply flared vane on the Lotus. An extreme feature compared with those seen on the other cars.

McLAREN ZELTWEG

The McLaren short nose debuted only in Friday testing on Alonso's car. A feature that is a combination of others seen on the Red Bulls and the Williams. A completely differently and equally new wing arrived at Silverstone.

McLAREN

The high pressure zone ahead of the rear wheels increasingly became a site for new features. Following the dual longitudinal L-cuts of the Toro Rosso, McLaren presented no less than four longitudinally and two transversally, close to the rear wheel. The aim was to reduce the lifting effect generated at this point with the complicity of the rotation of the rear tyres.

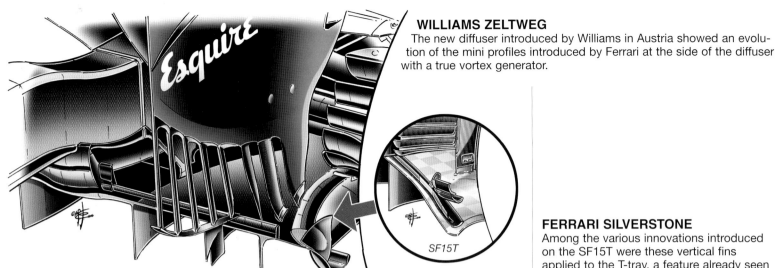

WILLIAMS ZELTWEG

The new diffuser introduced by Williams in Austria showed an evolution of the mini profiles introduced by Ferrari at the side of the diffuser with a true vortex generator.

SF15T

FERRARI SILVERSTONE

Among the various innovations introduced on the SF15T were these vertical fins applied to the T-tray, a feature already seen on other cars.

FERRARI REAR BRAKE INTAKE

A further modification to the rear brake intakes with three small vortex generators on the vertical fin introduced at Monaco. In the critical underbody area, ahead of the rear wheels, another small step in addition to the three cuts already seen in the preceding races and designed to improve the efficiency of the flow in this area.

WILLIAMS SILVERSTONE

The new diffuser introduced in Austria and illustrated in the technical notes was modified in the central section with this additional flap that renders the extractor profile more effective.

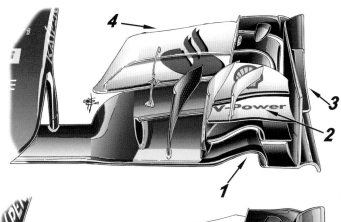

FERRARI FRONT WING

A completely different wing in all respects was fielded at Silverstone (bottom), from the main profile with an area much more sharply curving upwards (1). The cascades were wider and had an extra fin (2) directing the flow outside the front wheels. The end plate has lost the external fin (3) and the final flap has been modified (4).

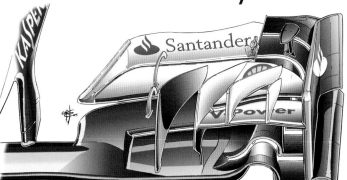

FORCE INDIA SILVERSTONE

The Force India "nostrils" were destined to set a trend. The design was based on the nose with the long finger from the previous season with two tubes being formed to feed the lower area of the car. The feature is perfectly legal because it respects the minimum and progressive section dimensions and above all because, in accordance with art. 3.7.8 the ground cannot be seen from a vertical observation point. The two ducts have an inclination of 45°. The view from above reveals a kind of spoon that not only prevents a view of the ground but also directs the flow towards the bottom of the car and increases the efficiency of the S-Duct.

COCKPIT PROTECTION

The incident involving Alonso's McLaren and Raikkonen's Ferrari at the Austrian GP brought attention to the theme of Formula 1 cars' cockpit protection. These drawings, taken from an animation, illustrate the study conducted by Mercedes on behalf of the Federation to safeguard the cockpit area in the case of intrusion by cars or other objects. A kind of ring-shaped structure in carbonfibre is fixed to a very slim vertical pylon that has to survive the same crash test as the roll-bar. Its rising configuration to the sides of the driver's head, evident in the side view, prevents the mirrors from being obstructed. Neither should frontal visibility be compromised. If approved by the Formula 1 technical working group, this study would become obligatory for all cars, with the shape being defined by the FIA.

Ciao JULES

Jules Bianchi dopo Ayrton Senna e Roland Ratzenberger. Sono trascorsi 21 anni dalla scomparsa del campione brasiliano e del pilota austriaco e la Formula 1, anche se in una situazione del tutto differente, si ritrova a piangere per la perdita di un altro suo pilota.

Una tragedia che si è consumata dopo nove mesi di dolore e di speranze.

Prima lo schianto della Marussia del francese contro il mezzo di soccorso che stava spostando un'altra monoposto, sotto una pioggia incessante, mentre la visibilità era ormai ridotta al lumicino, alla conclusione del Gp del Giappone 2014 a Suzuka. Poi, il buio.

Quello più profondo del dramma e del coma. Restava solo la speranza. Fede più che scienza. Jules respirava da solo, il corpo era integro ma il cervello non rispondeva per il danno assonale diffuso. Ma Jules continuava a lottare: a 25 anni il francese di Nizza non si era arreso.

Con la stessa determinazione con la quale aveva conquistato quel prodigioso punticino al Gp di Monaco, che per la Marussia voleva dire salvezza.

Un piccolo miracolo di un talento che sognava la Ferrari dopo essere stato il primo conduttore della FDA ad essere giunto alla F.1. Ce l'avrebbe fatta, ma ha preferito chiudere i conti con il destino il 17 luglio 2015, dopo mesi in cui è stato amorevolmente seguito dalla famiglia. Portandosi con sé il sogno. Ciao Jules…

Giorgio Nada Editore

Editorial manager
Leonardo Acerbi

Editorial coordination
Giorgio Nada Editore

Graphic design and cover
Aimone Bolliger

Contributors
Franco Nugnes (engines)
Ing. Giancarlo Bruno (gearbox and tyres)
Kazuhito Kawai (tyres)

Computer graphic
Alessia Bardino
Camillo Morande
Gisella Nicosia
Paolo Rondelli

3D Animations
Camillo Morande
Annunziata Generoso

Photo
Flavio Mazzi

Printed in Italy by
Tecnostampa - Pigini Group Printing Division
Loreto - Trevi
september 2015

© 2015 Giorgio Nada Editore, Vimodrone (Milan, Italy)

DESIGNED & MANUFACTURED IN ITALY

ALL RIGHTS RESERVED
All rights reserved. Apart from any fair dealing for the purpose of private study, research,
criticism or review, no part of this publication may be reproduced, stored in a retrieval system,
or transmitted, by any means, electronic, electrical, chemical, mechanical, optical photocopying,
recording or otherwise, without prior written permission. All enquiries should be addressed to:

Giorgio Nada Editore
Via Claudio Treves,15/17
I - 20090 VIMODRONE MI
Tel. +39 02 27301126
Fax +39 02 27301454
e-mail: info@giorgionadaeditore.it
www.giorgionadaeditore.it

Allo stesso indirizzo può essere richiesto il catalogo
di tutte le opere pubblicate dalla Casa Editrice.

Distribution
Giunti Editore Spa
via Bolognese 165
I - 50139 FIRENZE
www.giunti.it

Formula 1 2014-2015. Technical analysis
ISBN 978-88-7911-623-7